Cities of Refuge

Cities of Refuge

German Jews in London and New York, 1935–1945

Lori Gemeiner Bihler

Cover photo: United States Holocaust Memorial Museum, courtesy of Steven Pressman/PerlePress Productions

Published by State University of New York Press, Albany

© 2018 State University of New York

All rights reserved

No part of this book may be used or reproduced in any manner whatsoever without written permission. No part of this book may be stored in a retrieval system or transmitted in any form or by any means including electronic, electrostatic, magnetic tape, mechanical, photocopying, recording, or otherwise without the prior permission in writing of the publisher.

For information, contact State University of New York Press, Albany, NY
www.sunypress.edu

Library of Congress Cataloging-in-Publication Data

Names: Bihler, Lori Gemeiner, [date].
Title: Cities of refuge : German Jews in London and New York, 1935–1945 / Lori Gemeiner Bihler.
Description: Albany : State University of New York Press, [2018] | Includes bibliographical references and index.
Identifiers: LCCN 2017018232 (print) | LCCN 2017019431 (ebook) | ISBN 9781438468891 (ebook) | ISBN 9781438468877 (hardcover   ) | ISBN 9781438468884 (pbk.   )
Subjects: LCSH: Jews—England—London—History—20th century. | Jews, German—England—London—History—20th century. | Jews, German—New York (State)—New York—History—20th century. | Jews, German—England—London—Social life and customs. | Jews, German—New York (State)—New York—Social life and customs. | Jewish refugees—England—History—20th century. | Jewish refugees—New York (State)—History—20th century. | London (England)—Ethnic relations. | New York (N.Y.)—Ethnic relations.
Classification: LCC DS135.E55 (ebook) | LCC DS135.E55 L6626 2018 (print) | DDC 305.892/4042109043—dc23
LC record available at https://lccn.loc.gov/2017018232

10 9 8 7 6 5 4 3 2 1

Contents

List of Illustrations	vii
List of Abbreviations	ix
Preface	xi
Introduction	1
1. Arrival and Settlement	17
2. Family, Friendship, and Food	47
3. Dress and Names	65
4. Language and Mannerisms	91
5. Organizational Life	117
6. Identities	137
Conclusion	149
Notes	159
Bibliography	193
Index	209

Illustrations

Tables

1.1	New York City "Rooms for Rent" Advertisements in *Aufbau*, Rosh Hashanah Issues, 1935–1945	39

Maps

1.1.	Greater London, Borough of Hampstead	24
1.2.	*A-Z Map* of Hampstead with German Jewish points of interest	28
1.3.	*A-Z Map* of Hampstead with bomb sites	32
1.4.	New York City	37
1.5.	Washington Heights with German Jewish points of interest	44

Images

5.1.	Mastheads of refugee publications	130
5.2.	Couple reading *Aufbau*	131
C.3.	Hampstead street scene	151

Abbreviations

AJR	Association of Jewish Refugees
CGJS	Centre for German-Jewish Studies, University of Sussex
FDKB	Free German Culture League (*Freier Deutscher Kulturbund*)
HIAS	Hebrew Sheltering Immigrant Aid Society
LBI NY	Leo Baeck Institute, New York

Preface

As I began research for this book, I discovered that former German Jewish refugees on both sides of the Atlantic had specific assumptions about their counterparts' experiences. I was told repeatedly in London that New York German Jews became "immediately" American or immigration was "just part of the history" of New York. Likewise, when I visited New York, and spoke with former refugees about German Jews in London, many presumed the experience of refugees in London was similar to their own. Such perceptions, true or false, were also reflected in academic works on German Jewish migration to Great Britain, Israel, and the United States. For example, Steven Lowenstein wrote in *Frankfurt on the Hudson: The German-Jewish Community of Washington Heights*, "Most scholars view the integration process in the United States as easier, and more thoroughgoing than was the case in Israel or Great Britain. . . . In England, there was a dominant ethnic group. One did not become English; one was born English. . . . America today permits a much wider pluralism than do either Britain or Israel."[1] Similarly Marion Berghahn stated, "The refugees who emigrated to England instead of to the United States encountered a very homogenous society, one marked by sharply delineated boundaries of class and status but held together by a pervasive sense of 'Englishness.'"[2]

I have determined a need to reexamine these assumptions through a comparative analysis of refugee experience in each country. No work has been undertaken to date that systematically contrasts German Jewish refugee communities in the United States and Great Britain. This book challenges the widely held notion that immigrants integrated into American society because they were the recipients of a greater tradition of tolerance and diversity. It explores the concept of New York and London as "cities of refuge," in the actual and not the biblical sense, and allows us to look beyond national mythologies to explain the differences in refugee experience in each city.

Drawing on a wide range of published and unpublished sources, this work examines why Jewish refugees in London adopted local ways and customs more quickly than those in New York, yet identified less as British during this period than their counterparts in the United States did as American. Given that both groups of refugees derived from the same diverse yet distinct German Jewish community in Germany, the conclusions reached in this specific historical investigation have implications for the more general understanding of processes of migration and identity negotiation, not only for the Jewish Diaspora, but also for other displaced ethnic groups.

In planning this book, I drew from a relatively limited body of work of comparative migration histories, including Samuel Baily's *Immigrants in the Lands of Promise: Italians in Buenos Aires and New York City, 1870 to 1914*, which provided a structural model for the presentation of my findings.[3] Since I first began writing *Cities of Refuge*, several important works have been published whose findings and methodologies enhance and complement my own. Deborah Dwork and R. J. van Pelt's *Flight from the Reich: Refugee Jews, 1933–1946* offers a far-reaching and thorough study of the migration of German-speaking Jews.[4] This comprehensive volume establishes a historical context for *Cities of Refuge* and serves as a useful companion to it, especially for readers new to the topic. The authors successfully balance the use of oral history interviews, memoirs, letters, and refugee newspapers in presenting a narrative-style overview of the global Jewish refugee experience. Nancy Foner's *In a New Land: A Comparative View of Immigration* has been influential in allowing me to rethink the theoretical goals and direction of this work.[5] Foner ties the theory and approaches of social scientists to the historical analyses of nineteenth- and twentieth-century immigration. She successfully applies the "divergent comparison model" that Nancy Green offers and discusses concepts of "transnationalism" and "intergenerational transmission of culture." It is necessary for historians to draw on interdisciplinary approaches to better research the complexities and nuances of migration processes. Judith Gerson studies German Jewish history through a sociological lens and uses the term *identity practices*, while Lisa Silverman uses *performing Jewishness*.[6] As scholars of immigration history, it is vital that our understanding of historical context and its relation to migration today allows us to actively contribute as historians to the dynamic field of migration studies.

Many people helped and inspired me during the writing of this book. I would like to offer my special thanks to several of them. First, I would like to recognize Kristine Wern of the Jewish Museum of Frankfurt for her early encouragement, assistance, and friendship. Long discussions with Kathleen Fish helped me focus my thoughts and begin the writing process. I am also appreciative of Pauline Von Hellerman, Andrea Hammel, Deborah Schultz, Lisa Silverman, Cathy Gelbin, and Polly Beals for lending an ear and allowing me to formulate my ideas aloud with them in the early stages of this work.

Sincere thanks are especially due to the archivists and staff at various institutes who provided practical support and pointed me in the direction of valuable sources. I am particularly appreciative of the assistance of Marie Luise Hahn of the Exilarchiv at the German National Library in Frankfurt, Diane Spielman and the amazing archivists at the Centre for Jewish History in New York, Karen Robson at the Parkes Institute at Southampton University, and Samira Teutenberg, formerly at the Centre for German-Jewish Studies, University of Sussex. The librarians and archivists at the Imperial War Museum, the Wiener Library, and the New York Public Library were also especially helpful.

This research would not have been possible without the consideration and support of the following organizations: the Leo Baeck Institute, *Deutscher Akademischer Austauschdienst* (German Academic Exchange Service or DAAD), the Anglo-Jewish Association, the Ian Karten Trust, the Jewish Federation of Greater New Haven, the University of Sussex Chancellor's International Research Scholarship, and the Centre for German-Jewish Studies. I am especially appreciative of the generosity and kindness of Lilo and Gerry Leeds and to all of the individuals who shared their personal and sometimes painful memories with me in interviews.

I would also like to thank Marion Kaplan, and the late Ruth Gay and Julius Carlebach for their insightful suggestions, advice, and guidance early in my research. I thank Professor Edward Timms, my dissertation advisor, for his patience, encouragement, and belief in my work from the beginning. This book would not have been possible without his support. I very much appreciate the suggestions made by my examiners Professors Tony Kushner and Paul Betts. They have greatly informed this manuscript. My copy editor, Allison Jones, has been extremely patient and thorough. Many thanks go to Allison Greif Rentschler, Moni Beck, Miriam Reumann, and Tara Botelho for reading through various versions of this text. Their friendship and suggestions have been greatly appreciated.

Even with the help and encouragement of all of these people, I would have had a hard time finishing any task without the loving support of my family. Meredith Gemeiner and Joe Del Grosso, Robyn and Matt Wapner, and my parents, Yvonne and Howard Gemeiner have been a continual source of encouragement and inspiration. My daughters, Eva Marlena and Rebecca Johanna, have added tremendous joy to my life, while providing a happy distraction. Finally, I would like to thank my husband, Hermann, for his constant belief in me and his steadfast humor through all stages of this work. I am truly grateful for his love, patience, and support. This book is dedicated to all of Elli and Otto's great-grandchildren.

Introduction

IN LATE 2001, I WAS LIVING IN Great Britain and meeting members of the aging German Jewish refugee community through my doctoral work at the Centre for German-Jewish Studies at the University of Sussex. These former refugees from Nazi Germany were actively engaged in preserving German Jewish history. In impeccable English, they asked pointed questions regarding my research, which was still in its infancy. I did not know to what degree they were representative of typical German Jews from London and the south of England. Yet, it was evident that they were different from the German Jewish refugees I knew in New York City. My personal experience with this population, up until this point, had consisted of childhood weekends spent with my refugee grandparents and their social circle in Washington Heights in Upper Manhattan. There, German was the primary language heard among refugees on the street, in parks, and in homes. The weekly Jewish newspaper, *Aufbau*, literally translated as "build up," was published almost exclusively in German. Refugee manners, appearance, and habits reflected the retention of German Jewish culture, even after decades of living in the United States.

The longer I spent among former refugees in London, the greater my sense grew that they appeared more British than the refugees in New York seemed American. Their dress, leisure activities, and home décor, in addition to language and accent, supported this observation. Intrigued, I poured through current and back issues of the *AJR Information*, the Association of Jewish Refugees newsletter that had been in print in London since 1946. The articles, classifieds, and advertisements confirmed my suspicion that after the war German Jewish refugees had established a uniquely British refugee community in London; one that was unlike Washington Heights and the other refugee enclaves in New York, on the Upper West Side of Manhattan, and in Forest Hills, Queens. I became focused on comparing the London and New York communities but knew I would have to look back to the 1930s, the early years of their flight from Nazi Germany, to fully understand how they came to appear so dissimilar from one another. This was the beginning of *Cities of Refuge*.

To appreciate the extent to which German Jewish lives were transformed in London and New York in the 1930s and 1940s, it is useful to briefly review the long history of Jews in German-speaking lands. Providing a straightforward narrative, however, is no easy task. Since the end of World War II, there have been extensive efforts to understand the ways German Jews balanced *Deutschtum,* roughly translated as "Germanness" and *Judentum,* "Jewishness," prior to the rise of Hitler. In memoirs, former refugees have insisted that their own families were "assimilated" or "integrated."[1] Some historians have described a "symbiotic" relationship between separate Jewish and German culture. Others have argued that a German Jewish "subculture" or a "parallel associational life" existed as a response to antisemitism.[2] It is only in the past twenty or so years, as the approaches of Cultural Studies and Gender Studies, in particular, have become more widely utilized by historians, that a more nuanced and richer picture of German Jewish experience has developed.[3] Scholars are reconsidering meanings of "Germanness," "Jewishness," "citizenship," and "normality" through close analyses of individual lives.[4] The result is a more wide-ranging, diverse understanding of the history of German Jews and their identities.[5] *Cities of Refuge* draws on these developments to uncover the new patterns of identity practices among German Jews in London and New York.[6]

Millennia of Jewish Life in German-speaking Lands

Archaeological evidence indicates that Jews arrived in Central Europe with the ancient Romans as early as the first century CE.[7] By the fourth century, Jewish settlements with synagogues and ritual baths existed alongside newly Christianized Germanic peoples on the Rhine River.[8] For the next thousand years, Jewish communities developed near trading centers such as Hamburg, Frankfurt, and Cologne. Medieval Jews were restricted in their employment and housing options. They engaged in money lending and trade with Christians, but lived, studied, and prayed among themselves.[9] On the whole, however, Jews maintained a relatively low-profile day-to-day existence in the Middle Ages, punctuated by episodes of antisemitic persecution. In the eleventh century, Jews were massacred by Crusaders in cities such as Worms and Mainz. Two hundred years later, Jews faced waves of antisemitism resulting in Jewish dress codes in some states that required the wearing of "Jew hats" by men or a yellow ring stitched onto their clothes. In cities such as Cologne and Trier, Jews lived in designated Jewish quarters.[10] Some ghettos were walled and gated like Frankfurt's *Judengasse* or "Jews Alley," where Jews had limited contact with Gentiles, outside of business interactions. Jewish communities often flourished in these quarters with their own newspapers, hospitals, and Yeshivas.[11] Hamburg and other Northern cities of the early modern era saw an influx of Sephardic Jews from Dutch and Belgian cities, whose ancestors had originally fled Spain in 1492. In the countryside, Jews tended to live in or on the outskirts of Christian villages, clustered with other Jewish families. Traditionally they engaged in the trade of cattle and textiles. Both urban and rural Jews remained active in commerce throughout the early modern period. Yet, they were still living on the margins and, on the whole, were prohibited from entering other professions.[12] It is estimated that by the mid-eighteenth century, three-fifths of Jews in German-speaking lands remained among the "poor classes."[13]

The Enlightenment of the eighteenth century and industrialization and urbanization in the nineteenth century transformed the social and political climate for Jews in German-speaking lands. By the 1830s, modern concepts of liberalism, citizenship, and secularism were embraced by a burgeoning German middle class. With a swiftly expanding and liberalized economy, Jews gained greater financial security and rose in social status. Along with the German Protestant and Catholic bourgeoisie, German Jews valued *Bürgertum,* "civic contribution" and *Bildung,* roughly translated as the "cultivation of secular culture," and participated in the development of a German liberal middle-class society.[14] Across the separate and competing German-speaking principalities, from Baden to Prussia, the idea of belonging to a greater German nation began to take hold. Efforts to create a unified and liberal Germany in the 1830s and 1840s overlapped with organized movements for Jewish emancipation. *Haskalah* or "Jewish Enlightenment" of the late-eighteenth and nineteenth century, was a Jewish intellectual movement that explored issues around reconciling Judaism with secularism.[15] *Haskalah* directly influenced the establishment of the *Wissenschaft des Judentums,* the scientific study of Judaism, the Reform Movement of Abraham Geiger, and the Modern Orthodox Movement led by Samson Raphael Hirsch, groups that were in support of emancipation for Jews.[16]

Germans of Jewish Descent:
Imperial Era, 1871–1914

In 1871, the German principalities were formally declared one nation under the reign of Wilhelm I, the former king of Prussia, who was now the emperor of Germany. Some liberal concessions were made, including the granting of universal male suffrage. Jews became citizens of this new nation with equal rights in the eyes of the law. The German Imperial Era began with the unification of Germany in 1871 and ended with the outbreak of World War I in 1914. With their newly acquired legal rights, Jewish small-business owners and tradespeople expanded their production and distribution of goods on a national and even global scale.[17] Between 1870 and 1920, 60 percent of Jews were living in cities. A small but significant number of Jews attended German universities. They could now enter previously prohibited professions such as law and medicine. Jews entered the growing German middle class. They strove for *Bildung,* an appreciation for German high culture in private and public life, while simultaneously preserving Jewish values and traditions within the home and community. As Robin Judd wrote, "*Bildung* appealed to many Jews because it transcended religious and national distinctions. Men of any background could achieve civil and moral betterment if they were familiar with a certain corpus of knowledge and exemplified ethical behavior."[18] Cultural signifiers such as dress, language, food, and décor expressed both German *Bildung* and Jewishness. Marion Kaplan illustrates in *The Making of the Jewish Middle Class: Women, Family, and Identity in Imperial Germany* how Jewish women played an integral role in shaping this culture.[19] She explores how wives, mothers, and daughters demonstrated loyalty to both the "Fatherland" and their Jewish heritage through everyday customs and rituals in the home. The finest furniture-filled homes, and bookcases lined with German classics, stood near mantels bearing silver menorahs and ceremonial candle holders. Daily meals were typical German fare, consisting of hot midday dishes and cold evening meals with dark bread. Kaplan estimates that approximately one-half of all Jewish homes kept Kosher, but did so within the framework of the German dining schedule. German standards of cleanliness and order were adhered to in Jewish homes. This was coordinated by the female head of household, with the employment of at least one domestic servant. Kaplan writes that for Jews, "Culture did not begin and end with the university or German classics. It included the creation of a model home life, a model family."[20] Kaplan also shows how

German Jewish women used parenting, household management, and leisure activities to maintain this balance between German *Bildung* and Judaism.

Dressing elegantly and in a refined manner emphasized one's social and financial standing, and helped gain respectability within the community. Yet, with their elegant clothes, they maintained a careful measure of understatement, some argue, to prevent antisemitic backlash.[21] German was the primary language spoken by middle-class Jews, and the use of Yiddish was discouraged. The newly formed *Liberale* synagogues had German-language sermons, texts, and prayer translations, and classical music was played. German first names such as Ludwig, Siegfried, and Liselotte were adopted by middle-class Jews, although obvious Christian names, such as Lukas and Maria, were avoided. Family names were more often, but not always, identifiable as Jewish.[22] Jewish social and cultural organizations and clubs proliferated. The leading umbrella organization representing Jews in Germany was called the Central Association of German Citizens of Jewish Faith.

World War I and the Weimar Republic: 1914–1933

Like their Christian compatriots, Jewish men served in the German army during World War I. More than one hundred thousand Jewish soldiers fought in the trenches against the Allied powers. An estimated twenty thousand German Jews were killed and another thirty thousand were decorated with military honors. Jewish participation in the Great War strengthened their loyalty and sense of belonging to the German nation.[23] With the establishment of the Weimar Republic, the first real modern democracy in German history, German Jews were members of a modern liberal nation-state made for and by its citizens.

Throughout the Weimar Era, Jews were well established in German trade and culture. There were Nobel Prize winners, prominent architects, and famous musicians among them. German Jewish families owned businesses of all sizes. Although most Jewish women focused on marriage and family, they had more educational and professional opportunities than ever before. Rates of Jewish-Christian intermarriage remained remarkably low. Out of 525,000 officially registered Jews in Germany, roughly 35,000 were in mixed marriages, or 6.6 percent. This statistic belies the prior accepted wisdom that Jews strove to assimilate wholesale as Germans and is supported by works on the "Jewish Renaissance" of the Weimar Era.[24]

Nazi Germany, 1933–1945

With the rise of Adolf Hitler and the National Socialist Party in January 1933, Jewish lives in Germany became severely restricted. Jews were systematically forced from their professions; Jewish-owned businesses were boycotted. By May 1933, Jewish migration out of Germany had begun. It is estimated that between 37,000 and 45,000 German Jews fled Germany in 1933.[25] The enactment of the Nuremberg Laws in 1935, which codified the antisemitic Nazi visions of "Germanness" and "Jewishness," rescinded the German citizenship of Jews. This prompted another wave of emigration. Jews were no longer officially German. By 1937, approximately 129,000 Jews had left Germany, out of an estimated pre-1933 population of 525,000. By paying high penalties, it was still possible for Jews to transfer money overseas prior to their departure. German Jewish men and women continued to pack furniture and family heirlooms in containers that were shipped to their destination countries.

On the evening of November 9, 1938, Nazis attacked Jewish communities throughout Germany in a pogrom they referred to as *Kristallnacht*, also known as the "Night of Broken Glass." They systematically destroyed 190 German synagogues, vandalized thousands of Jewish shops, and sent twenty thousand German Jewish men to concentration camps. In the days and weeks that followed, wives and mothers frantically sought visas from any country that would grant them.[26] Proof of emigration plans could expedite the release of a loved one. Foreign visa applications tripled between October 1938 and December 1938 and preparations to emigrate began on a massive scale.[27] Jewish communities and organizations across Germany offered classes in English, Spanish, and Hebrew. Training sessions in anticipated job skills such as sewing, plumbing, and farming were available. By 1939, Jews were permitted to transfer only ten *Reichsmark* out of Germany (equivalent to $150.00 today). In that year, an estimated 78,000 more Jews emigrated. In October 1941, the German government officially halted all Jewish emigration.[28]

Flight from Nazi Germany and the Challenge of Numbers

Despite the availability of immigration records, it has thus far been impossible to track the precise numbers and movement of German Jews around the world between 1935 and 1945. Nazi-maintained records of Jewish exit visa applications offer information on how many people tried to leave at any given time. In order to emigrate out of Germany, however, one needed to simultaneously hold a German exit visa and an entrance visa to another country. As has been explored by numerous historians, the number of immigration and transit visas granted to Jewish refugees by other nations was sharply restricted. Therefore, while hundreds of thousands of German Jews applied for exit visas, many were unable to actually leave Germany. Additionally, thousands of Jews left Germany on temporary student or tourist visas, only to reenter Germany within a year. By December 1939, desperate circumstances led to an unrecorded number of illegal entries and exits throughout the world with no official paper trails. Another difficulty in using Nazi records of emigration was that many refugees did not end up where they had initially planned to settle. In addition to looking at German emigration documents, historians have poured through immigration records of recipient countries. These also have proven to be limited in their use. For example, U.S. immigration visas were granted according to one's nation of origin, such as Germany or Poland, and not by religious affiliation. Germans and Austrians also were counted under one quota, making it difficult to differentiate nationalities between those immigrant records. Furthermore, it is possible to access the official number of German and Austrian immigrants in any given year, but not the percentage that were Jewish. Research conducted by Bat-Ami Zucker shows that U.S. consular staff in Germany were given some discretion in deciding who received or did not receive a U.S. visa.[29] Zucker also found significant evidence that antisemitism guided much of their decision making. Nevertheless, determining the precise number of German applicants who identified as Jewish remains elusive. As Louise London argues in *Whitehall and the Jews*, Britain willfully chose not to track the number of visas granted to refugees from Nazi Germany. She wrote, "The Home Office studiously avoided keeping its own statistics on the highly sensitive issue of Jewish immigration to Britain. This saved it from having to give precise answers to embarrassing questions asked in Parliament and the press about the numbers of Jewish refugees in the country."[30]

The best way thus far for historians to track the movement of German Jews has been to look at the number of visas granted per country, and then try to corroborate those with social service records, refugee organizations, and synagogue records. This, of course, excludes the significant number of refugees who neither sought formal assistance nor joined refugee-related groups. Historians could also examine ship manifests, and cross-check the names of people who traveled through more than one country. By 1940, evacuations, internment, and military service made it even more difficult to establish the precise number of German Jews in any one place at any given time. Today there remain significant discrepancies between the numbers of German Jewish refugees calculated by various historians, demographers, and sociologists. To settle these differences, one would have to trace the individual paths of each of the 525,000 Germans who self-identified as Jews in 1933, and those who were identified as being "racially" Jewish by the Nazis after 1933. This in itself would be a gargantuan and likely futile task. However, the burgeoning field of digital history has opened the door to the possibility of someday developing software to cull multiple archival databases, access the appropriate information, and then plot out the migration patterns of German Jews during the Nazi era. In the meantime, however, Louise London's figures appear to be the most thoroughly investigated and accurate.

The number of Jews fleeing Germany between 1933 and 1945, as researched by Louise London, breaks down as follows: 18,000 German Jews escaped to Shanghai, 140,000 to Palestine, 85,000 to Latin America, and 6,500 to Australia. Approximately 30,000 refugees fled to continental European countries such as France, Holland, and Italy, which were eventually occupied by Nazis. Another 20,000 moved east to their country of birth, mainly Poland. By 1945, approximately 250,000 German Jews had entered the United States and more than 80,000 entered the United Kingdom.[31] By war's end, approximately 5,000 Jews survived in hiding in Germany and another 14,000 lived discreetly with Christian spouses. As to the number of Jews from Germany killed in concentration and extermination camps, estimates range between 150,000 and 170,000.

Great Britain granted temporary asylum in the form of transit visas to tens of thousands of German-speaking Jews. According to the Association of Jewish Refugees' anniversary publication of 1951, Great Britain saved more Jewish lives than any other country in the year between the November 1938 *Kristallnacht* pogrom and the outbreak of war in September 1939.[32] Approximately 4,000 financially solvent German-speaking Jewish refugees arrived in Britain between 1933 and 1934.[33] Another two thousand refugees were assisted by the Academic Assistance Council, formerly the Society for the Protection of Science and Learning, which placed German-speaking scholars in positions at UK universities. Additionally, the Special Areas Act of December 1934 was designed to attract German entrepreneurs to poorer regions of Britain. This resulted in the establishment of 1,000 refugee firms outside of London that employed more than a quarter of a million British citizens by the war's end. Some affluent German Jews sent their children to boarding school in Britain in the prewar years. Approximately 20,000 German Jews arrived on domestic service visas between 1935 and 1938. Such permits were offered by the British government to bolster the shrinking service class in Britain. While the vast majority of these visas were allocated to women, a limited number of men also traveled to Britain as gardeners and cleaners. The children and spouses of domestic servants were not guaranteed entry into Britain.

After the Nazi pogrom of 1938, Britain accepted approximately 60,000 Jews from Germany. One-sixth of this cohort was from the children's transport program, also known as the *Kindertransport*. This quickly organized endeavor provided visas and housing for 10,000 German-speaking Jewish youth aged two to eighteen years old. After arriving by train into London, unaccompanied by parents, the children were placed in hostels, boarding schools, with foster families, and, on occasion, into the homes of distant relatives. Approximately one-half of the children remained in London, while the rest were sent to homes and schools across the country. The entry of *Kindertransport* children was contingent upon proof of financial resources for their care and eventual emigration out of Britain. The nondenominational organization *Movement for the Care of Children from Germany* and the *British Committee for the Jews of Germany* took full financial responsibility for them. It is estimated that 30,000 refugees emigrated out of Britain between 1933 and 1939, mostly to the United States and Palestine. This left approximately seventy thousand German-speaking Jews living in Britain at the outbreak of war; although five times more than that had applied for asylum, according to Louise London.[34] Until the end of World War II, visa recipients had no reason to believe that Britain would permit them to stay beyond the date stamped in their passports.

During the first four years of Nazi rule in Germany, the United States' annual quota of 25,000 immigration visas allocated to German and Austrian nationals combined remained woefully unfilled due to too few applicants. As reported in Steven Lowenstein's *Frankfurt on the Hudson*, only 535 refugees came to the United States from Germany in 1933, and roughly 2,310 followed in 1934.[35] American efforts to bring refugees to the United States included the work of the Emergency Committee in Aid of Displaced German Scholars which brought 300 German academics to the United States between 1934 and 1939. Proof of financial sustainability or an affidavit from a U.S. citizen was all that was required to obtain a visa. Under a special provision, one thousand German Jewish children were permitted unaccompanied entry into the United States, sponsored by the German-Jewish Children's Aid organization in collaboration with the Hebrew Sheltering Immigrant Aid Society (HIAS). The Wagner-Rogers Bill called for the entry and placement of an additional 20,000 refugee children in the United States, similar to the British *Kindertransport* program. The bill died before making it to the floor of Congress in February 1939, despite the support of first lady Eleanor Roosevelt.[36] By the end of 1938 an estimated 33,000 additional German-speaking refugees entered the United States. In 1943 the total number of German-born Jews living in the United States was close to 197,000. The majority held permanent resident immigration visas that carried few employment restrictions.[37]

Nonetheless, for many, the road to a new home in the United States was a long one. German Jews often spent months or even years in exile in places such as Cuba, the Dominican Republic, Shanghai, or Lisbon, awaiting the American affidavits and papers that would allow them entry to the United States. Some refugees who settled in Britain came via stints on the Continent, in countries such as France, Belgium, and Holland. Other Jews went directly from Germany to Britain, such as the *Kindertransport* children and those who arrived on domestic visas. In the immediate years after the war there was a reshuffling of German Jews on a global scale. This included German Jews in Great Britain who emigrated out of Britain again, as well as refugees in Shanghai, South America, the Caribbean Islands, and across the African continent, who left for the United States or Palestine after 1945.

London and New York as "Cities of Refuge"

Cities have traditionally been points of settlement for immigrants, yet only a few historians have compared studies of migration patterns across multiple cities. In *Migrants, Emigrants, and Immigrants: A Social History*, Colin Pooley noted, "through the work of local historians, we know something about migration into particular villages or small towns, but we know much less about migration into and out of large towns and cities and very few studies have made a genuine attempt to compare different places and time periods."[38] Over the past decade, sociologists and anthropologists have developed new theoretical constructs for investigating the role of urban life on processes of migration. For example, the concept of translocal communities recognizes the mobility of immigrants in cities. It sees houses of worship and social clubs as communal spaces, at the same time that their members lived dispersed throughout a city. A translocal approach looks beyond the traditional concept of immigrant "ghettos," while drawing on urban studies scholarship of "unbounded" communities.[39]

As of yet, nothing has been published that focuses entirely on either New York or London as places of refuge for German Jews. Steven Lowenstein's *Frankfurt on the Hudson: The German-Jewish Community of Washington Heights, 1933–1983* centers on a particular neighborhood in New York, and Marion Berghahn's aforementioned *Continental Britons* was based on interviews with refugees across Great Britain.[40] A limited number of comparative studies of immigrants in New York and London exist, such as A. C. Godley's book, *Jewish Immigrant Entrepreneurship in London and New York, 1880–1914: Enterprise and Culture*, Nancy Foner's article, "West Indians in New York City and London: A Comparative Analysis," Andrew Reutlinger's article, "Reflections on Anglo-American Jewish Experience: New York and London, 1870–1914," and Selma Berrol's *East Side / East End*.[41] Although these works consider different periods of immigration and ethnic groups from *Cities of Refuge*, they are useful in providing ways of comparing London and New York as host cities. Moreover, they provide a historical context for immigrant experiences there.

Due to certain common traits, New York and London are ideal cities for comparison. They both experienced an influx of tens of thousands of German Jewish refugees between 1933 and 1941 and the subsequent development of immigrant networks and neighborhoods.[42] Many of the refugees came from German urban centers such as Berlin, Frankfurt, Hamburg, and Cologne. It is not surprising that they would initially relocate to another city.[43] Additionally, because London and New York were perceived as "Western" metropolises, they may have seemed more familiar to the refugees than the "exotic" cities of Shanghai, Buenos Aires, and Jerusalem. The use of English in the United States and Great Britain eliminated a potential unfair advantage one city may have had over the other in terms of language. The fact that both countries were predominately Christian, as had been the case in Germany, also affected identity development. Additionally, comparable social, religious, professional, and political organizations created by German Jews in both cities continue to function today, such as the Association of Jewish Refugees in London and Selfhelp in New York. Their newsletters and newspapers offer primary source material that might not have been as accessible in more temporary locations. The fact that German Jews continued to live in these cities into the twentieth century adds to their desirability as areas of study.

A Comparative Approach

Nancy Green deftly explains why a comparative approach to migration studies is imperative. First, she writes that the very nature of the immigrant experience is inherently a comparative one. For most, it entails a constant contrast of past life to present that can be recognized and utilized by practitioners of migration studies. Second, comparison allows one to explore the universals inherent in the refugee process. For example, formation of informal networks and the readjustment of family dynamics are often presented as processes unique to a particular group, when in fact they are not. Case studies provide the necessary details of a distinct migration. Yet, the comparative approach places those migrations within a broader context, one that presents opportunities for further analysis and insight. Third, it leads to a more analytical, rather than descriptive, investigation, thereby giving migration history a more "scientific" edge.[44] In her work, *In a New Land: A Comparative View of Immigration*, Nancy Foner explores the many new approaches to comparative immigration studies across time and place.[45] *Cities of Refuge* is informed by similar comparative immigrant histories, such as Samuel Baily's *Immigrants in the Lands of Promise* and Selma Berrol's *East Side / East End*.[46] Both books are structural studies of employment, education, and demographics, and have challenged the widely accepted notion of the United States as a "melting pot," particularly at the turn of the twentieth century.[47] As mentioned in the Preface, these works are similar to my own, in that they compare a single migrant population from one country of origin that settled in New York City and another comparable city. They employ a useful design that fits Nancy Green's idea of "divergent" comparisons, those that look at one original population in two different settings.[48] These tend to focus on cities as points of comparison, rather than whole nation-states or national policies. *Cities of Refuge*, however, compares immigrant experiences in two places against the backdrop of Nazi Germany and World War II, broader contextual factors that significantly shaped processes of integration, cultural adaptation, and identity practices. This work is unique in that it reveals an unexpected discrepancy in cultural integration and identity development. Namely, it asks why German Jews in London felt pressure to appear British but did not self-identify as such, while, at the same time, German Jews in New York looked and sounded German Jewish, but identified as American. It considers the role of broader national policy as well as more localized employment and housing opportunities in both settings.

Another advantage to the comparative approach is that it can potentially shift paradigms in the field of Jewish history. Werner Mosse notes that comparison "can throw light on the interaction between internal Jewish developments and external factors. . . . A regional pattern can be superimposed on what is often an overly Judeo-centric approach, while at the same time national compartmentalization can be transcended."[49] Although case studies of specific Jewish communities are critical, comparative research recognizes that the Diaspora transforms over time and place. It questions traditionally held beliefs; in particular, national stereotypes. A comparative approach identifies the factors underlying assumptions about absolute specificity and uniqueness of particular Jewish groups or regions, such as Sephardim and Ashkenazi or Eastern European and German Jews. One particular comparative study, Rainer Liedtke's *Jewish Welfare in Hamburg and Manchester, c. 1850–1914* provides a useful theoretical framework for *Cities of Refuge*.[50] In this work, Liedtke analyzes the historical development of self-formed Jewish welfare organizations in these two cities. In doing so, Liedtke addresses broader questions of how Jews perceived their place in British and German society and the external and internal factors that affected this. It does not, however, focus on two immigrant populations.

Research on diasporas continues to flourish in the fields of sociology and anthropology. This work is inherently comparative in nature. For example, Donna Gabbaccia's *Italy's Many Diasporas* was one of the first to apply social scientific concepts of diaspora and transnationalism to the study of historical Italian immigrant networks.[51] A challenge for historians who compare immigrant groups is in quantifying rates of cultural adaptation and identity formation. These processes are, by nature, fluid and dependent on multiple variables as described earlier in the introduction.

In this book, I have deliberately veered away from traditional notions of wholesale assimilation. Rather, the terminology and language used here outlines the myriad ways in which German Jews retained, relinquished, and practiced their culture and identities. The emergence of this critical theoretical approach by historians of Jewish history allows for recognition of the transience, complexity, and subjectivity of migration processes. Discourse around identity practice and performance are now being applied to the concepts of "Jewishness" and "Otherness" in the same way that gender has become a theoretical framework for analysis.[52]

German Jewish Refugees as a Subject of Study

Since the flight of German Jewish refugees began in 1933, scholarship on this cohort has been prolific. Sociological studies out of Columbia University were published as early as the 1930s and 1940s.[53] Social service organizations and governmental committees also produced research findings with titles such as *Refugees in America: Report for the Committee for the Study of Recent Immigration from Europe* and *Experiences, Problems, and Attitudes of German-Jewish Refugees*.[54] Beginning in the 1950s, a steady stream of books came out that focused on prominent refugee groups. A sampling of well-known titles includes: *Illustrious Immigrants: The Intellectual Migration from Europe*; *Exiled in Paradise: German Refugee Artists and Intellectuals in America from the 1930s*; *Hitler's Gift: Scientists Who Fled Nazi Germany*; and *Jurists Uprooted: German-speaking Émigré Lawyers in Twentieth-Century Britain*.[55]

A body of scholarship has developed around the everyday experiences of the tens of thousands of so-called "typical" refugees. These studies differ from the previous group in that they closely examine the obstacles, both material and emotional, faced by immigrants.[56] Some research focuses on children and young adults, including studies of the *Kindertransport* program.[57] Case studies have been published on German Jewish refugee communities in locations across the globe, including the Dominican Republic, Bolivia, Brazil, Shanghai, Zambia, India, Australia, New York City, and upstate New York.[58] Nation-based studies of German Jewish refugees in Switzerland, Canada, Australia, France, Turkey, and Ireland have critically evaluated their immigration policies and governmental procedures.[59] Each nation that accepted refugees provided a unique set of conditions influencing identity practices including: national immigration policies, employment opportunities and prohibitions, and their proximity to and level of engagement in World War II. *Cities of Refuge* directly compares how these broader external factors affected German Jews in London and New York.

A historiographic debate has developed among scholars of refugee history in Great Britain, which needs to be considered in this transatlantic study. In *Remembering Refugees*, historian Tony Kushner raises serious concerns about the presentation of refugees in historical accounts.[60] Kushner maintains that scholars should apply a more critical and less "celebratory" approach to their study of past and present refugees in Britain. He argues that while there is value in recognizing the contributions of the mid-century European Jewish refugees to British culture, it is vital that historians avoid the pitfalls of wholly embracing Britain's national narrative of the United Kingdom as a historical place of asylum. In his own expansive body of work, Kushner has been unafraid to expose the antisemitism and xenophobia faced by Jewish immigrants throughout Britain's history.[61] Anthony Grenville has taken another tack. He is the author and editor of numerous publications, such as *The Experience and Achievement of German-speaking Exiles from Hitler in Britain, 1933 to Today* and *Jewish Refugees from Nazi Germany and Austria in Britain, 1933–1970: Their Image in AJR Information*.[62] In 2002, Grenville wrote that "the current preoccupation of historians and social scientists with attitudes to race and racial prejudice in Britain has led some academics to create what seems to me almost a counter-myth, projecting the tensions arising from Britain's transition to a multi-racial society back onto the history of the Jewish refugees from Hitler and systematically downplaying or even ignoring anything positive in the interaction between Britain and the Continental Jews."[63] The tendency in Britain for former refugees to express gratitude toward Britain in their memoirs and interviews is obvious. Yet, as Kushner indicates, it is imperative that historians of German Jewish refugees do not present this group as immune to the prejudices normally experienced by refugee populations. This cohort struggled in both Britain and the United States. As evidenced in their own testimony, they were not "welcomed with open arms," yet they had positive experiences in both London and New York. Rather than attempting to evaluate the motivations and accomplishments (or lack thereof) of the American and British Jewish communities to assist European refugees, I strive to compare the refugees' own perceptions of their integration in each city and their understandings of nation and its meaning in the United States and Great Britain in a time of war.

Debórah Dwork and Robert Jan van Pelt's *Flight from the Reich: Refugee Jews, 1933–1948* is the most comprehensive work to date on the fate of German Jewish refugees.[64] The authors successfully acknowledge refugee achievements while critically analyzing the obstacles they encountered in Germany and around the globe. Methodologically, Dwork and van Pelt draw on a diverse range of sources including oral history testimony, memoirs, letters, and refugee newspapers. As stated in the preface, *Flight from the Reich* offers a broader historical context to the more narrow scope of this comparative study of German Jews in London and New York. In her 2003 article on her own personal connections to the community, Atina Grossmann observed that there is an ever-expanding body of German Jewish personal papers, such as letters, diaries, and other memorabilia, filling the archives of institutions around the world.[65] In recent years much of this has been digitized and made available online. This has become a treasure trove for historians. Hopefully, as worldwide archives synchronize their collection of metadata, many more avenues of investigation will open to historians of German Jewry.

The findings in this book come from a careful analysis of a wide range of sources. It draws on the archived collections of thirty-four individual refugees, including hundreds of letters, ten diaries, and more than twenty mostly unpublished memoirs archived in Britain, the United States, and Germany. Refugee publications such as *Aufbau, AJR Information*, and the Free German Cultural League's *FDKB Nachrichten*, and the documents and records of refugee and government organizations have been extremely useful. In addition, I conducted ten interviews with former refugees who had written unpublished memoirs, diaries, or articles. The ongoing discourse over the meaning and use of survivor/refugee testimony is part of an entire subfield on memory and the Holocaust.[66] My approach to refugee testimony is grounded in a consciousness of this dialogue. It would be wrong to assume that distinct collective refugee experiences existed in London and New York. Rather, I look for patterns that arise in the content and language of individual testimony on both sides of the Atlantic. I find myself nodding my head in agreement with Judith Gerson, when she writes,

> Although I initially treat each memoir as a case, I also am interested in aggregate patterns—something one can only discern by comparing these memoirs to one another. What at first appears to be an individual experience or reaction may also prove an illustration of a more generalizable pattern. Thus the most obvious form of comparison I rely on when reading these memoirs is contrasting them with each other. Closely related to this form of comparison is my reading of them with a larger socio-historical context.[67]

In the same way, my analysis of interviews, memoirs, diaries, letters, organizational documents, and newspapers reveals clear differences in identity practices and performance of German Jewish refugees in these two cities. It shows how specific policies and perceptions of the host countries affected this.[68] Distinct and divergent patterns arise. Refugee testimony of everyday life in London differs markedly from testimony in New York. German Jews were forced under the Nazi regime to rethink their identity as Germans of Jewish descent. It is the subsequent practices of German Jewish identity development and cultural adaptation in Great Britain and the United States that are the focus of *Cities of Refuge*.

1

Arrival and Settlement

BETWEEN 1935 AND 1939, MOST Jewish refugees en route to Great Britain or the United States fled Germany by rail to major European cities, such as Paris and Amsterdam, or by steamship from Hamburg. Once immigration papers and ship tickets were obtained, a process that could take weeks or months, they would depart on the next leg of their journey from ports such as Lisbon, Antwerp, or LeHavre. Refugee accounts of first impressions upon arrival in London and New York reveal some of the differences in expectations in both cities, and the host nations.

Most German Jews arriving in Britain disembarked at Harwich, and the sight of the White Cliffs of Dover evoked a sense of relief for some. C. C. Aronsfeld wrote, for example:

> I landed in England on 19 May 1933 at Parkeston Quay, Harwich. It was a somewhat drab and prosaic sight, and the first human being I espied happened to be a policeman, but to me the view seemed hardly less bright, romantic and dramatic than the White Cliffs of Dover on which my mind saw emblazoned the word *Freedom*. "Freedom all solace to man giffith"—this 14th-century poem was among the earliest I had learnt, and now I came in search of the reality.[1]

Another wrote, "It is very hard to describe our feelings of happiness and liberty when the chalk cliffs of Dover came in sight."[2] Also common among refugee accounts, however, were laments on the British weather. An interviewee at the Museum of London recalled, "England for me in my mind as a child was always something that was drab, grey, and foggy and wet. . . . I was not particularly happy or keen about going to England. Sure enough, when we arrived at Southampton on the 10th of March 1939, it was grey and musty and wet, and expectations were fulfilled."[3] A refugee child's father wrote, "On 30 December 1938 at 8pm, Marianne with her Mummy and Daddy arrived in Harwich port, and on this day we had found our new home . . . the arrival in England was not very pleasant. It was a cold, rainy, windy December evening."[4]

Of the European refugees who arrived in the United States between 1933 and 1941, it is estimated that 90 percent landed in New York harbor. They docked on the banks of the Hudson River on ocean liners such as the *Queen Mary* and the *Normandie*, disembarking at Hoboken Pier, the 46th Street Pier, Staten Island, or, on occasion, at Ellis Island. Refugees landing in the United States chronicled these first moments using powerful language, laden with drama and emotion. One wrote, "We were bursting with anticipation, curiosity, and emotion, glued to the ship's railing . . . people around us were shouting, pointing out again and again the Statue of Liberty."[5] This symbol of freedom and discussions of liberty, appeared frequently in refugee accounts. Another remembered that she "stood in awe of that great symbol of freedom," and claimed that the passengers on her ship cheered at the sight of it, while a woman sang the *Star Spangled Banner* as it came into view.[6] The Manhattan skyline also elicited awe. A teenage refugee wrote, "Coming into New York harbor was the most amazing sight I had ever seen. A setting red winter sun outlined the skyscrapers of downtown Manhattan to make them appear to us like the most enormous fairy castle in the world." Similarly, another remembered, "The excitement was immense. The Manhattan skyscrapers seemed magnificent. It was a sight I shall never forget."[7] A young woman described the promise this sight elicited: "We were spellbound by the view of Manhattan, by the zig zag of its tall buildings up against a clear golden afternoon sky. Hope for a happy, active future welled up in us."[8] The expanse of electric lights over New York City surprised the newcomers. Gerhard Saenger wrote in his 1947 study, *Today's Refugees, Tomorrow's Citizens*, that the refugees "were amazed at the flood of light in the city, unequalled in Europe, even before the war's blackout."[9] Walter Baum, a young refugee, recalled of his arrival in 1938, "As we approached the lower bay of New York harbor, we began to see lights along the shore and when we reached the upper bay and our anchoring place near Ellis Island, the lights of Brooklyn, Staten Island, and the tip of Manhattan seemed to form a festive garland welcoming us to a New World and a new 'City of Lights.'"[10] Baum's use of the term *New World* was poignant. This moniker took on a double meaning for the refugees of the 1930s. The New World meant more than a break from the traditional "Old World" of Europe. For many, this distant, foreign, and exciting land represented a new beginning. They had fled the stifling Nazi racially defined nation of Germany to enter what they perceived to be the ideal "melting pot" nation-state of the United States of America. German Jewish refugees swiftly inserted themselves into the historical narrative of American immigration. One woman described the first few moments upon arrival being "like thousands of immigrants before us—[taking in] the first sights of the New World."[11] Lilly Friedmann recalled, "The journey lasted five days, and because I knew we would enter a new world, a totally different life and environment, I was determined to make the most of those five days."[12] Rabbi Manfred Swarensky remembered, "Everyone was joyful or at least full of expectations. Now we were in America! For every Jew in Germany today has this image, like a gate to salvation, the harbor to heaven, the way to the final liberty."[13]

There are various possibilities why refugee accounts of arrival in the United States used more emotionally powerful language than those in Great Britain, which go beyond the usual tropes about America as the land of immigration. First, in the collective imagination of early-twentieth-century Germans, the United States represented immigration and economic opportunity and was home to many supposedly successful "uncles in America." It may also have had something to do with the fact that they held permanent immigrant visas, rather than transit ones. Second, refugees who arrived in British ports such as Harwich or Southampton may have missed particular symbolic sites, such as the White Cliffs of Dover, if they arrived at night or under heavy fog. The British harbors might not have appeared as strikingly different from their own ports of departure. New York's harbor was particularly unique in its appearance, with the Statue of Liberty and the skyscrapers. There is also little description of arrival into London proper. Perhaps the atmosphere of railway stations such as Liverpool Street, Kings Cross, and Victoria was not notably different from the *Hauptbahnhöfe*, or main train stations, of Frankfurt and Berlin. Third, while separated by the English Channel, Britain was still part of Europe. For many refugees, it remained too close to Hitler. Great Britain provided immediate escape from Nazi control for those arriving between 1933 and 1937. By 1938, however, Hitler had invaded sovereign nations outside of Germany. After the fall of Paris in June 1940, the possibility of a Nazi invasion of England seemed all too real. Additionally, the thousands of miles between Germany and the United States may have brought a greater sense of security for many German Jews arriving in New York. The journey across the Atlantic, ranging between five days and three weeks, signified a solid break from Europe, and their first impressions reflect this. German Jews in the United States were more likely to have spent months or even years in places such as Havana, Shanghai, or Lisbon awaiting their American affidavits and papers. The time between leaving Germany and arriving in New York was long and full of anticipation.[14] Lastly, German Jewish refugees in Britain held "for transit only" visas that severely limited employment opportunities and their hope of a permanent settlement. As many as 21,000 refugees in Britain had plans to emigrate once more to the United States, Palestine, or elsewhere before the outbreak of war halted this. Most German Jews arriving in New York, on the other hand, held permanent immigration visas that would culminate in U.S. citizenship.

Other more internal and perhaps subconscious perceptions affected their accounts of their first impressions. While some refugees in Britain recalled feeling relief to be out of Nazi Germany, the majority of descriptions did not reveal the same sense of belonging to a greater historical tradition of immigration, as reflected in the accounts of New York arrivals. Britain had, and still has, a notable history as a sanctuary for persecuted peoples. It did not, in the 1930s and early 1940s, hold the same weight as a place of refuge as the United States did for German Jews. I believe this discrepancy comes from a subconscious set of beliefs around the type of nations the refugees perceived Great Britain and the United States to be. Compared to Germany, Britain had a long and established history as a nation of liberal ideals with a representative Parliament and a constitutional monarchy. There still seemed to be traces of the belief among refugees that being British, and even more so being English, was somehow racially defined. The fact that the nation's religion was officially the Church of England may have further reinforced this sense of exclusion.

The melting pot narrative of the United States matched nicely with the concept of the United States as a political nation-state of citizens. At this time, German Jews in the United States could embrace the narrative of "liberty and justice for all." The American belief in "separation of church and state" contributed to the feeling that being Jewish would not interfere in their ability to become American. Antisemitism certainly persisted in 1930s and 1940s American society. There were arenas where Jews were not welcome.[15]

There were refugees who did not like living in New York City. Laqueur described that some refugees reported feeling overwhelmed by New York City and were eager to leave as soon as possible. Some returned to Europe, others moved to California or upstate New York. The majority of German Jews who arrived in New York, however, remained there until the conclusion of the war, some as long as fifty years.

Early Accommodation

Hotels, hostels, and bedsits throughout London provided temporary lodging for newly arrived German Jews. Reservations could be arranged prior to arrival by post or through a contact in Britain. Rooms had sparse furnishings with limited or no cooking facilities. Guests were fed breakfast and dinner by the hotel or hostel kitchen staff, taking meals downstairs with other tenants. The rooms were often cold and the shared bathrooms lacked privacy. Refugee-frequented hotel lobbies reportedly had a social atmosphere—the conversations were in German and centered on the worsening situation in Germany. Alice Schwab wrote that she took her father "to that lovely hostel in Wimbledon Parkside, where he was very well received by the other refugees. . . . I remember going there on Sunday afternoons, when lectures were given by people who had just come out of Germany, providing us with the latest information."[16] In her autobiographical novel *The Other Way Round*, Judith Kerr wrote that the hostel they stayed in was filled with German, Austrian, and other Central European refugees, which she believed helped ease her parents' transition.[17] The range of individual experiences in these hostels varied. One refugee wrote that when her parents arrived, they all "lived for three weeks in a hostel in London's East End—a horror that is unforgettable. So much unhappy humanity in one place, no one caring about anyone else—someone even stole two of our suitcases and we had arrived with little enough."[18] In addition, refugee hotels and hostels were not especially conducive to integration into British life. Refugees there had minimal contact with "real" English people in their first few months after arrival.

Most of the ten thousand refugee children who arrived in Britain between 1938 and September 1939 through the *Kindertransport*—literally translated as "children's transport"—program were met by relatives, foster parents, or organizational representatives at Liverpool Street Station.[19] Roughly half of them remained in London, finding temporary accommodation in hostels such as the Refugee Boys Hostel at Minster Road, Woodberry Down Hostel of North London, and the Jews' Temporary Shelter in Mansell

Street. Hostels in Hackney, Tylers Green, Shoot-up Hill, Cricklewood, and Turnbridge Wells also appear frequently in *Kindertransport* accounts.[20] Some children entered English boarding schools outside of London, if their parents or the refugee assistance program could arrange for it in advance.

Refugees in the United States were greeted at the New York piers by either relatives, organizational representatives from HIAS (Hebrew Sheltering Immigrant Aid Society), or the German-Jewish Children's Aid Organization, who had arranged for temporary housing in charity hostels, shelters provided by HIAS, or children's homes. Gerhart Saenger wrote in 1941:

> Some of them are housed temporarily in the "Congress Houses" or other shelters maintained by charitable organizations, many of which are situated in midtown or downtown Manhattan near the docks. Here they are taken care of without cost over a period of four weeks, until they can find some place to go and other means of support. Since all guests in these houses are refugees, the atmosphere is distinctly European, and a part of the old homeland reaches into the new life.[21]

Refugee hostels/shelters in London and New York served similar purposes: to provide temporary accommodation and to allow newly arrived refugees to meet one another. Roughly one-quarter of the one thousand children brought to the United States by the German-Jewish Children's Aid Organization found accommodation in New York City. Greeted by women from the organization, most refugee children were given a period of "reception care" immediately upon arrival, before being sent to a foster family or group home. Some of these thousand children stayed at the George Washington Hotel on Lexington Avenue.[22] In a period of a few days, they received medical attention and an opportunity to find their "land legs" with the other children. They were then placed either with relatives, Jewish foster families, or in temporary housing, such as the Clara De Hirsch Home, the Gould Foundation, the Hebrew Orphans Asylum, or the Pleasantville College School.[23]

Other refugees found early accommodation in upscale hotels such as the Barbizon, the Salisbury, and the Forrest Hotel, and less expensive hotels, such as Hotel Paris.[24] In some cases, refugees landing in New York were met by relatives or friends, who provided temporary shelter within the five boroughs of New York City. Inge Heiman recalled that upon arrival, she went to the apartment of her great aunt: "She had a very small apartment and Edgar lived with her, but she took the four of us in anyway. My aunt, Bertha, my mother, and I slept in one bed; my father and my brother,

Walter, slept on a couch and my uncle, Edgar Marx, slept on a cot in the hall."[25] Walter Baum wrote, "Those first days in New York were an adventure. Rose and her husband, Jack, with whom I would stay, lived in the far reaches of the East Bronx, on Castle Hill Avenue, where small-town looks predominated and only the El reminded you of the connection to a great metropolis."[26] Living with relatives did not guarantee a pleasant experience. Ilse Gutman, arriving alone as a teenager, was poorly treated by an uncle who, after two days, sent her to an orthodox Jewish family to be a nanny for six children.[27] Temporary quarters with relatives were often cramped. Most new arrivals in New York and London sought their own accommodations as quickly as possible.

Refugee Enclaves: London

After brief stays in London hotels and hostels, and the requisite visit to the local police station, the majority of German Jews deliberately sought housing in the Northwest London area of Hampstead and Swiss Cottage. They were drawn to the quaint streets, which reminded them of German middle class residential districts, such as Berlin's Grünewald and Tiergarten. Many German Jews chose to live in oneroom bedsits and shared flats in order to remain in this part of London. Werner Rosenstock wrote in *Britain's New Citizens* in 1951, "Though most of them arrived without means, they could not forget their middle-class background and preferred a bedsitting room with a gas ring in a more or less 'bourgeois' neighborhood to less expensive but roomier accommodation in other parts of London."[28]

The early twentieth century saw an influx of Jewish immigrants from Eastern Europe and Russia, who settled in the East End of London. They spoke Yiddish, were active in the labor movement, identified as working class. Meanwhile, the more-established middle-class Jewish community lived in Northwest London. The tensions between the two communities are explored in Miri Freud-Kandel's book on orthodox Jewry in Britain.[29] Mirroring the tensions between *Ostjuden*, Eastern European Jews, and German Jews that existed in Germany, it is not surprising that in the 1930s and 1940s most refugees identified with the middle-class West End Jews and chose to settle in their neighborhoods. One refugee organization's newspaper, *FDKB Nachrichten* (*FDKB* is an abbreviation of *Freier Deutscher Kulturbund* or "Free German Culture League"; *Nachrichten* means "news"), advertised accommodations throughout the 1930s and 1940s. A typical advertisement for accommodations in the *FDKB* newsletter read, "comfy living/sleeping room that includes lunch and dinner, near Belsize Park and Swiss Cottage," using the more upscale northwest London neighborhoods as a selling point.[30]

Rented rooms and bedsits in London provided basic utilities in tight quarters. Ilse Jacoby described her furnished room in Northwest London: "It had a gas ring for cooking and a basin with running hot and cold water, which served as our bath, sink, and washtub for our clothes. There were a lot of refugees living in similar circumstances. . . . I borrowed only a few dishes, silverware, and cooking utensils, because I had no place for storage." When having guests, seating was limited and she "pushed the gate leg table to the bed, where two of us could sit. Then we had a big trunk, which served as seating for two more, and an armchair provided another seat. We managed."[31] One young woman recalled, "My parents set me the example for survival and adaptation by making the best of things. If they could tolerate sharing a house and bathroom with strangers, then so could I."[32] Another refugee remembered that after a stay in a temporary hostel,

> We found a furnished room and in July of that year we were able to bring my brother over from Holland. Our landlady allowed my brother to stay on the understanding that he cleans the house every Friday. Often, that first winter, we sat in my

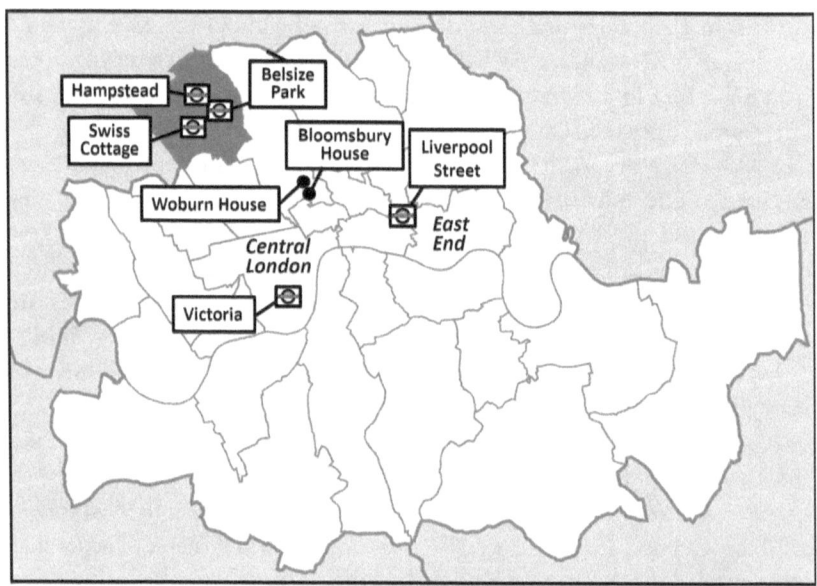

Map 1.1. Greater London, Borough of Hampstead (shaded in dark gray).

parents' bed to keep warm. Every week my father queued up at Woburn House for his week's allowance, which often ran out before more money was due. But we were happy, we were free, we were together, we were human again.[33]

By the 1930s, many Victorian single family homes in London had been divided into rentable flats. This concept was unfamiliar to refugees who had lived in single family homes or predesigned apartment blocks in German cities and towns. The bedsits and flats of the Northwest neighborhoods had hardly retained the look or form of the original structure. Gabriele Tergit thought her fellow German Jews got a false impression of British life by living in these rooms. She wrote:

> The refugees took a furnished room in Hampstead, one room, that is, for the whole family; if they were lucky they had water in the room, if unlucky it was on the landing. They put their books on Victorian sideboards; one paper lampshade hung down in the middle of the room. Divans represented a better class than beds. Many rooms had little gas cookers and wash basins and shelves for china and cutlery concealed in a cupboard; the cheaper ones had only a gas-ring near the fireplace on which to cook. They shared a bathroom with a dozen people. The rooms were cold, the fireplaces a mystery. They did not know how to lay a fire. . . . They got a distorted picture of English life. They compared the comfort of their former middle-class flat with their wretched makeshift standard. Some, of course, learnt that draughty windows and unheated homes were no yardstick for a civilization, that their bed-sitting room had, in former times, been one of the living rooms of a one-family house, that the English have kitchens for cooking and not gas rings in sitting rooms.[34]

Refugee domestics often lived in servants' quarters at their place of employment. Given second-class English food and basic accommodations, they were exposed to the class disparity of Britain. While they learned the proper way to make tea, they did not have the chance to genuinely adopt British ways beyond the role of maid or nanny. In his article on refugee domestics, historian Tony Kushner wrote, "The nature of domestic service, which depended on the absolute division of employer and servant, denied the refugee domestic the basic requirements to adjust to normal society."[35]

Of course, the range of experiences varied and while some were treated solely as employees, others were considered part of the family. Elli Bickart, for example, lived as a maid with a Jewish family that provided piano lessons for her and allowed her free time to socialize with other young refugees.[36] Living in British households, even as servants, they experienced more British culture than unemployed refugees living in hostels. Live-out domestics stayed in bedsits, boarding houses, or in specially designated domestic refugee hostels. Kushner also noted, "In the cities several hostels were set up by Bloomsbury House for refugee domestics looking for work. Regulations were harsh, training compulsory and stay . . . limited to six weeks maximum."[37] While they lived among fellow refugees, they were encouraged to adopt British ways. Between 1938 and 1939, refugee domestics overwhelmingly requested postings in London. Kushner and Katharine Knox point out in *Refugees in the Age of Genocide* that the national refugee organizations and the Home Office focused on dispersing the refugee women throughout Britain, perhaps in order to draw less attention to them and to stave off antisemitism. The domestics, however, often wanted to remain in London to have greater access to fellow refugees and to be closer to national offices where they could try to obtain the proper papers to bring family over from Germany.[38] The lure of London was great for many refugees, whose displacement was eased by social and familial ties with one another.

A smaller number of refugees found accommodation in the East End of London with distant relatives, foster parents, or at the Jews' Temporary Shelter at 63 Mansell Street. Here they found themselves immersed in a Jewish neighborhood that had been established by East European immigrants two generations earlier. They saw Hebrew letters spelling Yiddish words on the newsstands and on storefronts. Their hosts kept Kosher and celebrated the Sabbath. For some, this was more exposure to Jewish traditions than they had had in Germany. The look of residential East London was also unfamiliar to many young German refugees. Housing in the East End contrasted sharply with most middle-class Jewish homes in Germany. *Kindertransport* children in London, prior to evacuations, were sometimes placed with foster families in the East End. Charles Leigh, for example, recalled:

> I was quickly introduced to my foster parents, Mr. and Mrs. Burns, who then showed me to my room in the basement of the building. It was dark, and when I started to go down the steps something suddenly jumped past me, frightening the life out of me. It was a black cat that belonged to the household.

My first impression of my new home didn't please me one bit, especially as I had never seen a basement before, and the whole experience gave me the creeps.[39]

A girl who arrived through the *Kindertransport* program described her first impression of her new neighborhood:

The road we lived in, Plashet Road, was a very very long terraced houses road, they all looked alike which was something that I couldn't understand at all. Rows and rows of houses that all looked alike, little front gardens, and it was very strange. That was one of the strangest things that struck me about London; all these streets that looked the same and all very similar, and all these rows and rows and rows of little houses, which is quite unknown on the Continent. . . . And I suppose that's why London was so terribly spread out, because every family's aim was to have a house of their own and a garden, which was completely new to me. No, I can't say I liked it very much; I found it a bit depressing.[40]

In the East End, people lived in close quarters, living spaces tended to be cramped, and as Walter Laqueur wrote in *Generation Exodus,* there was no central heating and indoor toilets were not found in working-class neighborhoods.[41] One *Kindertransport* child wrote:

As a girl of fourteen, I was taken in by a family in the East End of London. Looking back now I realize that they were very kind, generous, and well-meaning people. At the time it was for me rather shattering. They lived in a tiny terrace house in a dreadful little road. There was a workroom at the back where some sort of tailoring work was done. There was no bathroom and I shared a bed with one of the daughters. We washed in the sink in the kitchen or went to a public bath. I had never seen such conditions and so felt rather awful.[42]

Refugees who found temporary housing in the East End, often sought to move to Northwest London, where the German Jewish community was based. This desire became more intense when British fascists gained traction in the East End of London in the 1930s and 1940s.[43] The Battle of Cable Street in 1936 and later street rallies of the British National Front were reminiscent of the Nazi marches through German streets. Eventually, the wartime evacuations and the bombing of the East End also contributed to the decline of the Anglo-Jewish population there.[44]

By 1939, more than 14,000 refugees had found accommodations in Northwest London neighborhoods such as Hampstead, Swiss Cottage, and Belsize Park.[45] For this limited time between their arrival and the outbreak of war, a distinctly German Jewish community existed there. The sights and sounds of these Northwest London neighborhoods became indelibly imprinted on the memories of the postwar refugee community that settled there, particularly in the Swiss Cottage section.

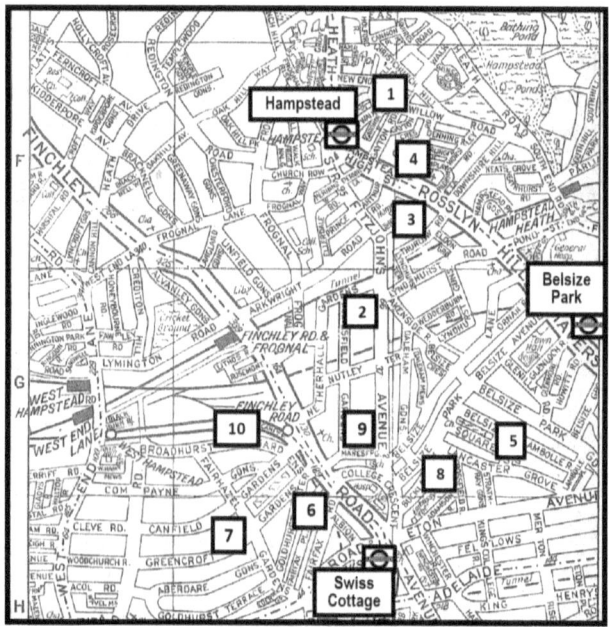

1. Hampstead Public Library, site of Enemy Alien roundup for internment in September 1940
2. Refugee Hostel for Domestic Servants on Fitzjohn's Avenue
3. 28 Thurlow Road (Advertisement for "Continental Food")
4. Embassy Theater Swiss Cottage, *FDKB* venue
5. 36 Upper Park Road, *FDKB* Headquarters (Originally 47 Downshire Hill)
6. Fairfax Mansions, Association of Jewish Refugees Headquarters (Originally on Finchley Rd)
7. 1 & 5 Fairhazel Gardens (Advertisement for "Continental Foods")
8. 20–30 Bucknell Crescent, Liberal Jewish Congregation during the war
9. Leo Baeck Lodge
10. Club 43

Original map reproduced by permission of Geographers' A-Z Map Co. Ltd. License No. B7958. ©Crown copyright and database rights 2017 OS 100017302. Labels added by author.

Map 1.2. *A-Z Map* of Hampstead with German Jewish points of interest.

In *Generation Exodus*, Walter Laqueur wrote of the teenagers and young adults who lived in London:

> At this time certain territorial refugee concentrations developed for instance in Swiss Cottage, London, behind the department store then known as John Barnes. If they had money, and many did not, they could frequent the continental restaurants and coffee houses that had opened in this neighborhood. . . . And then the war broke out and everything changed.⁴⁶

A community of refugees that formed their own congregation, Belsize Square Synagogue, was studied by anthropologist Bea Lewkowicz. She wrote, "Culture shock lessened for those who lived as part of the refugee community around Swiss Cottage."⁴⁷ Adult German Jews, unemployed and living in bedsits and flats, had little direct contact with ordinary Britons beyond what they observed reading the newspaper, listening to the radio, and the brief interactions with their landladies. They spent their early days wandering around London visiting museums, libraries, and parks and making a weekly visit to the Jewish Refugee Committee's headquarters at Woburn House to collect the "allowance" provided by the organization. By February 1939, the committee had moved to Bloomsbury House at Tavistock Square in Central London, where it continued to offer a wide range of services.

In refugee accounts, there is little mention of hostility from their British neighbors in Northwest London, other than the occasional note from an overly attentive landlady. Evidence indicates, however, that there was indeed a substantive backlash against their arrival, at least in the local press. Tony Kushner describes it in *The Persistence of Prejudice*:

> Refugees were supposed to have been rude and aggressive, especially in the local shops. It was a feeling supported by local papers—the *Hampstead and Highgate Express*, the *Hendon, Finchley and Golders Green Times* and the *Kilburn Times*. . . . Despite close personal contact, local refugees were accused of being foreign agents. . . . Internment was both urged and then welcomed in 1940. The *Hampstead Express* went as far as saying it was a "blessing in disguise" as it gave a chance to clear the area of refugees.⁴⁸

While Northwest London had become a refugee enclave, it was not immune to antisemitism and xenophobia. Anti-alien petitions circulated around Hampstead in October 1945 as the refugees continued to draw the ire of their British neighbors even at the end of the war.

War

Germany's invasion of Poland and Britain's immediate declaration of war in September 1939 marked a turning point for London's German Jewish community. Refugees became "enemy aliens" and were required to register with the police and stand before an enemy alien tribunal. There, German refugees were classified into one of three categories A, B, and C, with A deemed the greatest threat to British security and C the least. Within a year, these categories determined which refugees would be interned by the British government. Further work and movement restrictions were placed on the refugees in the early months of the war. While it was mainly men above the age of seventeen who were interned, there were also internment camps for women, although they tended to be released after a shorter period of time. The mass internment of "enemy aliens" by the British government that followed had a significant impact on the German Jewish community in Northwest London. Between May 1940 and the end of 1941, approximately twenty thousand German-speaking Jewish refugees were imprisoned by the British government; one-quarter came from London.[49] Northwest neighborhoods were no longer a refuge for German Jews. For example, there were reports of mass arrests targeting unsuspecting refugees on July 13, 1940, at the Hampstead Public Library and on Hampstead High Street. Anthony Grenville of the AJR wrote, "Refugees were often detained in the early morning—some suffered the dawn knock on the door that would carry them off to an uncertain fate—while others adopted the simple expedient of leaving home early to avoid arrest. The police notoriously raided Hampstead Public Library on 13 July 1940 to detain its refugee readers, but failed to round up those who congregated for an early breakfast at Lyons Corner House at Marble Arch. After their arrest, most refugees were held first in temporary camps, such as the racecourses of Kempton Park and Lingfield for those in the London area."[50] Men and women who appeared "foreign" to police officers and whose documentation then proved that they were, in fact, from

Germany were arrested. Traumatic and hurried separations were recalled by spouses, parents, and children. Refugees taken from temporary camps were then sent to established internment camps and prisons throughout Britain. The largest internment was on the Isle of Man. One thousand teenagers from the *Kindertransports* were interned. Four hundred were sent on prison ships along with another one thousand adult refugees, to the dominions of Canada and Australia.[51] Relatives who avoided internment appealed to the British government for the release of loved ones. A new level of uncertainty and anxiety afflicted German Jews in Britain. In later years, former refugees reported a range of feelings about the long-term effects of their internment. Some individuals emphasized the cultural and educational activities of the camps and the eagerness of German Jews to serve in the British armed forces upon release. Others spoke bitterly about their treatment as enemy aliens. At the very least, internment disrupted family life and stability for German Jews in Great Britain.

In addition to internment, refugee families were separated during the mass evacuation of women and children out of London. Between August 1939 and the end of the war, a total of 1.5 million people were moved to the Home Counties, East Anglia, and the Lake District. It is estimated that fourteen thousand Jewish refugee children were evacuated.[52] Evacuations came in waves, the first in September 1939. The period between September 1939 and the spring of 1940 was referred to as the "Phoney" war by many Britons, because it seemed as though there were no direct effects on British life. By May 1940, many of the evacuee British women and refugee women had returned to London. More refugees were looking for housing in Northwest London, reflected by the uptick in advertisements in the *FDKB Nachrichten* for bedsits in the neighborhoods of Belsize Park and Hampstead during this time.[53] This was most likely due to several factors: evacuees were returning to London, refugee domestics often lost their jobs once the war began and sought housing with other refugees, and those who had lived temporarily in the East End were now looking to the Northwest neighborhoods.

The Nazi air attack on London began in August 1940, prompting a second wave of evacuations. Between 1942 and 1944, the small refugee community began to rebuild again in Northwest London. In June 1944, a third and final evacuation on a smaller scale began with the landing of flying bombs on London.

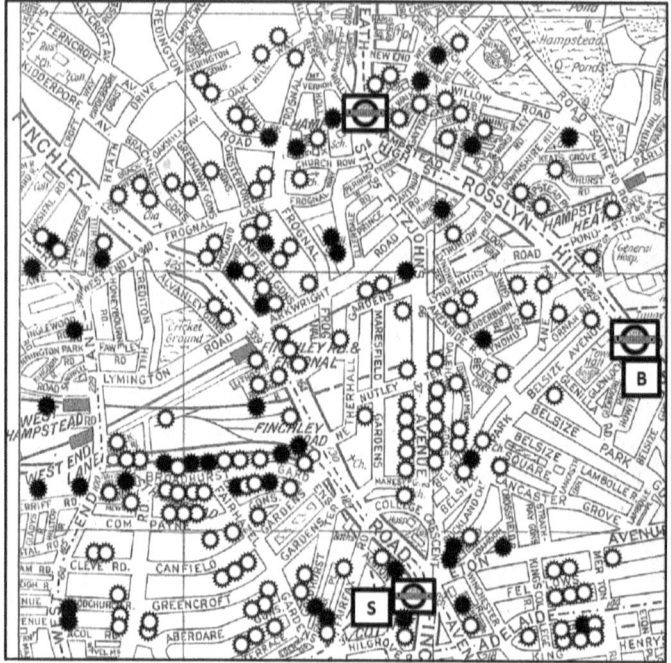

- Building destroyed
- Building severely damaged

S Swiss Cottage Underground Station; Used as Air Raid Shelter
B Belsize Park Underground Station; Deep-level Air Raid Shelter added in 1941

Original street map reproduced by permission of Geographers' A-Z Map Co. Ltd. License No. B7958. ©Crown copyright and database rights 2017 OS 100017302. Bomb sites and labels added by author. Sources of bomb damage sites: Ann Saunders, ed. *Bomb Damage Maps, 1939–1945*. London Topographical Society and London Metropolitan Archives: 2005 and *Hampstead at War, Hampstead 1939–1945*. Camden History Society, first edition 1946, updated edition, 1995.

Map 1.3. *A-Z Map* of Hampstead with bomb sites.

For the refugees in the United Kingdom, both free and interned, the fear of a Nazi invasion of Britain was all too real, especially after the fall of Paris in June 1940. Widely distributed government pamphlets, such as "If the Invader Comes: What to Do and How to Do It" and "Personal Protection against Gas" further fueled their anxiety.[54] From September 1940 to May 1941 London and southern England were under Nazi air attack. The Jewish refugees who remained in London were directly impacted. More than forty thousand civilians, including refugees, were killed during "the Blitz" and roughly one million buildings were destroyed. As recounted in numerous memoirs and interviews, refugees participated in neighborhood fire watches, adhered to the curfews, and spent hours in underground air raid shelters. Articles in the refugee press, such as the *FDKB Nachrichten*, provided instructions such as, "If you are missing a person after an air raid, go to the Citizens Advice Bureau."[55] For some refugees in London, the integration and cultural adaptation into British life accelerated during the Blitz because of the time spent in shelters and in civil duty with locals.

Refugee family members and friends of internees continued their efforts to procure their release. A national campaign led to a White Paper in July 1940 stating that certain categories of internees were now eligible for release. The first fifty refugee internees were freed on August 5, 1940. By August 1941, roughly 1,300 refugees remained interned.[56] According to the *FDKB Nachrichten*, the refugee community continued their efforts to send care packages to internees.[57] Upon release from internment, more than nine thousand refugee men enlisted in the British armed forces, mainly into the Pioneer Corps. This noncombatant army unit was one of the only service options for former "enemy aliens" at that time. But by the end of 1942 they were officially permitted to transfer to fighting units.[58] Some used their German fluency and knowledge of German life and geography to work in the Intelligence Corps. Freed internees who returned to London found a different city awaiting them. Some described it as especially loud from bombardment and physically devastated by bombs.[59] Refugees in London, including dependents of soldiers in the Pioneer Corps, still had to adhere to curfews and radio rules of internee dependents.[60] While refugee families took great pride in their members who enlisted, it meant a further disruption to family life, and constant worry for their safety.

According to Austin Stevens in *The Dispossessed*, the most significant result of Britain's entry into war for German Jews was the abrupt end to any thought of emigrating out of Britain. Stevens argues that 27,000 refugees in Britain had definite plans to leave prior to the war. He wrote:

> It is hard to exaggerate the sense of insecurity induced by thus finding themselves caught in a country which they had hitherto regarded as a mere stopping-off place or halfway house. . . . The practical results of the cancellation of thousands of re-emigration plans were certainly harsh and immediate. The refugee organization were faced with the prospect of maintaining a multitude of people who had never intended to stay in Britain at all. Those who had been able to bring some money out of Germany and

were still living on it might soon find themselves destitute; the employment position of the refugees was unchanged; the young and fit could not join the Services and civilian employment remained severely restricted. In theory, of course, one could still go to the United States, but shipping was disrupted by the outbreak of war. Thousands of refugees held steamship tickets which had been bought with German marks and were therefore useless now.[61]

Unable to leave Britain, refugees focused their energy on contributing to the British war effort against the Nazis.

Work in London

Upon arrival in Great Britain, none but the most prestigious and well-connected academics and artists could work in their former professions. British visa restrictions prohibited most employment. Thousands of refugees were reliant upon Woburn House for financial support and spent their days waiting in embassy lines trying to acquire visas for family and friends still in Germany. Unemployed male refugees described wandering the city rather than remaining in their small single rooms. Many recall visiting museums and libraries to help pass the time. There were opportunities to sell their personal goods, such as linens and cameras, for extra income, as revealed in the regular advertisements in the *FDKB* at the time. Some refugees retrained for British qualifications, learned English, or tutored German. Refugee writers, in particular, faced tremendous difficulty in resuming their profession because of language barriers, although some, such as Alfred Kerr, continued to write in German.

Between 1933 and 1939, refugee women in London were more likely than refugee men to be officially employed. There are several reasons for this. First, a majority of refugees who entered Britain had been granted temporary visas that prohibited employment of any kind in the United Kingdom. Of the twenty thousand domestic service visas granted to German Jews, the majority were held by women, who were quickly employed as maids, cooks, and nannies. Men were occasionally hired as gardeners and servants, but it was presumed that women would have more experience, or even innate abilities, in cooking and cleaning. With the outbreak of war, the employment outlook for refugees shifted as employment restrictions were loosened. In his article entitled "An Alien Occupation—Jewish Refugees and Domestic Service in Britain, 1933–1948," Tony Kushner noted that thousands of refugee domestics were fired from their jobs during the first week of war because of their employers' reluctance to have Germans in their homes.[62] German Jews, both men and women, then found work alongside Britons in shops, factories, and offices. The *FDKB Nachrichten* posted offers of help for newly released domestic servants.[63]

Once in London, German Jews with previous experience in textiles and design strove to reenter these fields. Jane Dorner wrote:

> The use of sub-contractors and outworkers (in the textile industry) was given a further stimulus in the thirties by the new influx of refugees from Europe, especially from Germany and Austria as the Hitler regime gained force and Jewish persecutions reached a new ferocity. Many of these immigrants were, as in the past, skilled tailors and dressmakers and they were readily absorbed into the industry . . . Many of them were expert in women's fashion-making, especially in Continental styling.[64]

Ulrike Walton-Jordan researched German-speaking refugees in the field of textile design, including the creators of *The Ambassador*, one of the top textile magazines in Britain.[65]

When the air attacks on London began, some German Jewish refugees working alongside British nationals reported a developing sense of camaraderie. For example, after the bombing of the Marks & Spencer department store where she worked, Alice Schwab was surprised to see her colleagues again: " 'We couldn't leave you alone,' said the girls, 'we just had to come and see what we could do to help.' So we carried on for a bit in the bombed-out store, clearing up, until there was absolutely nothing more we could do. It was heart-breaking because there had been such a wonderful spirit in the store."[66] For many refugees, this was the first time they had extended direct contact with "native" Britons. In a 2002 article, Anthony Grenville describes the connections between the department store Marks & Spencer and the German Jewish refugees. He writes that Simon Marks donated more than one million pounds of his own money to help the Central British Fund for German-Jewry and that the stores hired numerous refugees.[67] Ulrike Walton-Jordan wrote in that same volume that Marks & Spencer worked with refugee company owners and designers to improve their own stores, such as Eric Kann of Schocken, who implemented scientific quality control and product testing for two hundred Marks & Spencer stores, and Leonard Deeds (formerly Tietz) of Tietz Department Store, who helped "modernize" them. Walton-Jordan also wrote that many refugees found employment in Marks & Spencer once work restrictions were lifted in 1941.[68]

Throughout 1941, *FDKB Nachrichten* published regular notices for refugee employment opportunities and training programs. The first issue of 1941 reported the news of a December 19, 1940, House of Commons ruling that seven thousand work permits would be given to foreigners to work as machinists, clerks, or in regional labor exchanges. The announcement called for refugees to sign up through the auxiliary war service at Bloomsbury House, where there was a training center for men to learn metal works for three to five months, with a pay of thirty shillings weekly, adding, "Families will be supported."[69] The February issue posted an announcement from the Ministry of Labor and National Service requiring refugees to apply for jobs through the Training Centre for International Labour Branch.[70] In March, the newsletter announced a "meeting for ex-internees for job possibilities and release possibilities for those still interned."[71] The April newsletter of 1941 seemed most optimistic regarding work opportunities. It stated, under the heading *Work Possibilities for Refugees*, "The time has come that Great Britain needs all working power. Outside of domestic work and farming there are great and growing opportunities in hotels, restaurants, factories, and offices. . . . Now healthcare and teachers are needed, especially math, physics, and chemistry. While it may not be your old profession and could be exhausting, the earnings are small, it is a small step."[72] Four months later, the *FDKB Nachrichten* announced, "The Ministry of Labour orders men 16–65 and women 16–50 to register for industrial work at Hannover House in High Holburn, the only exceptions are Pioneer Corps, interned, British Military duty and women's auxiliary."[73] Up to 30 percent of all refugees were working in the British armament industry.[74]

The constant mobility of refugees in London, whether due to employment, evacuations, internment, or military duty, meant that German Jews had difficulty creating a stable home environment for their families. *Kindertransport* children and evacuees lived in foster homes or hostels. By 1942, after internees were released and employment restrictions eased, a small community of refugees in London remained linked through self-formed organizations such as the *FDKB* and Belsize Square Synagogue.

Refugee Enclaves: New York

The formation of German Jewish neighborhoods in New York City began early and continued throughout the duration of the war. By the end of the 1930s, most German Jews in New York City lived in a furnished room or small apartment with a private bathroom and kitchenette. Apartments were acquired through word of mouth or advertisements in the refugee press; as a result, many refugees found themselves living in close proximity to other German Jews. Just as London refugees generally avoided the East End of London as a place of settlement, most German Jews in New York chose not to settle on the Lower East Side of Manhattan, the neighborhood traditionally home to East European Jewish immigrants.[75] Instead, they sought housing in middle-class neighborhoods uptown.

By 1939, approximately 25,000 German Jewish refugees had settled in Washington Heights. The second highest concentration was on the Upper West Side/Riverside section of Manhattan, which drew many refugees from Berlin and Vienna. Forest Hills and Kew Gardens in Queens also attracted refugee families.

Map 1.4. New York City.

German Jews in New York moved to middle-class neighborhoods for the same reasons as their counterparts in Northwest London. The leafy and well-kept streets reminded them of their middle-class neighborhoods in Germany. Manfred Kirchheimer wrote about Washington Heights' Fort Tryon Park, "The park commands spectacular views of the Hudson River vista so like the Rhine that it was one of the main reasons that led my people, when they fled Germany, to settle in Washington Heights."[76] Others likened Washington Heights to Grünewald, Berlin (just as refugees did Northwest London), or Frankfurt am Main, hence the nickname "Frankfurt on the Hudson," also the title of Steven Lowenstein's sociological study of German Jewish Washington Heights. Other names used included "The Fourth Reich" and the *Deutsch-Jüdisches Viertel*, German-Jewish quarter. In Steven Lowenstein's analysis of obituaries in the refugee newspaper *Aufbau*, he estimates that more than one-half of the German Jewish refugees in the New York region came from German cities with populations greater than one hundred thousand.[77] Washington Heights drew refugees from Central and Southern Germany cities such as Frankfurt, Stuttgart, and Ulm, who tended to be more religious, middle-class, small business owners. The Riverside/Upper West Side attracted a more cosmopolitan and literary population, many of whom had come from Berlin. For a closer look at the demographic shifts and settlement of refugees by borough and neighborhood, I tabulated the housing advertisements of every first week of September issue of *Aufbau* between 1936 and 1945.[78]

The findings were not particularly surprising. For example, there were only four rooms advertised in the 1936 issue, which correlates to the limited number of German Jews who arrived in New York at this early date. By 1939, the number of available rooms in the first September issue totaled 120. Out of these, 35 (29 percent) were on the Upper West Side of Manhattan (West 60th to West 129th Street) and 71 (59 percent) were in Washington Heights (West 130th to 204th Street). Only 13 (11 percent) rooms for rent were advertised in boroughs other than Manhattan. The total numbers of rooms advertised in Queens, the Bronx, and Brooklyn dropped further in the last three years of the war. The peak of available rooms to rent appears to have been in 1942 when out of 218 advertisements, 50 (23 percent) were for rooms on the Upper West Side, and 102 (47 percent) were in Washington Heights. Between 1943 and 1945 the number of rooms available significantly lowered across New York. This reflects the housing shortage that occurred in New York City during those years.

Despite the burgeoning of Washington Heights and the Upper West Side as refugee enclaves in the late 1930s and early 1940s, German Jews

Table 1.1. New York City "Rooms for Rent" Advertisements in *Aufbau*, Rosh Hashanah Issues, 1935–1945

Year Early Sept.	Manhattan Upper West Side W.60th–129th	Manhattan Lower Washington Heights W.130th–160th	Manhattan Washington Heights / Inwood W.161st–204th	Manhattan Downtown Midtown East Side Harlem	Queens	The Bronx	Brooklyn
1935	0	0	0	0	0	0	0
1936	1	1	3	0	0	0	0
1937	2	5	10	2	0	0	1
1938	18	24	20	2	0	5	1
1939	35	26	45	1	4	4	5
1940	48	32	52	0	2	1	2
1941	50	40	62	0	7	2	3
1942	64	30	70	0	1	0	1
1943	26	8	21	0	9	0	1
1944	24	15	20	0	1	0	0
1945	15	7	9	0	0	1	0

lived across New York City's five boroughs. Some found accommodation with American Jewish relations or chose to live near job opportunities. Walter Baum, as mentioned earlier, stayed with cousins in the East Bronx until his parents arrived, at which point the three of them settled in Washington Heights. Rudolf Katz's cousin Else moved to Brooklyn to live with a relative who did not charge room and board. Another young refugee moved with his family out to "the leafy suburbs of Flushing" after having spent a short period in an Upper West Side hotel.[79] While only one-quarter of New York's German Jews actually lived in Washington Heights, the neighborhood developed a strong German look and feel, where continental products and services could be purchased by refugees across New York.

Compared to London, there was a swifter process of upward mobility for refugees in New York. From 1933 to 1942, most German Jews in New York moved at least once to a larger living space, to a more upscale neighborhood, or to be closer to friends and family. The Katzes, for example, briefly lived in a two-room apartment on 103rd Street, near Riverside Drive. They decided to stay only one week before moving into an apartment on 101st Street that was "not so elegant as before, but bugless and cheaper" and in the same building as friends. They eventually moved to a "very quiet nice one-room-apartment at 815 Riverside Drive, where most of the disagreabilities [sic] of the former residence—the kitchen sharing and noises—will quickly be forgotten. It really looks attractive and homely [sic]."[80] Ilse Jacoby found a furnished room rented out by fellow German Jews from Breslau, her hometown.[81] Those who arrived with sufficient funds prior to 1935 could buy less expensive real estate in Washington Heights, which experienced a housing surplus of Art Deco–style apartment buildings constructed in the 1910s and 1920s. If they were able, they advertised rooms to rent to other refugees in the *Aufbau*. Between 1935 and 1941, Washington Heights continued to thrive as a German Jewish enclave. This is evident in the multitude of organizations, synagogues, and social networks that emerged during this time. The *Aufbau,* written almost exclusively in German, advertised weekly social activities for refugees, young and old. These included weekly announcements for sports activities such as hiking, ping pong, soccer, tennis, swimming, or walks through Central Park, which will be explored further in chapter 5.

The United States' entry into the war in December 1941 brought relatively little change to German Jewish neighborhoods in New York. Unlike Londoners, New Yorkers did not face an immediate threat of Nazi bombs. There were no mass evacuations, no air raids with gas masks, and, most significantly, no internment. German Jewish refugees in the United States were not imprisoned en masse as they were in Britain. (Instead, Japanese Americans faced that particular injustice in the United States.) From 1939 to the end of 1941, there were significantly fewer disruptions for refugees in New York, compared to those in London, and the refugee networks there were more likely to remain intact.

Once the United States was fully immersed in fighting the Axis powers, refugees in New York felt some effects of the war. Joshua Franklin found that 50 percent of all eligible refugee men joined the armed services, a total of 9,500 German Jewish soldiers.[82] By 1942, German Jews were also restricted in their movement out of New York City. According to Davie, between 1942 and 1944, German Jews held enemy alien status in the United States and could not be naturalized as U.S. citizens unless they enlisted in the armed forces.[83] The *Aufbau* published updates regarding government restrictions on refugee life. They urged non-U.S. citizens to report to authorities and informed them of travel and photography restrictions.

Due to the wartime housing shortage mentioned previously, refugees often had to remain in the same apartment for years at a time. Enclaves such as Washington Heights flourished. Their homes' interiors more clearly reflected aspects of their German past. Some New York refugees, especially those who had left Germany before 1938, retrieved their furniture and belongings from prepacked containers or "lifts," which enabled them to retain elements of their prior lives. This was especially true once the war ended and lifts held in European harbors when war broke out in September 1939 were finally shipped to New York. Ernest Stock described a German Jewish apartment in New York in 1951:

> Many families are still using the heavy German furniture they brought over in their packing crates. . . . The center of the traditional living room is a massive table with straight-backed chairs around it; along one wall stretches the so-called "buffet," a two-story cabinet used to store linen, china, and silver. In the top half, a glass showcase, knick-knacks and small antiques are exhibited. Part of another wall may then be taken up by a bookcase almost ceiling high, with the books protected from dust and the mere browser by a locked, glass-paneled door. . . . Where space permits, the vast German twin beds—each bed almost the size of an American double bed—have remained in the bedroom. They may not look very up to date, but they are

too comfortable to be thrown out, and besides a bedroom is not meant to be a showplace anyway.[84]

Refugees who left Germany after 1938 invariably came with fewer personal belongings. Nonetheless, they, too, accumulated furniture and created *gemütlich,* or cozy, homes relatively quickly. Because most refugees remained in the same apartment throughout the war, they were also more likely to invest time and money into decorating it. Liselotte Kahn recalled that she furnished her apartment "in an amusing way." She wrote:

> In Manhattan one day I passed an auction gallery just as an auction was in progress. I went in and watched for a long time, fascinated. . . . Toward the end, a drop-leaf desk came up for sale. It was an enormous mahogany desk, standing on heavily carved lion feet . . . I got it for twenty-five dollars. . . . This huge piece was put into our bedroom-living room-dining room. It served as a writing desk, storage place for papers, as a silver chest, and as a linen closet.[85]

In addition to stores and auctions throughout New York, local shops advertising in *Aufbau* in Washington Heights and Forest Hills sold "Continental" furniture. Even during wartime, refugee homes in New York seemed more up-to-date than those in Germany or Britain. In his study, Maurice Davie observed, "The apartment houses with all modern conveniences, the kitchen facilities and appliances in the home, the delivery service, refrigeration, even soap that floats, all these available even to lower paid workers were things to be remarked about."[86]

Work in New York

In New York, German Jews began seeking work soon after arrival. While most did not immediately resume their former professions, they could still earn a living more easily than their counterparts in London. Those who arrived empty-handed took whatever work was available to them. As early as September 1936, the refugee newspaper *Aufbau* was asking readers for "*Stellenvermittlungen*" or work opportunities for refugees.[87] In 1938, the German-Jewish Club advertised open hours to discuss job opportunities on Monday and Thursday mornings from 9:30 a.m. to noon and Wednesday evenings from 8:30 p.m. to 9:15 p.m. on West 91st Street.[88] Some refugees found temporary work in factories or other labor-intensive posts. Melitta Hess recalled, "My husband had a slip of paper. It said 'I'm looking for work. I have three children to support.' And he went wherever he was told to go. He worked unloading barges for a few months at the docks in Brooklyn. Then he went to work as a dishwasher at the Éclair."[89]

Under U.S. immigration law, it was permissible for German Jews to find employment and to start their own businesses. With an extensive refugee network, it was easy to find fellow refugees to fill positions. Growing German Jewish enclaves became a reliable customer base and clientele. From its inception, *Aufbau* ran advertisements for German Jewish–owned bakeries, butchers, clothing stores, beauty salons, travel agencies, translation services, and furniture shops. Professional services offered in the September 1936 issue came from German Jewish lawyers, insurance brokers, photographers, dentists, and doctors.[90] In Sophia Robison's 1942 study entitled *Refugees at Work*, she reported that out of 304 refugee-owned retail stores in New York City, fifty were located in Washington Heights. Another forty-seven were located on the Upper West Side, owned by refugees who lived there or in Washington Heights.[91]

Those who could learn English, naturally, had a better chance of getting their German qualifications recognized and securing employment in their prior fields. A former doctor resumed practicing medicine once he passed his English language exam and, later, the New York Medical Exam, all of which he did within his first year of arrival in the United States.[92] Walter Baum recalled that his father was unable to return to sales because his English was insufficient.[93] There were ways of overcoming this, as Bert Kirchheimer recalled: "I started freelancing with cartoons. I sold to the leading magazines: *Colliers, Journal American*. To them I sold a whole Sunday page of cartoons in August or September 1936. They were German gags that my brother translated into English for me."[94]

Many refugee women in New York found brief work as maids and nannies in the first few months upon arrival. Some lived with Orthodox Jewish families on the Lower East Side; others worked in wealthy uptown homes of established American Jews. There is little evidence that refugees found long-term domestic work with non-Jews. After a few months in domestic service, many reported seeking work in an office, factory, or shop. Liselotte Kahn recalled that for refugee doctors' wives like herself, "Some worked in factories; many worked as maids and cleaning women. The ones who spoke English got jobs as sales women in the five and ten cent stores."[95] Due to

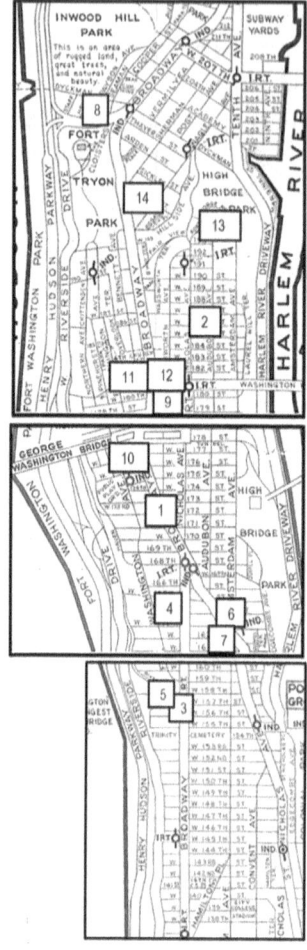

1. Bloch and Falk Butchers
2. Prospect Unity Club
3. Lublo's Palm Garden
4. New World Club
5. Maccabi Athletic Club
6. New York State Employment Service—Washington Heights Office
7. Synagogue Gemeinde Washington Heights
8. Stern Kindergarten
9. Book and Card Store (Advertised as "Formerly *Modern Booksellers* in Berlin")
10. Berko Beauty Salon (Advertised as "Formerly of Frankfurt am Main")
11. RKO Coliseum
12. Heights Beauty Salon (Advertised as "Formerly of Wiesbaden")
13. George Washington High School
14. YMHA and YWHA

Original street map: ©*Norman's Simplified Maps of New York City* (Norman Garbush, New York Lithographic Corporation, 1945). Number labels added by author.

Map 1.5. Washington Heights with German Jewish points of interest.

an absence of employment restrictions, German Jewish women in New York did not remain in domestic posts for as long as refugee women in Britain.

As this chapter demonstrates, the conditions under which German Jews lived in London compared to New York directly affected their experience. Refugees in London were initially prohibited from seeking employment, excepting those who arrived on domestic service visas. The likelihood that German Jews in London would own property in those early years was slim, especially since most arrived with limited funds and were not permitted to work. Once the war began, refugees faced internment and evacuations during and after the Battle of Britain. Meanwhile, refugees in New York came primarily on immigration visas with no employment restriction. They eagerly opened their own shops and offices and hired other newly arrived refugees. German Jews living interspersed throughout the city had close connections to other refugees and spent time in refugee enclaves such as Washington Heights shopping, working, or socializing. While many refugees in London found housing in Northwest neighborhoods such as Hampstead and Swiss Cottage, the brutal disruptions of war and internment meant that they could not establish firm ties. Internalized refugee perceptions about the United States and Great Britain as different kinds of nations of refuge influenced their early impressions of each country. More potent, though, were the external and circumstantial factors, including immigration policies, the proximity to and timing of the war, the bombing of Northwest London, and the British internment of enemy aliens. The availability of accommodation and work opportunities in New York and London also led to differences in identity formation and cultural adaptation in the two cities.

2

Family, Friendship, and Food

IN HER ANALYSIS OF MORE THAN three dozen memoirs of German Jewish men in New York, Judith Gerson observed that family was the "modal frame and the most frequently mentioned category of analysis."[1] In my own research of refugee letters, diaries, interviews, and memoirs, I, too, found the consistent focus on extended family relations prior to emigration to be particularly striking. Many accounts inevitably compared the former familial networks to the sparse connections of extended family in exile. Perhaps, as Gerson argues, writing the histories of their own extended families going back generations gave refugees the opportunity to reclaim a sense of belonging to a larger long-standing community, one that no longer existed. In this chapter, I demonstrate that familial networks and "friendship families" developed by refugees in both cities were spaces of new cultural and identity negotiation. Identity practices within refugee homes and community are further played out in discourse around food. Their descriptions of the accessibility of certain food items and how, where, and with whom they were consumed illuminate the differences.

Gender and Family Dynamics

There is extensive scholarship on the challenges immigrant families face as a result of shifting gender roles and expectations for men and women.[2] As explored in the introduction, prior to emigration married German Jewish women were primarily responsible for running the household and bringing up well-educated children. At the same time, they supported their husbands both socially and professionally. A small percentage of German Jewish women worked outside of the home in family businesses or as independent professionals.[3] After 1933, women prepared for emigration by enrolling in English, Spanish, and Hebrew language classes and strengthening traditionally female-designated skills, such as sewing and stenography.[4] Those who were able to procure visas packed up their homes and, when circumstances permitted, gathered the items they imagined would be most important abroad including tokens of their middle-class lives in Germany such as photos, china, linens, and furniture. Jewish families with the means to leave Germany promptly sold businesses, property, and personal belongings. The process of fleeing was often piecemeal, with one or two family members preparing to emigrate before their visas expired, planning to bring the rest of the family over soon after. They made arrangements to care for family and friends who were unable to emigrate. Familial and social networks were inevitably strained, but at the same time were relied upon in exile and in Germany.

Although middle-class Jewish women in Imperial and Weimar Germany generally did not engage hands-on in the daily household chores, in Nazi Germany, with the advent of the 1935 Nuremberg Laws, they were responsible for undertaking the household chores that their former servants once did. This was little preparation for those who arrived in Britain on domestic visas. German Jewish refugee women were employed in traditional female-designated jobs like maids and nannies, under this scheme. However, many reported gaining a sense of independence and self-sufficiency that they had not previously experienced. In postwar refugee accounts, women were heralded as the financial and emotional backbone of the refugee family in Britain. This is exemplified in an article by refugee Gabriele Tergit in the Association of Jewish Refugees' Anniversary Edition of 1951:

> It was easier for the women to find work. The highly-specialized men seemed suddenly to be worthless, and the sad psychological fact is that whatever may happen later, will never eradicate the sense of frustration and bitterness once it takes root in the individual's heart. The women could take on their ancient jobs, looking after the young, the old, the sick, cooking and mending. The woman as breadwinner makes married life very difficult. Women off to factory work or trying to sell their handicrafts to the buyers of great stores, men brooding in depressing rooms—only a strong moral tradition prevented the disruption of married life.[5]

Gabrielle Tergit, herself a refugee, demonstrates in this article that the role of women in these traditional "female" positions was seen as necessary. Joseph Adler's account uses similar language. He wrote:

Now the roles through the immigration changed our life. Mieze was a moral force. She represented the centre and the home of the family. Mieze was the one who threw in her vitality, knowledge, and perseverance, and kept the household going. She was the bread provider for all of us. We two had, in the beginning, very often to go to bed without dinner. The kids had to eat. She never lost the hope that we would make it one day.[6]

While German Jewish women in London labored outside the home, they also worked in the home. For example, Ilse Jacoby recalled that she cooked meals for all five of the unemployed refugee men in the building in which she lived.[7] Accounts describe refugee women in London as providing a safe haven from the foreign and unpredictable world, using décor, food, and other tangible signs of the past, all the while providing emotional support for their families. Jillian Davidson notes that among members of this group, there was "a juxtaposition between the old 'matriarchal' style of the German-Jewish community, and the new meaning given to the status of the independent woman in the exiled German-Jewish community in England."[8] Working as a domestic servant, Eva Reichmann's experience as the primary earner in her family reflected these difficulties:

> Another girl and myself were billeted on [our landlady] for bed, breakfast and one meal a day, and during her absence my husband did the cooking. When he was doing the chores in his apron, and the landlady had a chance to see him, she used to say "He's a scream," so funny did he look and with such good spirits did he perform his menial tasks. And yet, he suffered greatly from the idea that, at the time, I was the "breadwinner" and he was condemned to do nothing. He explored every chance to use his—and for that matter, also my—potentialities for a better purpose. So he begot the idea to write a book on the Jewish catastrophe in Germany.[9]

Many men felt that they could be doing something more "important." The realities consisted of unemployable older men, with time to reflect on what they no longer had in terms of status and purpose. Judith Gerson's work on the expressions of German Jewish refugee masculinity in New York was particularly illuminative.[10] She argues that immigration is comparative; the primary comparison is between extended family prior to emigration and the lack of extended family in exile. Rebuilding of kin and social networks was of primary importance.

German Jewish families in London were repeatedly separated by evacuations, employment, internment, and then enlistment. They endured constant upheaval and disruption due to war. Men were more likely to remain in internment camps, while refugee women returned to London and tried to get their interned family members released, although there were women who were interned.[11] As mentioned previously, interned men under forty years of age were more likely to enlist upon release immediately in the Pioneer Corps. Women were left to "hold down the fort"; they continued to find work, maintained ties with loved ones left in Germany, and created social networks of support.

The circumstances under which German Jews arrived in New York significantly affected gender relations. By 1941, the number of German Jewish men and women in New York was almost evenly divided. Davie reported that only 5 percent of married German Jewish refugee men and women in the United States lived apart from their spouses.[12] Full-time employment of New York refugee women dramatically changed their status within the family, as it had for refugee domestics in London. There were a range of fields that refugee women entered into in the United States.[13] Davie wrote of refugee women, "Their main economic adjustment consisted in becoming wage earners for the first time. And here they took jobs chiefly in the household or domestic field, with which they were already familiar. They met the change in status with more equanimity than the men, who experienced a greater sense of loss and frustration. The role of husband and wife in the European household frequently became reversed, with the women becoming, for a time, the main support of the family, which increased the discomfiture of the men."[14] It seems that, even when unemployed, some German Jewish men did not increase their domestic contributions and had a difficult time switching roles. This meant that many women carried the double burden of working outside of the home and "keeping house," circumstances common for refugee women universally.[15]

Historian and former refugee Peter Gay wrote, "I do not want to intimate that all, or most, refugee men lived in exile in a permanent state of collapse. Many landed on their feet. But the dislocations, the narcissistic injuries, were often overwhelming."[16] This seemed to be the case in both cities. Nevertheless, women's contributions were sometimes recognized and appreciated by German Jewish men. For example, former refugee Leo Grebler wrote:

I believe the real heroes of the early struggles for an economic foothold were the women—all the more remarkable since most of them came from a middle-class milieu where wives or grown daughters adorned and possibly organized the household but did not do household chores, and where education had prepared relatively few for professional or semi-professional work. The ladies hired themselves out as domestics, cooks, governesses, kindergarten assistants, sales clerks, or used the skills acquired in Hitler Germany to run bakeries or lampshade workshops, or sold Avon products door-to-door while the men were seeking ways to enter the system. And they were doing so without loss of dignity and in the conviction that this was only a temporary expedient, so it involved no sense of social degradation.[17]

While men were trying to restart their professional lives, either through applying for American qualifications or preparing for a new career, women traditionally bore the financial and emotional responsibility for the refugee family and home. The relatively small percentage of professional refugee women in medicine, law, or academia were often the first to sacrifice their careers.

Through her analysis of male refugee memoirs, Judith Gerson finds that there is "unquestionable evidence that the German Jewish practices of memory and identity are family centered."[18] In fact, she found that in memoirs of refugees in New York, family was the most commonly discussed topic, with employment and former military service as other prominent themes. Gerson argues that the very process of writing a memoir for future generations allowed refugee men to serve as vital caretakers of their family history, while mourning and preserving their extended families who remained in Germany or in exile around the globe.[19] Writing memoirs was also a way for refugee men to recuperate the respect and authority that they might have felt was lost upon emigration. Gerson shows that nationhood was tied to masculinity, as was a tradition of military service. Stripped of their nationhood and with their masculinity degraded, men revealed through memoirs their own efforts to reestablish validity as Germans. Gerson found that refugee men emphasized extended genealogical connections to Germany, and their own, or their fathers', German military service.[20] The key difference for those in New York was that the men had legal permission to work and had realistic hopes to reenter their former professions. They had the potential to retain their professional status in the United States. Those in Britain were on temporary visas, were interned and evacuated, and were not permitted to work when they first arrived. Refugee families in both London and New York experienced shifts in gender roles and husband/wife dynamics, and families in London were more likely to face separation and upheaval than those in New York.

Of all the Jews who fled Germany between June 1933 and September 1939, approximately 62 percent were under forty years of age.[21] In her article "Child Exiles: A New Research Area?" Marianne Kröger explores the growing body of work on the effects of migration on children and, in particular, the child refugees from Nazi Germany.[22] Current scholarship, such as the essays in Rumbaut and Portes's *Ethnicities: Children of Immigrants in America*, reveal the uniqueness of the child's experience of migration.[23] The transformation of parent/child relationships in immigration and the intergenerational transmissions of culture are gaining attention across the disciplines.[24] The extenuating circumstances of German Jewish refugee life in London compared to New York between 1935 and 1945 resulted in divergent patterns of intergenerational cultural transmission and changes in family dynamics.

German Jewish children in Britain often lived apart from their parents. Whether they arrived on a *Kindertransport*, were sent to boarding school, or were later separated because of internment, evacuations, or military service, child/parent relations were severely disrupted. German Jewish children experienced ongoing concern for the well-being of parents either left behind in Germany or living apart from them in Britain, and parental roles were often reversed. By 1939, Kenneth Ambrose, already an older teenager, had arranged for his parents' visas and housing, and supported them financially though he was still a student.[25] The improbability that a child's rescue efforts would bear any fruit, particularly once the war began, weighed heavily. Although they may have lived with foster families, German Jewish children were forced to take on adult responsibilities and concerns.[26] For children living with their own family in London, the realization that parents were struggling often led to role reversal. Children quickly became "experts" on British culture in the eyes of their parents, hence the title of Judith Kerr's book *The Other Way Round*.[27] Refugee parents often came to depend on their children's mastery of English and children often became the conduits of British culture for the refugee family.[28] The education of refugee children was frequently interrupted or postponed. Those who were interned sometimes obtained an informal education within the internment camps. Others were evacuated or were placed in refugee hostels and schools such as the Bunce Court School.

German Jewish nuclear families were more likely to remain intact in New York than in London. Refugee children arriving in New York were more likely to be accompanied by at least one parent.[29] Robison's study showed that by the latter part of 1941, "three out of four refugee families in New York City had two or more members, the majority of which both parents resided in the home."[30] Those in New York lived in small apartments and the children attended local public schools. As Gerhart Saenger found in his 1941 study, refugee families in America remained emotionally close. He wrote, "The improvement of relationships within refugee families, developed during these times (of persecution in Germany), does not lose its importance over here. While different problems have to be faced, reliance upon the family remains the same. The refugee arriving in America with his family will find it easier in many ways than the single man or woman."[31] Saenger continued, "The old formal relations existing particularly between father and children vanish and are replaced by the closer bonds of friendship and comradeship between parent and child."[32] This may be true, but intergenerational tension arose in German Jewish households, as well.

Despite the likelihood of a New York refugee nuclear family remaining intact, traditional German Jewish family roles were challenged. Children, and most notably girls, were perceived to have more personal freedom in the United States than in Europe. In 1945, Davie wrote, "The male head of the family has tended to lose authority and status, and the women and children have experienced something approaching emancipation."[33] For working mothers, the need for child care was met by self-formed day care cooperatives and help from grandparents. Similarly, for a brief period, an Austrian refugee day care was established in London. Yet, the instability in Britain due to war meant that this program was short-lived. Davie also observed that "while admiring the independent and natural behavior of American women and girls, some refugees are critical of the amount of freedom allowed young girls; their seeming preoccupation with 'dates,' clothes, and light entertainment; and the amount of make-up both women and girls use."[34] Even Saenger observed, "There is little doubt that the younger girls of the upper classes in America have more freedom than do their European sisters."[35] This difference in gender expectations among American youth affected parent/child relations among German Jewish refugees. Occasionally, teenage refugees arrived alone in the United States, the sole recipient of a relative's affidavit. Sometimes their mothers and fathers joined them later, as was the case for Walter Baum, but other parents remained trapped in Germany, like Inge Gutman's.[36] Older male teenagers often lived with relatives and then joined the United States' armed forces after 1941.

In both London and New York, German Jewish parent/child dynamics were transformed. German Jewish children in London, more often than not separated from their families, were forced to integrate more quickly than refugee children in New York and thereby may have gained a greater sense of independence. In New York, parental and communal pressure to retain German Jewish behaviors was more direct. Refugee children often led split lives: German Jews at home and Americans at school. London refugee children had more freedom to wholly adopt British culture. This is explored in more depth in chapters on dress, language, names, and identity.

As the field of childhood studies has grown, so has the interest in older immigrants and their role in cultural retention within immigrant families.[37] While historically migrant peoples have tended to be made up of predominately young adult males, German Jewish refugees comprised an unusually high percentage of middle-aged and elderly men and women in both London and New York. This was perhaps because financially established German Jews tended to be older. Senior German Jews had the means and connections to obtain entry visas into Great Britain and the United States. According to a 1945 Jewish Central Information Office report, approximately 35 percent of all German-speaking refugees in the United Kingdom were older than fifty years of age.[38] Whether arriving alone or with family, they experienced the same upheavals of internment, evacuations, and the bombing of London. Some senior refugees in Britain recalled that in internment camps, they retained a part of their former status among their peers and organized numerous intellectual and social activities. Most of the older refugees, especially the men, who had built careers in Germany, had to effectively "start from scratch" once released from internment camps. Learning English was a particular obstacle for older refugees to overcome, and many took language classes through Woburn House. At the start of the war, Woburn House and then Bloomsbury House offered classes in skills that were needed during the war effort. Employment was encouraged in certain fields and older refugees who were physically capable found work. Women worked as seamstresses and in necessary fields once war began. The sudden loss of social and economic status for the majority of refugees in their fifties, sixties, and seventies was devastating. It was uncommon for refugee grandparents to live with their grandchildren in London. This slowed the intergenerational transmission of culture and led to the reduction of German Jewish ways among younger refugees. Elderly refugees in New York tended to live with their adult children and grandchildren, where they could speak German, meet fellow refugees on the street, and surround themselves with German Jewish ways of life. This was especially true for those who chose to live in refugee enclaves such as Washington Heights. They remained active in the German Jewish community and were less likely than younger refugees to try and "Americanize." The housing shortage meant that most remained in these homes for the duration of the war and often longer. The most significant result of the cohesiveness of the refugee family in New York was that grandparents and parents were able to pass on aspects of German Jewish life to their children. At the same time, grandchildren and young adults were trying to adopt American ways. As a result, a kind of hybrid culture developed in the New York refugee home that negotiated aspects of German Jewish and American life, yet certainly revealed a more German Jewish flavor.

Prior to 1945, there were not many opportunities to place incapacitated parents and grandparents into institutionalized care. Eventually, refugee communities created homes for the aged, but in the first ten years after arrival, adult children had to provide twenty-four hour care. Independent elderly refugees continued to live with their families in flats and apartments and formed their own social networks. Their presence ensured that German language and behaviors were not lost. The connections between refugees in London and New York and their elderly relatives were, for the most part, maintained over distances. In most cases, the parents and grandparents of refugees remained in Germany and, until war broke out in 1939, they exchanged letters and parcels, and called on friends and family who remained behind to check on them. There was still hope that older family members would survive the war and be reunited with the refugees. Many refugees wrote about the constant worry about their parents and older relatives left behind. One refugee soldier in the U.S. Army had his elderly mother's name engraved on his dog tags as next of kin with a Brooklyn address, in case she was able to escape. He did not know that while he served in the South Pacific, his mother had been shipped out of Frankfurt to Theresienstadt and from there was killed in Maly Trostenec.[39] By the end of 1941, refugees in New York and London had no further contact with family members left in Germany.

Friendship and Food

The role of foodways in migration processes has been well established by scholars such as Hasia Diner in *Hungering for America: Italian, Irish, and Jewish Foodways in the Age of Migration* and Donna Gabaccia in *We Are What*

We Eat: Ethnic Food and the Making of Americans.[40] These works provide a nuanced understanding of integration processes that occur within the immigrant family and across social networks. In studying the eating habits of German Jewish refugees between 1935 and 1945, it becomes clear that these processes reveal distinct patterns in London and New York. Besides providing nourishment, food choices reflected how one negotiated and practiced their ethnic, class, and national identities. It also allows for the study of women's roles in family expressions of identity. There has been some research on the role of friendship and social networks in the German Jewish community.[41] For many immigrants, friendship networks filled in for family left in Germany or scattered around the world. The evidence indicates that German Jews in both London and New York maintained supportive social networks.

In these early years, German Jews living in London maintained close contact with other refugees by living near one another. Numerous refugee accounts describe evenings spent talking with new and old European friends. For example, Alice Schwab recalled, "I met a Professor Wolpe through the crowd I mixed with in Hampstead; we had quite a social life there. There was Natalie Gurney, one of the Gurney family, who used to arrange a sort of get together for refugees on Monday evenings."[42] Refugee women working as domestic servants socialized with fellow refugees during their weekly afternoon off. In her article "A Woman's Place . . . ? German-speaking Women in Exile in Britain, 1933–1945," Charmian Brinson mentions refugee women meeting on Wednesday afternoons to discuss work and offer support to one another.[43] Ilse Jacoby wrote, "Many of the women in the family had come to England on a domestic permit, so they worked as maids in different families. Since Wednesday was an afternoon off for all of us, they either came to our room or to Alfred and Ruth's room for coffee and a get together."[44] Until the middle of 1939, there was a social club on Fitzjohn's Avenue organized especially for refugee domestics to gather and socialize. These translocal meetings gave them a direct link to the German Jewish community. Gabrielle Tergit recalled, "Many of those girls, who had been between twenty and thirty when they arrived in 1938, still did not know anybody in this country. They were straphangers [subway riders] twice a day. They had waited for news of their parents and relatives in Germany. On Saturday evenings they went to the cinema."[45]

It was difficult to procure German foodstuffs in London after the outbreak of war in September 1939. This was due to the halt on trade with Germany, and, in later years, rationing. Work restrictions and a lack of stability and funds meant fewer opportunities for refugees to open stores and stock the shelves with goods that catered to German Jewish tastes. A handful of small shops sold Continental foods such as pastries and *Wurst*, but they relied mainly on imported goods. Evacuations, air raids, and the internment of German Jews outside of London naturally led to a decline in customers. On the whole, German Jews were restricted to whatever products were available in local neighborhood shops or served in refugee hostels. Still, pockets of refugees in London had access to Continental food. Early in 1940, refugee newspapers such as the *FDKB Nachrichten* had advertisements including: "Fairhazel Stores at 1 Fairhazel Gardens NW6—All Continental goods, all fresh in the store," "Raben Stein, Ltd at 5 Fairhazel Gardens, best Continental Kosher *Wurst*—our own factory," and "Kallir Swiss Cottage: Continental Goods and Coffee at Swiss Terrace"[46] Even throughout 1941, there were some advertisements for Continental baked goods such as *"Bienenstich and Pfannkuchen at the Wiener and Berliner Bäckereien"* (sweet pastries and pancakes in the Viennese and Berlin bakery) in Swiss Cottage.[47] The *FDKB* itself had a café where they advertised, "meet your friends in our restaurant—cold and warm meals from 1–2:30 and *Kaffee* daily at 7 am/pm."[48]

There is no doubt that refugee women working as domestics in English homes would come into direct contact with typical British fare. Often they were responsible for the shopping and cooking of meals for their employers. As servants, they would usually be relegated to eating what other domestics ate—generally typical English food such as porridge and toast. Lucy Bettelheim wrote in a letter that when she had to cook for her visiting boyfriend, she planned that "we will have porridge and then lemon jelly with sweet cream," evidence that she attempted to make some British specialties when cooking at home.[49] Socializing allowed them to introduce their fellow refugees to aspects of British life they learned at work. Through this, refugee domestics played an important role in facilitating the adoption of British ways. They also spent their days off, usually Wednesdays, socializing with other refugee domestics eating German food. The *FDKB Nachrichten* advertised in 1940 a Wednesday *Frauennachmittag,* a women's afternoon, from four to six in the evening with "loud voices, clanging of tea cups, to quickly forget about cabbage, toast, and fireplaces and that these *Tasse Tee*, cup of tea, get-togethers included *Allen Deutschen Dialekten*, in all German dialects."[50] There was also an advertisement for *Kasperl Theatre*, or puppet show, on a Sunday afternoon offering tea and biscuits, calling on members to "bring English and German children ages three to ten."[51]

The *FDKB Nachrichten* included regular information on internment and rations in their 1941 issues. In January, for example, it advertised that there were to be "no rationed goods in packages to interned."[52] In June 1941, they published the restrictions laid out by the British Food Control Office, stating, "Do not send rationed food to the Isle of Man: butter, ham, tea, cheese, meat, sugar, or cooking fat."[53] Specially designed cookbooks issued by the Home Office and other organizations provided ration recipes with titles such as *Your Food in Wartime*, *Food Facts for the Kitchen Front: A Book of Wartime Recipes and Hints*, and *Daily Express War Time Cookery Book: Practical Advice and Recipes Specially Prepared for War Time Conditions*.[54] Such government booklets provided examples of many different ways that Londoners could join in the war effort from their own homes. Some refugees grew "victory gardens" outside of their London flats. Rudolf Apt wrote, "During the war we would grow tomatoes, beans, peas, onions, and parsley in abundance. 'Digging for Victory' was a wartime slogan. After the war we changed from vegetables to flower beds, and only the parsley remained."[55] These efforts allowed refugees to participate in the war effort at a personal level. Even in October 1941, Continental delicacies could be prepared using rationed food. The *FDKB* wrote, "Do you know that our restaurant gets rationed portions of goods now and you have a richer choice on offer? Daily 12:30pm–9pm main dish meat or fish with potatoes, veggies or salad. Assorted Continental specialties homemade cakes, order a cake to take out."[56]

Anne Koppel, who arrived in January 1939, temporarily stayed with a foster family and then moved into a refugee children's hostel. She was especially impressed by the food in prewar England, "We arrived at the boys hostel just in time for tea, and we were astonished to find butter, eggs, and other delicacies on the long table. We had never heard of having three eggs in two days in times like these."[57] Children evacuated out of London were introduced to typical British food and mealtime manners. One wrote that his foster parents "were kind, quite unselfish, and anxious to make me feel one of them, though I never quite got over the feeling of being a guest. Particularly the first year I would never dare to ask for a second helping—unless they asked me first—fearing that I might prove too expensive for them."[58] Another recalled, "I was given margarine when the rest of the family ate butter, on only one slice of bread was I allowed to put jam—the very jam for which I had collected the brambles. When visitors came I was banished to the kitchen where I also had my meals."[59] Not all refugee children were treated as outsiders. Charles Leigh wrote:

On Sundays we would sit down to a traditional lunch of roast beef and Yorkshire pudding, after a member of the family said grace. As a sweet that followed, Mrs. Gray excelled herself by producing the most delicious home-made apple or blackberry pie and custard. The pastry was her specialty. In the evenings before going to bed, we children had the choice of two sweet biscuits from a biscuit barrel, and a glass of milk. I must admit that it wasn't enough for me, and I was generally hungry going to bed, but I did realize that sacrifices had to be made, and that the family wasn't able to afford any more.[60]

Staying with foster families provided a swift immersion into British home life, just as it had for refugee evacuees during the air raids. These children were unable to recreate familiar German Jewish surroundings. Leigh described the food he was given at his first foster home, which also happened to be a guest-house, "For breakfast we had the traditional cornflakes and fried food, something that was completely strange to me. All the streets nearby, where hotels, guest-houses and restaurants were situated, smelled of porridge, fried bacon, toast, and kippers. A very pleasant odor indeed." He also looked forward to hearing the milkman "yodeling 'Mihilk'" at the door every morning and remembered that the first time he tried a Cadbury's chocolate bar he "never tasted anything so delicious before."[61] For the small number who met up with their parents later, food was just another obstacle that separated them. One remembered, "Of course it was a relief to see them safe and well, but I saw them now as foreigners and intruders. I objected to the salami sandwiches made with German bread, which they'd specially saved for me. I'd only just got used to English toast, marmalade, and grapefruit for breakfast."[62] Every detail appeared strange to these children. Another recalled, "I remember writing home to Germany: the windows are different, the light switches, the food, and the way the beds are made, school hours . . ."[63] Out of necessity, London refugees quickly adapted to British food. They had limited access to Continental basics such as German bread and sausages and later faced war shortages and food rations. As a result, German Jews of all ages in London adopted local eating habits and tastes much sooner than their New York counterparts.

In New York, refugees found a wide array of food available, including typical German fare. An article on healthy eating published in the *Aufbau Almanac* advised eating dark bread whenever possible because the "ubiquitous white bread here, although cheap, gives your teeth too little to do and leads to cavities." The author continued, "Don't forget to include raw fruit, vegetables, salad, and regular exercises to keep the insides working properly . . . if you adhere to a general diet, don't eat pork that is not fully cooked breaded is not enough. Many cold cuts and sausages, in particular *Teewurst,* include uncooked pork, even the beloved Frankfurters and Hamburgers do as well."[64] One may presume from this article that German foods such as *Teewurst* and dark bread were available in New York. This was partially due to the existing Christian German community in the Yorkville section of Manhattan. This food was either self-produced or, until the war broke out, directly imported from Germany. Some refugees were impressed by the Kosher food on offer on the Lower East Side and in Brooklyn. Leo Grebler and his wife enjoyed their first meal—a Jewish delicatessen sandwich and a bottle of Coke—"a proper introduction to the US."[65] It is interesting that a Jewish deli sandwich was perceived by Grebler to be typically American, when in fact, it had fairly recent European origins.[66]

Throughout the 1930s and 1940s, stores in New York sold German food specialties. In *Aufbau*, there was an advertisement for Stern Brothers on East 47th street for *Wurst und Fleischwaren,* sausage and meat, and boasted the company's hundred-year history in Germany.[67] *Aufbau* also frequently advertised wholesale tea and coffee.[68] Butchers, such as Bloch and Falk, and numerous refugee-owned *Konditoreien,* confectioners and sweet bakeries, made familiar foods easily available for those used to German tastes. Ernest Stock wrote in 1951, "These bakeries are among the most tangible manifestations of the German-Jewish hold on Washington Heights; although they dutifully turn out a certain quota of sweet and fluffy American-style *challah* on Fridays, they devote their main efforts on that day to the production of the German *barches,* which has a hard crust covered with poppy seed and is not sweet in taste."[69] Less frequent in the refugee press were advertisements for German food in Yorkville, but they could be spotted on occasion.[70] Despite rationing in the United States, German Jews in New York had greater access than their London counterparts to a range of foods and materials to surround themselves with familiar comforts.

In New York, there were constant references made to the adherence to Kosher law, in particular in *Aufbau* advertisements for vacation destinations, room rentals, and restaurants where *"streng Kashrut,"* or strictly Kosher, was included. Outside of the refugee enclaves, Kosher butchers, bakeries, and delicatessens were plentiful across the five boroughs of New York City. Although they catered to the general American Jewish community, who were mostly of East European descent, these businesses provided German Jews with familiar cuts of meat, except those made from pork, which could still be found in Washington Heights. It was not possible to adhere to German eating habits and mealtimes in New York. First, the traditional hot lunch was eliminated because of the fact that both men and women worked outside the home. They learned quickly that the American work schedule did not allow for an extended lunch break. Second, kitchen appliances, measurements, and some food products were different from those in Germany. Elsa Heineman wrote an article entitled "Your Household" for the *Aufbau Almanac* aimed at newly arrived refugees. In it, she explained the standard measuring units used in the United States as well as the different styles of cooking, such as broiling and grilling. She also described the different vegetables available in America, such as squash and sweet potatoes, two foods associated with Thanksgiving.[71] Secular holidays like Thanksgiving and the Fourth of July gave refugees the opportunity to experiment with American food and add their own German elements. For example, one Thanksgiving Rudolf Katz and his wife enjoyed a "heavy turkey dinner" with their friends the Memelsdorffs. Two days later, they had turkey again with the Brauers, where they met for *Skat,* a German card game, and French red wine.[72] One woman recalled that her first Thanksgiving in New York was shared with another refugee couple: "At dinner I encountered for the first time pumpkin pie and mince pie."[73] Inge Heiman remembered that at her first Thanksgiving dinner served by her Great Aunt Bertha, "we received our first lesson in American history."[74]

German Jewish children mainly lived with their parents, yet most were eager to adopt American foodways. Children were able to teach their parents about American cuisine. One mother recalled, "The children now were on the way to becoming real Americans. We learned a lot from them. They bought us gadgets for the house and utensils for the kitchen, and Ulrich baked pies and taught me to prepare many American dishes."[75] Most German Jewish homes eventually served a mix of German and American foods. Compared to London, refugees in New York had the time and the resources to slowly adopt American ways in the kitchen, while still retaining some of their German traditions.

German Jews were also intrigued by the casual nature of American eating habits. Liselotte Kahn recalled that on the first morning after her arrival in New York:

> We were taken by my sister for breakfast in a nearby cafeteria. . . .
> We were delighted. Everything looked appetizing and seemed so

inexpensive to us. Five cents for a cup of coffee! I intended from now on to eat only in cafeterias and never to start a household of my own again. I did not own a single cup or plate or pot, and purchasing everything from scratch struck me as an impossible task.[76]

Anne Koppel was surprised by the iced water that was served at American restaurants, which she had "never had before, because it was considered harmful in Europe." She also found that, after buying ice cream cones in a drugstore, "We ate our ice cream cones in the street. I was amused to see even my uncle do it. In Europe, eating anything in the street just isn't done."[77] For those refugees coming either directly from Germany or via England, this informal attitude toward food was peculiar and perhaps even liberating. Yet, it represented one more difference to overcome.

German Jews in New York had few intimate friendships with "real" Americans and instead spent their limited leisure time with fellow German Jews engaging in familiar activities, such as visiting for *Kaffee und Kuchen*, coffee and cake. Ilse Jacoby recalled, "Since my trip to work by subway took three hours back and forth, I was really glad to be in our room when Sunday came. We ate, slept, and spent our time in one ten feet by twelve room. . . . Our one pleasure was visiting our friends, who were immigrants also in New York."[78] Rudolf Katz spent evenings visiting fellow refugees in their apartments, as well as entertaining in his and Agnes's two room apartment on the Upper West Side. After they moved into a new apartment in 1938, Katz wrote in his diary, "Had the first visitors in our new apartment already, Eric, Kaehler, Thomas family, Hedwig Wachenheim and Max Brauer. The apartment indeed is much superior to our Broadway room. Mendelsdorffs were our Sunday tea guests yesterday and the Hirschfields the night before."[79] On another occasion, he visited his friends for a dinner and birthday party, "where the Bandmanns, Memelsdorffs, and Gumprechts contributed to the success of a 'German party,' with much eating and wining."[80] Katz, in particular, frequently mentioned the importance of German-style activities in every gathering. Refugees made day trips out of visiting friends living in different boroughs, or by meeting at a New York beach or park.[81] *Aufbau* advertised such social events for refugees in every issue.[82] While it may seem that German Jews easily enjoyed themselves in New York, in reality, refugees maintained a constant level of worry and sadness for those left behind in Germany, particularly after the start of the war in Europe. Conversation among refugees focused on the situation overseas and updates on loved ones' circumstances. Granted, the most terrible and horrific news came after the end of the war, but the anxiety during this period was heavy. Perhaps the distractions and intensity of internment, air raids, and evacuations in London helped refugees there to focus their energy on everyday survival rather than thinking about loved ones in Nazi-occupied territory. In any case, German Jews around the world were overcome with worry.

Divergent patterns emerged for refugees in London and New York, with regard to home life, social networks, and family dynamics. In London, visa limitations and entry into World War II fractured family life. In New York, refugee families and social networks were consistently more cohesive.[83] It was through social and familial networks that refugees in London practiced their new British ways, while in New York, refugees reinforced their German Jewish lifestyles among friends and relatives. Home was a safe environment for refugees to experiment with cultural adaptation and identity. Additionally, the study of home life, as opposed to community or work environments, is inclusive of women, children, and the elderly. Their role in driving the cultural integration of the family was vital. As Judith Gerson writes, "Practices of memory and identity are family centered."[84]

Refugee homes in both London and New York provided a space for rest and replenishment, physical and psychological. German Jews in London were significantly more transient than their New York counterparts, and were thereby less likely to have German Jewish food or furnishings. Air raids, internment, and evacuation meant they adopted British foodstuffs and home furnishings out of necessity. Meanwhile, German Jews in New York had greater access to Continental goods. As mentioned previously, the New York housing shortage after 1941 prevented refugees there from moving frequently. German Jewish enclaves were filled with refugee-owned businesses. Plus, Jewish delicatessens were abundant throughout New York City. New York refugees retained much of their German Jewish lifestyle in the home. With limited exposure to "typical" American homes, they were slower to adopt American food and furnishings than refugees in London adopted British ways. The close examination of décor, food, and leisure reveals discrepancies in cultural adaptation and identity formation in the two cities.

3

Dress and Names

GERMAN JEWS' PRECONCEPTIONS OF British and American life, as well as the realities they faced upon arrival, shaped the ways in which they negotiated and renegotiated their identities. Some of the clearest indicators of the process of self-identification among immigrants are the use of dress, names, and language. In her work on early-twentieth-century Jewish immigrant women in the United States, Barbara Schreier writes of "the adaptability of dress and its ability to transcend and alter an image . . . their appearance and self-image were inextricably linked, and both were in constant renewal."[1] In examining German Jewish refugee testimony and source material, it becomes apparent that the ways in which German Jews identified themselves through their dress and names differed in London and New York.

In *The Making of the Jewish Middle Class: Women, Family and Identity in Imperial Germany*, Marion Kaplan wrote of German Jews at the end of the nineteenth century and beginning of the twentieth century, "Women needed to raise the family to a new social level to exhibit and maintain its economic achievements. Since class formation demanded visible means of distinguishing those belonging to different classes, Jews needed to be visibly middle-class. But they also needed to be invisibly Jewish."[2] This balancing act was well practiced by German Jews by the early 1930s. Dressing in a refined manner emphasized one's social and financial standing, and helped gain respectability within the community. At the same time, German Jews maintained a careful measure of understatement to prevent antisemitic backlash. Their everyday styles were formal; hats and well-made coats, suits, and dresses were the norm. Germans took great pride in the durability and high quality of their apparel.

Despite centuries of restrictions across Europe on the types of work Jews were allowed to undertake, the trade of fabric, fur, and clothes remained a legal and feasible option for them. Strong family and professional networks in this industry had developed and by the 1920s and early 1930s, most German Jews had some member of their extended family in textile design, manufacturing, or sales. Once in exile, many refugees reestablished and developed these connections.

London: Dress and Appearance

From 1933 through the autumn of 1938, Jews fleeing Germany faced fewer restrictions on what they could take with them. Meticulous records kept by the Nazis show detailed, itemized lists of objects taken out of Germany by emigrants, revealing the extent to which German Jews packed their finest items. One example included eleven suitcases containing fur coats, winter, summer, day and evening clothes, towels, tablecloths, hats, bed sheets, blankets, shoes, and some silver house wares.[3] By 1939, Jewish emigrants could take no more than ten *Reichsmark* and one suitcase out of Germany. As a result, energy was focused on packing well-made and potentially valuable clothing. In their memoirs, refugees recalled using their remaining *Reichsmark* prior to leaving Germany to purchase tailor-made suits and coats that would, hopefully, last until they could afford to buy new ones. Weekly advertisements in the refugee press in London and New York throughout the 1930s and 1940s show a strong demand for furs, leather, and fabrics that were brought over from Germany to be sold as a side income.

Refugees in London regularly remarked that they had brought the wrong kind of clothes for the reality of their situation. Herbert Jonas commented that his friend had dinner suits custom made that were of no use, and Marianne Berel describes an unworn satin dress.[4] Gabriele Tergit wrote of young refugee women, "They had brought a party frock, but it never left the trunk."[5] Kenneth Ambrose, who found a domestic job for his sister in England, wrote, "My mother seems to have had an altogether inflated idea of the circumstances of the Director who had applied for Ilse as their domestic, and who lives in a pleasant suburban three-bedroom house. . . . She was equally far off beam with another query, 'Will Ilse need long gloves with her evening dress?'"[6] Perhaps holding on to the idea that they might need these clothes was a way for refugees to maintain a sense of dignity during difficult times or a means to demonstrate their former middle-class status. In any case, due to the limitations on what Jews were permitted to take out of Germany, clothes came to represent the primary material connection with their former lives.

Once in London, German Jewish refugees were swiftly taught the expectations of the Anglo-Jewish community, in terms of their visibility as foreigners, and even as Jews. The German-Jewish Aid Committee, founded and funded primarily by prominent British Jews, published the widely distributed pamphlet *While You Are in England* for refugees. It stated:

> Do not make yourself conspicuous by speaking loudly, nor by your manner or dress. The Englishman greatly dislikes ostentation, loudness of dress or manner, or unconventionality of dress or manner. The Englishman attaches very great importance to modesty, understatement in speech rather than overstatement and quietness of dress and manner. He values good manners far more than he values the evidence of wealth.[7]

By encouraging refugees to maintain a low profile, the existing British Jewish community may have hoped to stem a rise of antisemitism in Britain. What is clear is that newly arrived refugees read this booklet and immediately understood that they were expected to blend in. This could prove challenging, especially since they were mostly unfamiliar with British norms of dress and the class differences that shaped them. In 1945, Crane Brinton, an American historian living in London, wrote that the English upper class was particularly conspicuous, so that it was "easy even for a foreigner to tell who is a gentleman and who is not . . . clothes for instance, which are not always tweeds, and a whole set of ritual responses in the day-to-day routine of life, which only can be made properly automatic, unconscious, by early training."[8] Of course, German Jewish refugees did not have access to this "early training." The small number of refugees who were prominent in a specific field and continued to work within a profession were generally accepted into their equivalent class even if their manners and looks may have seemed quaintly Continental.

German Jews may still have felt middle-class, but the reality was that most were now working as servants, manual laborers, or were unemployed. For the approximately twenty thousand refugees who worked as domestics, their class demotion could not have been more obvious, as they wore servants' uniforms or plain clothes to work. Unemployed men with work restrictions stamped into their passports spent much of their time dressed in formal coats and ties and standing in queues at the various embassies throughout London trying to get visas for their friends and family still in Germany or for themselves to another destination.

Once in the workforce, German Jews were well aware that they appeared different and even out of place to their British co-workers. Lilly Friedmann wrote:

> The forelady soon realized that I had never "worked" before and gave me a hard time. She couldn't quite figure me out. I seemed so strange to the girls I worked with . . . my clothes were too elegant—custom-made and totally out of place—my background was too different to find anything in common, and nothing had prepared me to work efficiently in a "sweatshop" environment.[9]

Gabrielle Tergit wrote in the tenth anniversary of the *AJR Information*:

> In 1941, training centers were opened. Former lawyers and writers, salesmen, and agents learned to be fitters and frazers at four pounds a week, a payment which many of them couldn't have hoped for even with full-time toy painting or feather making. Some went to work with overalls and sandwiches in suitcases, which were covered in hotel labels from Nice, to St. Moritz, from Westerland to Florence. . . . Foreladies were less tolerant than foremen, girls often hostile against the better groomed strange newcomer.[10]

For Britons, the refugees' appearance often led to confusion. These foreigners were not easily identifiable and did not fit into the traditional social order they knew.

The outbreak of World War II led to a sudden increase in pressure on refugees to become even more invisible as Germans in Great Britain. As mentioned in the previous chapter, German Jews were sometimes subjected to the hostility of British citizens who did not distinguish between Nazi Germans and German Jews, even in Northwest London. Eileen Erlund wrote that she received a friendly response upon meeting her London neighbors, but that "a very short while after, all that changed. The war started and somebody mentioned something about spies, and now it was their turn to be afraid. One morning, when I drew the curtains aside, I saw the whole road filled with threatening fists. It took Mr. Smith ages to pacify the roaring crowd!"[11] Others also reported negative encounters with British nationals who wrongly assumed refugees would be in favor of a German occupation of Britain. The official designation of Germans Jews as enemy aliens and their subsequent internment did not help allay these fears.

When refugees described the air raids on London in 1940, discussion of dress was limited to how they could keep warm in the air raid shelters. For example, Ilse Jacoby wrote, "The air raids continued night after night. As soon as the alert sounded, we went to the shelter, which was a garage under an apartment house. We had to dress warmly and sleep on deck chairs."[12] London refugee accounts frequently mention the gas masks that had to be carried by everyone at all times. War rations placed severe restrictions on the kinds of materials Londoners could purchase. Clothes remained basic and practical; to dress otherwise would appear unpatriotic. Most German Jews could not afford new clothes, or the wardrobe space, so this simplicity of wartime dress made their integration easier.

Eligible German Jewish men enlisted in the Pioneer Corps and later into other military units and were issued soldiers' uniforms, which helped them forge a new identity as British soldiers. Their foreign-looking parents were conscious of the advantages this brought. Victor Ehrenberg wrote to his son Ludwig, "When you have to travel on the nineteenth don't you think it may be useful to travel in uniform?"[13] The full participation of German Jews in the war effort, both as soldiers and civilians in air raid warden gear, significantly increased their integration into British society, at least during the war.[14]

Refugee children adapted more swiftly to British dress than their elders, for numerous reasons. First, by the 1920s all British state schools had adopted the tradition of school uniforms for boys and girls. German Jewish youth received the same uniforms as their classmates, immediately easing this transition. Children living with foster families were usually provided a simple outfit for weekends. Charles Leigh's German-looking knickerbockers were transformed by a relative of his English foster parents into the typical short trousers favored in Britain.[15] Refugee youth hostels and group homes often provided a basic uniform and sometimes a weekend outfit. One child recalled, "I was asked to empty my suitcases and it was explained to me that it was the home's policy to pool most of the clothing such as trousers and jackets. The rest was going to be labeled for identification after laundering. Every boy was given a grey flannelette suit, the trousers being short ones, and a school cap to match."[16] Some German Jewish children, such as Kenneth Ambrose, were sent to British boarding schools in the 1930s while their parents stayed behind in Germany, planning to join them later in the UK. Ambrose wrote in his memoirs, "A photograph taken a month after my arrival shows me wearing my new long German winter coat, and with no idea how to sport a straw boater. However, wearing the weekday and Sunday school uniform, I could pass for an ordinary King's College boy."[17] As in Germany, boys wore short pants until their late teens. These factors led to an easier transition clothing-wise for schoolchildren in Britain.

Mothers in Germany whose children arrived on *Kindertransports* prior to the outbreak of war would send new clothes and sometimes even clean laundry for their children. Ambrose also recalled, "My mother was concerned about the tennis shoes I had asked for.... She wrote, 'I could buy these at Zadek's shoe shop, but you must send me your foot measurements and you must do it soon, because Zadek will be selling his shop shortly and emigrating to Palestine.'"[18] Eva Ehrenberg seemed to place a great deal of importance on her sons' clothing, repeatedly asking in her letters who was darning their socks, and inquiring into their laundry and tailors.[19] When children lived with their parents, the close quarters and tense circumstances often led to family arguments over appearance. Clothes from Germany began to symbolize the past, and children were eager to leave that behind, a typical reaction of immigrant youth. One *Kindertransport* child, who was later joined by her parents, wrote, "Getting rid of the last of my German clothes was both a symbolic and a practical gesture. As I gained confidence, I went out more and more on my own and so did not have to put up with the loud, foreign ways of my parents."[20] The wearing of school uniforms, combined with the desire of youth to fit into their peer group, meant that German Jewish children and teenagers tended to adopt and embrace British styles at a faster rate than refugee adults.

Refugee accounts note subtle distinctions between German and British dress. For example, Marianne Walter observed, "Men in dark striped trousers with folded umbrellas under their arms were hurrying to the station. In Germany, only women carried umbrellas; a man would have thought it effeminate [*sic*]. Here men in well-tailored suits wore little flowers in their buttonholes. German men would have thought this sissy."[21] Phineas May, who kept a more or less official diary of daily happenings at Kitchener Camp for refugee men, noted that a group of new arrivals looked particularly German because they wore the German peaked *chapeau* caps, and he drew a little picture of it for emphasis.[22] A *Kindertransport* teenager, Anne Koppel, wrote that upon her arrival in London, "What grieved us girls most were the black stockings some of the English girls were wearing."[23] These slight variations between British and German dress, mostly in the form of accessories, were easily overcome by refugees trying to adopt a more British look. In Britain, it was a relatively smooth transition from German to British dress style. The similarity in mainstays of clothing, the desire to blend into British society out of a fear of antisemitism or a Nazi invasion, and the perpetual separation of families meant that German Jews were more inclined to adapt to local dress habits. As recommended in the "While You Are Here" pamphlet, London refugees aimed for understatement. Once the war began, it was crucial not to stand out as foreigners.

New York: Dress and Appearance

While German Jews in London considered the British understated and modest in dress and manner, German Jews in New York considered Americans overstated and "showy." For example, Anne Marie Grebler wrote in New York, "What do I dislike? Fundamentally what I always imagined: the superficiality of it all. Everything presents a beautiful exterior designed to impress, the houses with imposing lobbies but small and ugly apartments; the people in fine clothes, neat, elegant, and for the most part, dressed in good taste. How they are underneath I don't know; we have met only a few people."[24] German Jews in New York were surprised by the amount of make-up Americans wore; one even noted that in Germany make-up was only for the stage.[25] A refugee who arrived as a child with her parents remembered, "A few days after arriving, we were enrolled in school. It was strange and interesting. Little girls no older than I, were allowed to wear red nail polish on dirty finger nails and spent much time in class peeling off the hardened polish."[26] An *Aufbau Almanac* article explained that one hardly saw warts or birthmarks on American women because "everything was easily taken off by a doctor." It further stated, "The American woman is a master of make-up, which is characteristic for her, because she tends to be superficial, which foreign observers speak of as a kind of uniform."[27] Refugees may have perceived Americans as overfocused on their appearance, but, German Jews were also conscious of their looks and the upkeep of them as evidenced by the frequent advertisements in the *Aufbau* from 1936 through 1945 for beauty salons offering permanent waves and electrolysis.[28] Unlike their counterparts in London, they were under little pressure to blend in. As this section will show, German Jewish adults in New York did not feel it necessary to hide their German background, and at times even took pride in what they perceived as their own refined European tastes.

As in London, most refugees in New York did not have appropriate work clothes upon arrival. Men worked blue-collar jobs and women worked in domestic service or in factories. Alice Oppenheimer, one of the founders of the Congregation of Washington Heights, recalled:

> People were still allowed to bring their good clothes with them from Germany and, of course, it was understandable that they brought only good clothes. But since they had to work on the lowest level in America, doing housework for example, they needed work clothes. So we established this office, a room where everybody could come on a Sunday morning and get clothing. . . . It was our policy never to write down any names, because it was very hard for these people to take charity. They were very proud. They didn't want to depend on charity even though they were willing to work on the lowest level.[29]

Without the disruptions of internment and evacuations, and with few employment restrictions, New York refugees found jobs in offices and shops at a faster rate than their counterparts in London, and could return to their more "dignified" attire sooner. This allowed them to wear the clothes they brought with them.

Although rationing of fabric occurred in the United States, it had less impact on American life since it came at a later date and entailed fewer restrictions. Caroline Rennolds Milbank wrote in her book *New York Fashion* that as a result of a 1943 rationing regulation, "manufacturers made do without certain materials and minimalist styles were made popular." She quoted an article from the February 1943 issue of *Vogue Magazine*, "The British, who have felt the pinch of fabric shortages longer than we, practically live in slim coat-dresses."[30] For refugees who had spent time in London during the war and then arrived in New York by 1941, the amount of available material goods was overwhelming. Bridget Stross Laky wrote, for example:

> In the morning the sun was shining, and I strolled along Fifth Avenue. I had no money to spend, but gorged my eyes on dresses and coats, evening wear and nylons. And shoes! I had a passion for shoes and thought that owning four pairs, bought with scarce clothing coupons in England, was a hoard. For a long time I could not afford coupons for the fourth pair, but after my father's death, I used some of his leftover ones. . . . In New York, I could only look at the plethora of shoes and other goods,

but the anticipation of future purchases was enough. . . . Most striking of all was the absence of uniforms still prominent in England and an integral part of my environment since childhood. . . . I admired the chic women in high heels, hats and white gloves. . . . I felt once again an outsider in my drab wartime clothes, flats, and without make-up.[31]

Kenneth Ambrose's cousin, Jenny, wrote from New York, "Shopping is a joy here, everything is in plenty, so long as you have a bit of money. . . . Everyone has to work and work, time is money, and they are all pleased to have a bit of peace in the evening—altogether different from England."[32] She was familiar with the employment restrictions placed on refugees in Britain, food and clothing shortages, and the nightly bombings endured by all Londoners. Refugee accounts show that World War II influenced the dress and appearance of German Jews in New York to a much lesser degree than in London.

Living between two worlds, refugee children felt simultaneous pressure to adopt American ways while satisfying their parents, who continued to embrace their German Jewish heritage. For the most part, though, refugee youth wanted to look like their American classmates. One recalled, "We wanted to assimilate as quickly as possible, to learn American customs and to fit in. . . . In Germany we wore short pants until fifteen, sixteen, seventeen years of age. I was fifteen when I arrived. I adapted. I started wearing long pants."[33] Another, who came through Britain, remembered, "English students wore knee length coats over Bermuda-like shorts and knee length high woolen socks with shirts, ties, caps, but in America you had to be 'with-it.' You had to have jackets. So, one of my first errands was to a department store."[34] The lack of school uniforms created extra pressure on struggling refugees to provide appropriate clothing for their children. Consequently, clothing became an object of contention at home. Refugee parents often believed one could be American and still wear German Jewish clothes, while children were much more attuned to the differences between American and European dress. Compared to refugee children in London who wore uniforms to school and were, more often than not, unable to wear their German-style clothes, New York children had to balance parental expectations with their own desire to look American.

Most peculiar about American dress for German Jewish parents was its casual informality. Adults, who equated elegant and formal clothes with dignity and respectability, were frustrated by the outfits their children preferred to wear. Walter Baum remembered:

> My parents had outfitted me very well with lots of stuff. But the stuff was German which meant I had a raincoat that looked like a policeman's. Now that wasn't what kids wore . . . I felt it gave me an appearance that people could tell immediately that I wasn't native born. . . . The coloring of the clothes was different and American styles were much more relaxed. You didn't have to wear a tie and jacket and everything. So when my parents saw me when they came, they felt I had become sloppy. An American wore a sweatshirt and a pair of pants and that was good enough. Refugees went to the movies and had to dress with a tie.[35]

Younger refugee men considered neckties too formal for everyday wear, but those who worked among fellow German Jews, in refugee-owned shops and offices, obliged their employers. One child who grew up in Washington Heights recalled that her father always wore a tie, even when he went out to buy milk.[36]

American clothing was more casual and less traditional than European styles, even among wealthier Americans.[37] These styles were noticeably different for newly arrived refugees, who tended to dress in a more formal and tailored fashion. Clothes in the United States were generally not custom made, but rather purchased ready to wear off the shop rack. Nonetheless, in the 1930s and 1940s, refugee-frequented shops such as S. Klein did a solid business in the formal tailored style of clothes the refugees were accustomed to in Germany. Clothing shops and individual refugees sold their wares in Washington Heights or downtown and advertised in German in *Aufbau* throughout the 1930s and 1940s. For example, in the January 1936 issue there was an advertisement for F. Bader Tailor, "in the club's [New World Club] neighborhood" on West 90th Street and another for "Crawford Custom Quality clothes—*Deutschsprachige Bedienung in unserem Laden* E86th St. [German-speaking staff in our store on East 86th St.]."[38] In September that year were ads for furriers and men's clothes and hats on West 85th Street.[39] Some refugees hoped to have clothing made out of fabric they brought over from Germany. There were tailors who did alterations and updates, but getting bespoke outfits was generally too expensive for most refugees. Liselotte Kahn remarked disappointedly that the high cost of getting clothes custom made in New York forced her to leave the fabric and leather she had brought with her untouched and unused.[40] The German tradition of updating one's fall outfit at the end of spring was continued in New York. Former specialty manufacturers often restarted watered-down versions of their German businesses using fabric and materials they brought to the United States. This included hat makers, furriers, upholsterers, shirt makers, and those who made bespoke suits. These smaller outlets provided places for refugees to purchase specialty items. European styles were still popular among adult refugees, especially on weekends when they socialized. Lowenstein wrote that:

> persons describing the way German Jews dressed both at the time of their first arrival and later speak about conservative style, elegance and an absence of flashiness. . . . The immigrants tended to look down on the nouveau riche style of show and flashiness and preferred a more dignified style of dressing. Of course, some of the clothes brought from Europe were unfashionable, and often even outlandish, in America.[41]

Lowenstein described the refugees as arriving with "their formerly fashionable bourgeois German clothing. These possessions not only made it difficult for many refugees to convince American Jews and others that they were really poor, they also helped reinforce old German-Jewish cultural attitudes and to orient the immigrants in their new surroundings."[42] Refugees tended to preserve the one formal piece of clothing they brought with them and to wear it repeatedly outside of work. By the late 1930s, *Aufbau* was filled with weekly advertisements for clothing stores and individual retailers either repairing or selling apparel directly from their apartments in Washington Heights or on the Upper West Side. These ads were primarily in German and geared toward refugee customers. Examples in the September 6, 1940, issue of *Aufbau* include an advertisement that stated, "Hat Salon of Madame Hermy, formerly of Vienna, finest individual handwork."[43] That same issue had another advertisement for a private tailor and seamstress. In addition, each week in *Aufbau* there was a section called "We Rebuild" and it listed the names and descriptions of newly opened refugee-owned businesses, usually transplanted from Germany or Austria. A close look reveals a steady rise in the number of these from 1935 to 1945. What began as a cottage industry of individual refugees selling items out of their apartments developed into a network of businesses across the city. Refugees in New York had more disposable income than their counterparts in London and also more places to purchase Continental-style clothes.

German Jewish formality of dress and manner could sometimes be perceived as snobbery by outsiders, as alluded to briefly in the Lowenstein quote above. In their 1945 study of German Jews, Davie and Koenig found that the refugees were accused of a "conspicuous display of wealth by the 'café society' among them, their arrogance, air of superiority and ungratefulness," but Davie also wrote that his study found this complaint to be exaggerated, and that "in most communities the number of refugees is so small that, unless attention is drawn to them, the community as a whole is hardly aware of their presence."[44] Their visibility as a foreign or immigrant group was, on the whole, not possible among typical Americans, and especially not in a diverse metropolis such as New York. Usually, it was refugees alone who noticed one another.

The Orthodox German refugees dressed differently from East European Orthodox Jews in both Germany and in New York. They had long ago adopted German-style clothing that complied with religious code. They generally did not look different from any other German Jews. Since hats were still common in the United States when they arrived, Orthodox German men could remain inconspicuous as long as they covered their heads with fashionable straw or felt hats. Lowenstein wrote:

> Separatist Orthodox congregations did not attempt to distinguish themselves from other Americans in their outward appearance. Though males wore head coverings at all times, and some of the women wore marriage wigs, neither sex wore a special Jewish costume. Except for the rabbis, virtually none of the German-born members of the Separatist Orthodox congregations were bearded. The point was not to stand out as a group obviously different from others, but rather to adhere strictly to Jewish religious law. If that could be accomplished in an inconspicuous manner, which did not hinder one's participation in the modern world, so much the better.[45]

Orthodox German Jews, unlike Eastern European Orthodox Jews in New York City, chose to follow German tradition by being clean shaven, wearing hats as head covering and fine suits and coats on the Sabbath.

To many refugees' surprise, the weather in New York, with its hot and humid summers and bitterly cold, snowy winters, was more severe than in Europe. With their German clothes, they arrived unprepared for these extremes in climate. Leo Grebler remarked, "This was July and August, the heat unbearable, our European summer wardrobe much too heavy."[46] Similarly, Sabor wrote, "My parents equipped themselves in England with warm clothing but . . . the American climate demanded long pants."[47] Walter

Baum described the trunk of clothes packed by his mother, "There were many other wardrobe items that never made it out of the trunk: long, heavy underwear; a *Kleppermantel,* which is a European version of a policeman's rubberized raincoat (someone had told my parents about the 'rainstorms' in New York); hats and heavy socks and all the paraphernalia which European misunderstanding associated with life in New York."[48] Rudolf Katz's diary also noted the weather and its effect on his daily activities: "Days are rather hot and sticky now and I wear my khaki shorts and a sport shirt only."[49] A doctor writing in the *Aufbau Almanac* reported:

> We are mostly too heavily dressed. In the summer it is as hot as we can take it and in winter the houses are so overheated that, with the surplus warmth that escapes through New York chimneys and windows, one could take care of a major European city. One can best protect them against the cold on the street by overdressing, which is unbearable indoors. Frequent changing of underclothes in summer is necessary and the daily bath is no luxury.[50]

The heat and humidity of a New York summer, along with the uncontrollable heat of their apartment buildings, was unexpected and unplanned for by most refugees. Their German clothes were not particularly suited for these extremes. Yet, they adapted.

Upon close examination of accounts from both cities, it becomes clear that most refugees in London relinquished their German dress practices, while those in New York retained them for the myriad of reasons explored in this chapter. The adaptability of dress provided a means for refugees to maintain a semblance of control over their situation. They could retain or renegotiate elements of their former identity through their appearance. The pressures to do this differed in London and New York. Those in Britain found that looking German, or just different, could be a liability, especially after September 1939. Meanwhile refugees in New York could choose to adapt to American dress or not, at their own pace.

Names

The changing of one's name is perhaps the clearest and most substantive means of self-expression and identity declaration available. German Jewish refugee accounts reveal greater pressure to Anglicize German-sounding names in London than in New York City. Nonetheless, the patterns for first and last name usage and titles were more familiar to German refugees in Britain than in the United States.

First Names

In both Germany and Great Britain, first names were traditionally reserved for close friends, family, and children, while last names were prefaced with *Mr., Mrs., Miss,* or *Dr.* for acquaintances, neighbors, colleagues, and employers. In a review of more than twenty private diaries and letters of German Jews in Britain, first names were not used for British acquaintances. Eva Reichmann, for instance, wrote extensively about Lady Gollanz and Dr. Weiner, but only mentioned their first names once.[51] Alice Schwab did the same with many of her colleagues, such as Mrs. Neuth, Professor Neuth, Mrs. Salomon, Mr. and Mrs. Dobbs, Professor Wolpe, and Mrs. Rathbone.[52] Marianne Walter continually referred to Mrs. and Mr. Lamb, her hosts, without ever mentioning their first names.[53] Resi Kohen wrote of a Miss Holingsworth and a Mr. and Mrs. Pomfrett, all of whom employed her as a maid. Later in her account, she referred to her colleague Mrs. Huxley, but it was only when she mentioned her "true friends," Margaret and Kathleen, and her boyfriend, Joe that she used first names.[54]

In both British and German Jewish circles, adults referred to children by their first name, a nickname or, in school, by their last name only. This is evident throughout refugee accounts. School-aged children used first names, nicknames, or just last names among themselves. Refugee children who attended British schools often Anglicized their first names. Charles Leigh, formerly Karl Levinsohn, chose to go by "Charlie" while living with a foster family in London. It was an old nickname his cousin teased him with back in Germany.[55] Although their parents continued to call them Ludwig and Gottfried, brothers Lewis and George Elton, formerly Ehrenberg, changed their names just prior to joining the British military in 1942, a common precautionary move for Pioneer Corps volunteers. Gottfried had planned to eliminate his German-sounding middle name of Otto in the process, but his father wrote, "Why oppress [*sic*] your second letter? Otto is not a bad name, you would keep the names of your two grandfathers, and it is in accordance with the English custom. I really don't see why you should restrict yourself to the G.!"[56] Prior to the outbreak of World War II, there was less pressure on refugees to change German-sounding names into English ones. Birth announcements in the refugee press continued to show the use of traditional German names, such as Renate, Daniela, and Hans. When Germany began to invade other countries across Europe, German names lost their appeal among most refugees.

In New York, refugees were taken by surprise when Americans they had just met used their first names. For example, Julius Cohn wrote in a letter that he was greeted at the Hoboken pier by "a real American, the kind you see in a book . . . he acted as if he had known me ten years, and from the first minute on, he only called me 'Julius.' "[57] This differed significantly from refugees' experiences in Britain, where they continued to use titles and last names with their British acquaintances. As in London, it was typical for refugee men in New York to refer to German Jewish friends solely by their last names. Yet, when they referred to their new American friends they tended to use only first names. Leo Grebler noted:

> Curiously, while I have easily adopted the first-name basis in professional and social contacts with "real" Americans, I have had much greater trouble extending it to old refugee friends from Germany who were much closer to me; for some time Franz Wolf, ex-colleague at the *Frankfurter Zeitung*, was *Herr* Wolf, then dropping the *Herr* became the climax of intimacy, and it took quite a long time for us to reach the first-name stage without self-consciousness.[58]

This reaction is seen throughout refugee letters and diaries.[59] They retained their German traditions within refugee circles, but adopted the American name procedures with "real" Americans. First names were more likely to be Anglicized than last names; the first names were often shortened, especially in the army. Ernest Stock found that while serving in the U.S. Army, "people started calling me 'Ernie,' everybody had a nickname, and that sort of stuck with me for the rest of my life."[60] Otto Bickart adopted the name "Robert" when he joined the U.S. Army and was subsequently referred to as "Bob" by his fellow soldiers, but remained "Otto" among his Washington Heights friends and family.[61] In general, first names were more likely to be altered by refugees in the United States, regardless of whether they changed their last name or not. The common use in America of first names in both social and professional environments may have contributed to this. In his 1958 study on Jewish refugee name changes, Ernest Maass questioned, "Is it too far-fetched to suppose that such changes were, at least in part, prompted by the great use of first names in this country, which is much more customary here than in Europe and renders the possession of a given name that is pleasant to the bearer of greater importance?"[62] Refugee first names were often unofficially exchanged for their English equivalent, such as Hermann-Herman, Franz-Frank, Gerhard-Gerry, and Georg-George. This was especially true for younger refugees, who were more eager to blend in. In some cases, women's first names were Americanized by their employers or co-workers, who had difficulty with German names. In any case, most German Jews in New York retained their German first name within refugee circles, while using American versions of their names outside of the refugee community.

The majority of German Jewish refugees in both cities gave their newborn babies Anglicized names. In Britain, giving Anglicized first names to newborns had become more prominent by 1940. Prior to this, the given names tended to be German. Perhaps because they held temporary visas, these new parents did not anticipate remaining in Great Britain. German Jewish parents in New York City gave their children typical American names quite early—especially those used by American Jews at the time.[63] Lowenstein observed that in Washington Heights:

> [w]hile most of the older generation kept their German first names or still used them privately, even when they changed them officially, virtually all gave their children American first names. Among the German-born in Washington Heights common names included Ludwig, Julius, Max . . . mixed with a smaller number of more typically Jewish names such as Simon, Moses. . . . The German Jews of Washington Heights generally followed American-Jewish naming patterns for their children. Children were given the Hebrew name of a deceased relative for religious functions but were called by their English names on all other occasions. . . . The most common first names given to the children of German Jews born in Washington Heights in the 1940s, 1950s, and 1960s were very similar to those typical of American Jews of the same period. They included Stuart, Steven, Milton, Howard, Allan, Jeffrey, Arthur, Joan, Susan, Judy, Carol, Helen, and Linda. Such names as John and Mary, which were considered too Christian for most American Jews, were likewise avoided by most German-Jewish parents. The only possible exception to this was the large number of boys born in

the 1940s who were named Frank or Franklin after Franklin D. Roosevelt. . . . The cases of children given German names like Ludwig or Arno were very rare.[64]

The use of first names in London and New York had an impact on how easily refugees integrated into the society there. It took some time for German Jews in the United States to get used to being called by their first names by Americans. In Britain, the practice of using courtesy titles for acquaintances and first names exclusively among family and intimate friends was more familiar. They understood the practice and felt comfortable following it. It helped make integration into British culture swifter for the refugees in London.

Last Names and Surnames

By the summer of 1940, there was a very real fear that the Germans would invade London just as they had Paris and Amsterdam. This led many German Jews to feel the needed to adopt an English name. However, the elimination of an "enemy-sounding" name was more than just a precaution against possible invasion. There was a growing sense that xenophobic acts by Britons could be prevented with the Anglicization of one's name. Anne Marie Fortier wrote that Italians living in Britain experienced similar pressure: "The intense Italophobia pervading public discourses during the 1939–1945 war years in Britain compelled many to seek to hide their Italianness; avoiding speaking Italian in public, and Anglicizing their names or their trade."[65] The same could be said for German Jews during these years.

In London, air raids, internment, and employment restrictions meant that refugee neighborhoods were unable to flourish prior to 1945, and refugees were forced to integrate more quickly into British society. The growing anti-German sentiment refugees experienced firsthand in Britain, due to the proximity of the war, helped secure their decision to hide their German origins through name changes. The British armed forces strongly encouraged the nine thousand enlisted German Jewish soldiers to change their last names in case of capture by the Germans. For example, Kenneth Ambrose, formerly Kurt Abrahamsohn, recalled that "the RAF realized that I would be in a bad way if I ever fell into German hands with my name unchanged, and it was their policy to encourage former German nationals to adopt new names."[66] His name change document was legalized "under the procedure applicable to foreign nationals serving in the RAF or RAFVR who have been authorized by the Air Ministry to adopt an assumed name during the war for security reasons . . . for the duration of hostilities."[67] Although this was intended to last only through the war, the majority of German Jewish soldiers retained their Anglicized names. Their families usually adopted them as well.

German Jews unofficially Anglicized their names in London workplaces in order to ease everyday interactions with English staff and customers. Kenneth Ambrose wrote, "I had already become accustomed to respond to 'Ambrose' at my workplace, where 'Abrahamsohn' was thought to be too difficult for staff and customers."[68] Alice Schwab, formerly Liesel Rosenthal, kept part of her Jewish-sounding name while working as a manager for Marks & Spencer during the war. She wrote of her staff, "They knew me as 'Miss Rosen,' cutting the 'thal' off the end of my name. Mrs. Salomon [her boss] had decided that she thought that 'Rosen' was long enough."[69] Other German Jews working in London modified or changed their names for similar reasons. Some examples of changes I discovered in my research included: Karl Levinsohn to Charles Leigh, Gottfried and Ludwig Ehrenberg to George and Lewis Elton, Liesel Rosenthal to Alice Rosen, and Hans Menzinger to Ian Menzies. There was usually a pronunciation or origin connection between the old and new names. One way for women to Anglicize their names or disguise their German background was to marry a non-Jewish British man and take his last name or to marry a British Jewish man with a previously Anglicized name. For some female refugees, marrying out of the German Jewish community allowed them to leave their refugee status behind.

Ernest Maass examined refugee publications, synagogue documents, and German Jewish organizational files and found that in the 1940s and 1950s fewer than 15 percent of German Jewish refugees in the United States changed or altered their last names.[70] Several factors might account for this low rate of name changes in the United States. First, the development and longevity of German Jewish enclaves in New York meant that German cultural practices were maintained. Business and social networks relied on the use of family names and, once established, it was difficult to change them. Second, German Jewish names traditionally carried respectability in America since the nineteenth century. Many German Jews embraced the American melting pot narrative and believed that a foreign-sounding name could still be American. In their eyes, America's long history of immigration and a widely held faith in the American Dream went hand in hand with retaining one's "old world" name.[71] Throughout the country, but particularly in New

York, most proprietors of shops and restaurants used their Italian, Polish, German, or Jewish names for their businesses. The visible diversity of New York also made it easier for many refugees to feel comfortable retaining their German names. In 1952, J. Alvin Kugelmass wrote:

> It is understandable in xenophobic France or homogeneous England that someone with an outlandish name should want to lose his "foreignness." But in the polyglot of United States alien names, like alien origin, are almost as much the rule as the exception, as a glance at the telephone book, a list of the honored war dead, names on a good football team or a list of contributors to the Red Cross will show.[72]

Some German Jews reported that they were sentimentally attached to their German last names and the status they held within the New York German Jewish community and did not wish to Anglicize them. This is particularly true for those who settled in German Jewish enclaves, or who worked and socialized mainly among fellow refugees. This was not hindered by the fear of a possible German invasion, as it was in Britain. While the majority of refugees in the United States retained their German names, it is interesting to examine the reasons why that 15 percent chose to alter their last names and how the justifications differed from those in Britain. According to Maass, the typical refugee who changed his/her name was married, well educated, and professional, and arrived in the United States in his/her late twenties.

German Jewish name changes in New York were usually done to increase professional opportunity, in anticipation of antisemitism rather than as a direct response to anti-German feeling. Evidence of this can be found in Maass's study, which revealed that identifiable Jewish names, such as Rosen, Cohen, Levi, and Solomon, were those most frequently altered among refugees. Some respondents in his survey claimed that they changed their Jewish-sounding names prior to arrival in the United States to prevent any type of discrimination. Kugelmass found that, among German Jews who changed their name in New York, most were doctors and dentists who felt that they might attract more gentile patients if their name did not give away their Jewish background. For some, the experience of persecution in Germany had strongly affected their sense of Jewish identity. One wrote:

> When I came to the United States in 1937, I was still suffering from my experiences in Germany. I was confused. Father

Coughlin and his Social Justice Movement and the German American Bund were all very active. American Jews were quite disturbed. It was at that time that I opened my first store and wanted to put my name, which is quite Jewish, on the roof in big letters. I changed it at that moment.[73]

Sometimes it was other Jews, already established in the United States, who encouraged or requested these name changes. Maass wrote of one respondent, "A secretary who had been put under pressure by her Jewish employer, a lawyer, to drop her Jewish name. He did not want a Jewish name to 'appear so often on legal documents to be witnessed,' tentatively decided to adopt Gordon instead."[74] Another refugee recalled, "At the time I was a travelling salesman, my Jewish boss asked me to change my name because it sounded Jewish. As I had thought of a name change before, I decided to go through with it."[75] Both Maass and Kugelmass asked their study participants whether, upon reflection, their name changes were warranted. The overwhelming majority regretted their decisions, stating that they soon realized it was unnecessary. Kugelmass reported, "All twenty-five said they had been fools and regretted it. Some felt it didn't better their situation and most would change back now if they could."[76] Louis Adamic wrote in 1942, "Of course, there is no reason to change Jewish names; for like Italian names, these are generally known and respected."[77] Overall, it appears that the persecution Jews experienced in Germany led to an anticipation of antisemitic discrimination in the United States. In the end, it turned out that they felt name changes may not have been necessary.

Further reasons for name changes in the United States included difficulty in pronunciation and spelling for native English speakers. Some German Jews felt they should simplify their name by making modifications favorable to the American ear. After typical Jewish names, the most common names to be changed were standard German-sounding ones, such as Hirschfeld and Hirschheimer, and those ending in "stein" or "thal," such as Katzenstein and Lowenthal. Whereas in Britain refugees often adopted completely Anglicized names, alterations in the United States took all shapes and forms. Name modifications among German Jews in New York also included many name shortenings that were not attempts to cover their German background, but rather to make spelling and pronunciation of their names easier for Americans. Complete or partial translation was common, such as Fuchs-Fox, Hertz-Hart, Wertheim-Worth, and Rosenberg-Hill. It was also easy to shorten names, such as Rothhirsch-Roth or Friedlander-Lander and to phonetically re-spell them, as in Treu-Troy. Similar to German Jews in London, some in New York chose English-sounding names that began with the same letter as their old name, such as Mandelbaum-Morton and Joachimsohn-Jackson.

In German Jewish enclaves such as Washington Heights, retaining one's German name was the norm. In fact, in his extensive social history of the neighborhood, Steven Lowenstein does not make a single mention of last name changes among this population. Even those who officially changed their names often used their former German names in refugee circles. Maass wrote of his study, "The old name came to life again when refugees met, exchanged information, relived common experiences and revived old memories. One of the people reached in the sample survey stated, 'I use the old name sometimes to identify myself as my father's son,' while another one wrote, 'Friends usually call me by my old name.'"[78] Some had already changed their name while living in the first country of exile and decided to keep their French, Italian, Spanish, or Portuguese name, such as Noir, Ferro, and Santos. German Jews serving in the U.S. military in the European theater were encouraged to Anglicize their names in case of capture by the Nazis, yet this practice does not appear to have been as widespread as it was in Britain. Occasionally, refugee parents in New York took it upon themselves to give their newborn children a completely new American-sounding first and last name. One birth announcement dated May 9, 1943 stated the arrival of a Danielle Louisa Franklin born to a Dr. Hans Alexander and Stella Fraenkel of New York City.[79] Perhaps the "Franklin" was also a tribute to Franklin Delano Roosevelt, as it also appeared frequently as a boy's first name at the time.

Changes in first and last names of German Jewish refugees in New York were less common than in London. In the United States, the later entry into the war and the distance of New York from the European front meant that anti-German sentiment never gained the momentum that it did in Britain. Also in New York, the perception of a more diverse and heterogeneous society meant that German Jews were more likely to retain their German name. The differences in naming patterns in London and New York further prove that refugees in the former city felt greater pressure to blend in than their counterparts in the latter.

Titles

In many ways, the British use of titles and names was similar to that of Germany in the early and mid-twentieth century. Germany and Britain both had stratified upper classes that were defined by titles such as *Herzog* and

Graf in German, and Duke and Duchess in English.[80] One difference was that nonaristocrats in Britain could become a Sir, Lord, or Lady regardless of their station at birth. This allowed some very prominent Jews to eventually achieve official upper-class status. Professional titles, such as *Frau Doktor* and *Herr Professor*, were used in Germany and remained extremely important to those who held them. Similarly, British society also used professional titles, although they differed somewhat from the German ones. For instance, the use of "Doctor" was reserved for doctors of medicine, and only occasionally for academics, and never for lawyers. Only when holding an academic position could one insert "Professor" in front of a first name. Additionally, teachers were called "Sir" and "Miss," regardless of their social or marital status, whereas in Germany they used "*Herr*" and "*Frau*" with the last name, sometimes with "Professor" inserted. New acquaintances, both German and English, were addressed with an English title, such as "Mr.," and a last name. In refugee circles, the continued use of "*Herr Doktor*" and "*Herr Professor*" was important in maintaining their self-esteem, especially if they were now unemployed or working as menial laborers.

Upon Britain's entry into war, most refugees stopped speaking German, even among themselves, and thereby relinquished this tradition of professional titles. In some circumstances, however, such as internment, these titles were retained. On the whole, though, most refugees swiftly adopted the appropriate English titles, using "Doctor" and "Professor," "Mister" and "Misses," when applicable. The infrequent use of titles in the United States was particularly difficult for refugees to fathom, especially since new acquaintances were instantly on a "first-name basis" with them. Professional titles for lawyers and scholars were generally not used in conversation. Gerhard Saenger wrote:

> Most academicians [*sic*] are surprised that the title "*Herr Doktor*" no longer serves as an introduction to society. . . . Professor K., formerly one of Germany's most distinguished scientists, shared this opinion and added that "educated people, and particularly university professors, do not occupy the same social position in America that they held in Europe." This difference finds expression in the European habit of using the academic degree with the name.[81]

Postcards from Europe to Oskar Bern in New York were addressed to "Herrn Architect Oskar Bern," yet postcards from local organizations were addressed to "Mr. and Mrs. Oskar Bern."[82] Among themselves, refugees in the United States retained their former titles for a longer time than those in Britain. Saenger also observed:

> This emotional need is the main reason why the recent newcomers seek each other's company. In refugee gatherings the old titles, *"Herr Doktor"* and *"Herr Kommerzienrat"* (commerce councilman) are still used and distinguish their bearers. Here *"Stadtrat Holzman"* (city councilman) is still known as the descendant "of this old and famous family from Burgenhausen," not as the immigrant X. In speaking of the old times, memories of past glory and achievement awaken anew. . . . The search for a lost prestige is an important reason for the formation of an isolated refugee community life.[83]

In Washington Heights, Gabriele Schiff noted, "In the beginning when I got the room there, it seemed to be a little bit like home and there were people who spoke German. And they called me 'Frau Doktor' in the store. It's this type of thing that makes for a cohesive neighborhood."[84] The importance of earlier titles is clearly revealed when examining the business cards of former refugees living in New York. The card of a Dr. Fr. W. Foerster included, "Former Professor of Philosophy and Pedagogy at the University of Munich," and a Manhattan address in the bottom corner.[85] Advertisements in the *Aufbau Almanac* during this time often included former titles alongside the German town or city they came from. For example, there is an advertisement for "the services of Hilde Nathan, Dr. rer. pol. (*früher* [formerly of] Berlin)" and another one for Assja L. Kadis, Diplom. Wien (Vienna).[86]

For many refugees, the loss of their former careers and businesses was the most difficult personal challenge they faced. As Saenger indicated, "One may almost say that while a scholar without a position and money is still a scholar, a businessman without a job and money is no longer a businessman."[87] Throughout his diaries, Rudolf Katz pointed out fellow refugees' prior professions, such as one acquaintance "who used to be an artist."[88] Maurice Davie wrote in his 1946 study:

> Some of the refugees find it difficult to get accustomed to the informality of Americans, the lack of distinctions in forms of address and the free use of first names. It is a jolt to the Herr

Doktor Professor to be called "Doc." On the other hand, once they are used to it, the refugees like the easygoing, informal manner of Americans, the common bond of the universal "you" instead of the formal "Sie" and informal "du" of the Germans. In response to the question as to what had changed most in his way of life, a German states, "From the very formal, very bourgeois businessman, Herr K., to the hardworking war worker, 'Fred'—and I like it."[89]

Individual expressions of identity such as dress, names, and titles are clear indicators of immigrant integration. Once Britain entered into war with Germany, refugees in London believed it was vital not to stand out as German. Evidence shows that they were highly conscious of differences between German and British dress. The formality of London attire made it easier for refugees to adopt these styles than in New York. Younger refugees were most likely to adapt, especially those who were fostered by British families as part of the *Kindertransport* program or evacuation. The informality of dress among Americans surprised many refugees and made it more of a challenge for older refugees to remain inconspicuous. It also led to tensions between parent and child. In New York, while younger refugees tried to blend in visually with their American classmates, living with their German Jewish parents in German Jewish enclaves meant they adapted at a slower rate. German Jews in New York were also more inclined to dress in their former styles because of a belief that to be American meant one could retain one's former ways. There is little evidence of anti-German sentiment in New York accounts. It seems that refugees there felt less pressure to hide their German roots.

These divergent patterns of cultural adaptation are repeated in the usage of first and last names of refugees in London compared to New York. The differences between German and American name and title customs were greater than German and British traditions. London refugees Anglicized their first and last names out of fears of anti-German sentiment and the possibility of a German invasion. Many name changes in Britain occurred among male refugees serving in the British army, where it was widely encouraged. Refugee soldiers in the U.S. armed services were more likely to Anglicize their first name but to retain their German last name. Since the mid-nineteenth century, German Jewish last names in the United States came to represent quality service, and many refugees retained their last name to benefit from this. However, in some cases, fears of antisemitism prompted name changes.

Overall, refugees in New York kept their names because they were tied to the German Jewish community either socially or professionally.

As with dress and manners, a British appreciation for titles and last names aided the cultural integration of German Jews in London. Informality of American culture again became obvious to German Jews living there, in terms of first-name familiarity. It seems that within the German Jewish community of New York, German titles and last name usage were retained. Those who worked among "real" Americans tended to follow the American custom in that particular setting, but returned to German patterns among their cohort. The distinct patterns of integration in London and New York, evident in the communal and family spheres, were replicated at the individual level. This is apparent in the differences in retention and relinquishing of German Jewish dress, names, and titles among refugees in the two cities.

4

Language and Mannerisms

By THE TURN OF THE TWENTIETH CENTURY, middle-class Jews in Germany spoke German as their primary language at home, in school, and at work.[1] Yiddish was considered the language of *Ostjuden,* Eastern European Jews, who, in German Jewish eyes, were unassimilated and not German. In synagogues, Hebrew usage varied, depending on the particular congregation's denomination. Liberal services tended to be held in German while Conservative or Orthodox ones included Hebrew, at least during the prayers and the reading of the Torah. Parents sent their sons to learn to read Hebrew for their Bar Mitzvahs, but daughters were generally excluded from learning more than the Hebrew alphabet. After Hitler came to power, German Jews began learning Modern Hebrew, not for religious reasons, but to prepare for a possible future in what was then Palestine. Those intending to emigrate elsewhere took lessons in English, Spanish, or other languages.

The field of migration studies has benefited from recent contributions of linguists who examine immigrant populations.[2] In this chapter, I look at the immediate pressures felt by refugees between 1935 and 1945 to use either German or English in certain situations in London and New York. I examine the distinct social and historical circumstances that directly affected language choices among refugees. Immigrant perceptions of British and American body language and mannerisms are also explored here, as an extension of verbal and written language.

Language

In the early years of emigration to Britain, prior to the outbreak of war in 1939, German Jews in London mainly spoke German among themselves, but used English in their interactions with native Britons. Work opportunities directly affected refugees' acquisition of English. Refugee women arriving on domestic service visas learned English at their place of employment. Those working as governesses could practice the language with their charges. Susanne Samson, for example, recalled, "My occupation at the time was to look after this little girl. And she actually taught me quite a lot of English, because children are very good language teachers, because if you don't understand, they willingly repeat things over and over again . . . so I learned quite a lot of English from her because she was quite a teacher."[3] Alice Schwab wrote of her nanny experience, "The youngest girl—she was only a toddler, taught me English and corrected my mistakes."[4] Refugee maids learned piecemeal English from the contact they had with other British domestics and directly from their employers.

Unemployed refugee men described days waiting in embassy queues, retraining for their professions, wandering around London, and reminiscing with fellow refugees while trying to learn as much English as possible from newspapers, radio, and evening classes. Congregating in hotel lobbies and in cafes, it was only natural to speak German with one another prior to the outbreak of war. In her autobiographically based novel, *The Other Way Round*, Judith Kerr describes her family's stay at a hotel that was frequented by newly arrived refugees; they were greeted by all, including the desk clerk, in German.[5]

The Woburn House booklet, *While You Are in England*, distributed to newly arrived refugees explicitly advised, "Spend your spare time immediately learning the English language and its correct pronunciation. Refrain from speaking German in the streets and in public conveyances and in public places such as restaurants. Talk halting English rather than fluent German—and *do not talk in a loud voice*. Do not read German newspapers in public."[6] The message was clear: do not allow yourself to be recognized as German, and try to blend in. In the same way that Anglo-Jews encouraged refugees to be understated in dress and appearance, they promoted inconspicuous use of language.

At the outbreak of war in 1939, and especially by late 1940 when a Nazi invasion was possible, it became imperative for German Jews to speak English. One respondent in Berghahn's study remembered, "When we came we could not speak German, one had to whisper; one was an enemy, one was treated as an enemy. . . . One certainly did not make any demands."[7] Accusations of being a German spy were not uncommon, as Eileen Erlund discovered:

One day Mother and I went for a walk. I had never been able to find my way about—no sense of locality whatsoever! I had to ask somebody where we were. Finally I stopped a pleasant-looking elderly gentleman, "Can you tell me the way to . . . ?" I did not finish the sentence—he looked suspiciously at me, "Just a minute, I'll be back." Mother and I waited patiently until he returned—accompanied by a Bobby. He threw out his hand: "There they are. These are the spies!"[8]

Internment in 1940 disrupted English language acquisition for refugees who had been living and working among native English speakers, such as those on domestic visas. Herbert Levy spoke English exclusively with his host family. Upon internment, Levy was swiftly re-immersed in the German language on the Isle of Man.[9] This was true for refugees on domestic service visas, who lived at their place of employment. For older unemployed refugee men, who had limited opportunities to learn English in London, their two hours of daily English lessons on the Isle of Man were beneficial. Eva Reichmann recalled that her husband had "joined a fellow inmate, who had set up a so-called 'Camp University' and acted as its secretary. They arranged language courses in nearly all the languages of the world, particularly for all stages of students of English, and as many retraining courses for future use as they could manage."[10] Women were interned separately and had limited access to English lessons and other classes for men in neighboring camps.[11] For former domestic servants and *Kindertransport* children, who had lived and worked with native Britons prior to internment, their English acquisition was slowed.

The ten thousand refugee men who enlisted in the British Army's Pioneer Corps after internment swiftly picked up English. Once restrictions were lifted and refugees could serve in the full armed forces, they quickly learned the British slang of their fellow soldiers. Charles Hannam, for example, wrote, "I found happiness in the army. I had mates. They may not have been very choice, but they were my mates, and they accepted and tolerated me with a generosity, which I still find moving. For the first time in my life it seemed to me that I belonged somewhere."[12] Some took advantage of the down time of army life. For example, Oliver Pond, formerly Otto Patriasz, asked his wife for weekly copies of *The Statesman, The Times of London,* and *The Manchester Guardian* to improve his English while serving with the Pioneer Corps in France.[13]

The evacuation of refugee children out of London accelerated their English language acquisition. For example, after spending months in St. Albans, Charles Leigh found that when he returned to his refugee hostel outside of London, his English was better than that of his friends. He wrote, "I was something of a novelty amongst the other boys in the hostel, as I was the only one who had experienced life on the outside, and in the company of English people. I was able to talk about the songs that I had learned and about the different table manners that Mrs. Gray had taught me."[14]

Opportunities for German Jewish daily contact with native English speakers expanded as wartime work restrictions were lifted. Previously unemployed men found work in factories, construction, and sales, as their German professional qualifications were, for the most part, not recognized in Britain. Peter William Johnson, formerly Wolfgang Joseph, worked for a London firm delivering goods where he picked up slang words such as *bastards* and *bloody*, which were sprinkled throughout letters to his father.[15] Charles Leigh worked for a furrier, where his colleagues, "tried their best to teach me some English. John thought that he could do this by naming the longest words in the dictionary. He came out with the word 'disestablishmentarianism.'"[16] Many refugees gained a sense of camaraderie with their fellow workers and this assisted in their adaptation to British life and the English language. Alice Schwab's father "got a job in a paint factory, accompanying the delivery van on its rounds. He was very happy and liked the job very much and it brought in a bit of money. He absolutely adored England; he liked the easy life; he liked going to the pub, the small talk—it suited him extremely well."[17] Refugee women, no longer limited to domestic service work, found employment in factories, offices, and shops where they continued to expand their English vocabulary. Ilse Abrahamson became a waitress after she quit her domestic post. There, she earned more money, practiced English, and could learn secretarial skills during the day. By February 1943, she found work as a shorthand typist in a British firm where she further improved her English.[18]

With the constant threat of a Nazi invasion, the refugees were under intense pressure to forsake German for English. For some, there was a desire to wholly exchange their German for English. One refugee wrote in a postcard, "Excuse please, Mistor Zensor, [*sic*] but sure, you have more difficulties with my English as with my German, though I would prefer the English for this letter and forever!" and another wrote in a letter to his sister: "I would like to change German into English. Is this your opinion too?"[19]

Without the opportunity to speak German, most young refugees adopted English out of necessity. The disruption in family cohesiveness meant individual family members learned English separately and in very different ways. There is a general assumption that children who arrived on *Kindertransports* had little difficulty learning English, because children naturally pick up languages more quickly than adults. In many cases this was true. Anne Koppel, for example, wrote of her first few days with her foster family in London:

> The next day we started going to school to learn English, so that we would soon be able to go to an English school and understand what it was all about. We met at the school and compared our "parents." The trouble with all of us was that we did not understand the people we stayed with, and they could not understand us. After a few days, however, we got over that and after a month I could talk with the Wimborne family just as if I were talking my own language. The things that aided me most in learning the language were the children, the movies and, of course, the school.[20]

One child recalled, "My command of the English language was slight on arrival, yet I can hardly remember now a transitional period of becoming gradually more proficient. I suddenly seemed to be able to speak and write English fluently."[21] Most children who lived with English families and attended local schools mastered English with the support of native speakers. Another wrote, "I was sent to school on the Monday following the Friday of our arrival. I could just speak and understand enough English not to be entirely lost. The teacher was nice and I got very childish readers in order to improve my English."[22] Nevertheless, one must avoid assumptions about children's natural linguistic capabilities. The constant moving in and out of London interrupted English acquisition. Herbert Levy, who arrived in London during the summer of 1939 at the age of ten, was evacuated to the country, and later interned. By the time he moved back to London two-and-a-half years later, he had only attended a British school for a total of three months.[23]

Despite challenges faced by refugee children, most eventually achieved English fluency. Eric Sheldon wrote of the typical refugee girl who lived with a British foster family and attended school "where she makes all the progress required of her, with the exception of German, at which subject she never seems to do well. She has forgotten her mother tongue and something in her subconscious seems to rebel against it."[24] Children's ability to adopt English depended on the stability of their foster home life, the degree to which they were immersed in English surroundings, and their own individual psychological mechanisms for dealing with trauma. In many cases, children's natural ability to acquire language coupled with their developmental desire to be inconspicuous, provided the impetus to convert entirely to English. A small number of German Jewish parents sent their children to English boarding schools, sometimes before they themselves were able to leave Germany. These children tended to pick up "proper" English from their classmates and teachers, because they were immersed in upper-class English culture and activities. Judith Kerr wrote in her semiautobiographical novel, "After four years of public school and nearly two terms at Cambridge, Max looked, sounded and felt English. It was maddening for him not to be legally English as well."[25] Weekend visits to parents in London allowed for limited practice speaking German. Refugee parents were awed by the speed with which their children adopted British English. Gabriele Tergit wrote in 1951:

> Meanwhile the children had become truly English. These schools, this state, this England had taken these little lost souls over lock, stock, and barrel and made them members of her community. They soon wrote verse "The Call to Go to Sea," or about King Arthur's knights. . . . They knew "the bad loser," the "understatement" and the "team spirit" before their parents could understand the words, let alone the meaning. . . . Unlike their fathers who had been rebels in Germany separated from their Christian school friends by being opposed to militarism and Sedan celebration, these children rapidly became ardent English patriots.[26]

Another refugee noted that his children's "acclimatization was no problem. They went to the local schools, made friends, and soon spoke an excellent Cockney English."[27] One refugee, Rudolf Apt observed, "The younger generation mastered [English], of course, much better than we old ones; but after the war we too were able to speak and write it quite well and could follow lectures and plays."[28]

While many *Kindertransport* children adopted the dialect of their foster families, learning English was not uncomplicated. Several accounts in Karen Gershon's *We Came as Children* reveal these difficulties. One recalled, "I hated England, refused to learn English, I always thought the teacher was cross with me because I did not understand."[29] Children fostered in strangers' homes were subject to the moods of their keepers, and some learned English out of pure fear. One girl, named Inge, wrote in her diary: "We have a governess, an English Miss like in a book. Mr. and Mrs. Roberts are very upset because she told them that I am lazy and don't learn English as well as I could. . . . Today Mr Roberts told me that he would send me to an institution if I wouldn't speak English."[30] Reunions between parent and child, particularly if the child arrived in Britain first, were sometimes tense. The child felt torn between two worlds, and this manifested itself in language selection. Gershon's collection of *Kindertransport* narratives confirm this. One respondent wrote, "In England, my mother's twin sister met me and I lived with her and her family. . . . Six months later my mother and father came over penniless. Suddenly I spoke English, and for many years it was as if I had never known German. More than anything in the world I wanted to be an English girl; I rejected my past and my parents."[31] Another recalled that once her parents arrived, "I could no longer speak proper German and my mother had to interpret for my father when he wanted to speak to me."[32]

Many refugee parents came to depend on their children's English assistance. As mentioned earlier, the title of Judith Kerr's book *The Other Way Round* reflects the altered nature of her relationship with her parents. Kerr's character Anna, helped her parents write English correspondences.[33] Kenneth Ambrose also remembered his father being "employed almost full-time drafting letters, talking to people, going for interviews on their behalf [to get relatives out of Germany]; I would translate the letters from German and my sister, when she was at home, or I, would type them."[34] Children could help in the family's struggle with mastering English. A respondent in *Continental Britons* recalled of her mother, "She wouldn't have got anything during the war. Shop owners said that things she wanted were sold out or made comments, 'Bloody foreigner, get out.' Sometimes I was very cruel; I refused to go shopping with my mother and she implored me in tears to go with her."[35] This quote reveals not only the parent/child role reversal, but also tensions typical within immigrant families. At the same time, it illustrates the kind of harassment some refugees endured because of their German accents.[36]

Elderly refugees, usually dependent on their adult children, had a particularly difficult time learning English. Those who could live with their families did so unless they were interned, while others resided in bedsits or refugee hotels living among fellow refugees. In most cases, elderly German Jews in London retained German longer than their children and grandchildren. Some refugees earned money by offering German lessons; however, this did not necessarily improve their English. For refugee writers in particular, language was everything. Alfred Kerr continued to write in German, and the PEN club gave some writers the opportunity to share their work in German. After the start of the war, a few refugees were employed by the BBC Monitoring Service to produce German-language radio programs to be broadcast abroad as propaganda. They, too, had limited chances to practice English at work.

Although German Jewish refugees in New York City were highly motivated to learn English, they were more likely to speak German in their daily lives than refugees in London. Numerous factors led to this disparity. Early refugee accounts describe a New York that was filled with foreign words and accents. Inge Heiman wrote of her first few days in New York, "What we had not expected is that almost no one on the crowded streets seemed to speak English. The streets of New York were like a horizontal tower of Babel. In our neighborhood, Washington Heights, German predominated. In other sections one could hear French, Yiddish, or Russian."[37] Julius Cohn wrote in a letter to his parents, "One sees all races of the world here mixed together. Here one sees blacks, browns, fair-haired, dark redheads, everything one could imagine, walking on these streets."[38] The German Jews, for the most part, embraced the historical narrative of the United States as a land of immigrants, and found proof of it all around them.

In New York, English acquisition tended to be a matter of individual initiative and opportunity. Specialized classes were listed in the *Aufbau*.[39] In an article in the *Aufbau Almanac* entitled "How to Become an American," E. K. Schwartz wrote, "One of the most obvious manifestations of this desire (to become American) is the adoption of English as the sole language of communication on the street, in the subway, and especially in the home. Moreover, there is a practical and realistic dollar-and-cents value in acquiring a basic facility with English."[40] Mastering English was encouraged by fellow refugees as advantageous to one's own success. Comparatively, London refugees were encouraged to speak English so as not to upset the local population. Although most German Jews in the United States could speak some English by the start of World War II, it was still widely acceptable to use German openly in refugee enclaves such as Washington Heights. Ilse Kaufherr recalled, "A lot of Jewish people you meet on the street [in Washington Heights] speak only German to you. You feel like an idiot if you want to answer them in English. [They'll think,] 'Oh, she wants to show off already. She can speak English.' "[41] Because of the predominance of German Jewish–owned businesses and shops in Washington Heights, it was possible for refugees to get by with little knowledge of English. Kenneth Ambrose wrote of his cousins in Washington Heights, "Martha's sister, Jenny, kept house in spite of having virtually no English. However, the latter did not matter, according to her, as everyone in their neighborhood understood German."[42] Davie wrote of Washington Heights and the other German Jewish enclaves, such as the Upper West Side, Forest Hills, and Kew Gardens, "The strain resulting from language problems was somewhat less severe for those living in refugee colonies where they could continue the use of their mother tongue than for those living in native American communities."[43] Northwest London, which was becoming the most German Jewish area in Britain, still did not compare to New York's Washington Heights in the 1940s, where the German language was heard throughout the streets and local establishments.

German was generally the language of choice in refugee-owned businesses when the customers were also refugees. Ernest Stock remembered that he spoke both German and English at his job in a refugee-owned office, "When I was working with other German Jews we would speak German . . . when other people were around we would speak English."[44] The clientele was mostly German-speaking and many of the business transactions were in German. Gerda Sabor wrote of her mother:

> While she was familiarizing herself with New York she went into the local butcher for the first time. It was a German store that had all the meats she was accustomed to and she pointed them out. The butcher told her that she could speak German with him and if she would "take the mosquito net off" [her hat's veil], he'd let her taste them all![45]

A former doctor found work in a home for the elderly where most of the patients were either German-speaking refugees or Yiddish speakers. He claimed that, because of this, his English never really improved.[46] German books and newspapers were easily accessible.[47]

For the 75,000 other German-speaking refugees who lived in New York City during the early years after their arrival, residing among the more general New York population helped their English. Those who opted to fully relinquish the German language avoided Washington Heights and other refugee enclaves altogether. One refugee wrote, "We are very glad we moved to Kansas City. In New York, they [refugees] stick too much together and speak too much German. For the first year in the United States I did not speak English."[48] Refugees who found employment beyond the refugee neighborhoods, naturally had more opportunities to speak English with customers and American co-workers. Nevertheless, their accents often betrayed their continental origins. Felix Pollak, an Austrian émigré, noticed that once he left New York City, "more people responded in English to my attempts to speak that language, for in New York they usually answered my efforts with Yiddish or German or a mixture of both, which retarded my linguistic learning process."[49] Those who lived and worked in Washington Heights or other refugee enclaves tended to primarily speak German.

Although German Jews faced limited employment restrictions in the United States, most were forced to take work as manual laborers or domestic servants due to their unrecognized German professional qualifications and the high unemployment rates of the 1930s. With their willingness to take on low-skilled work, women often mastered the language before their husbands. Those who were domestics learned English from the children they looked after, like their counterparts in England. Men who spoke limited English sometimes found temporary work in factories or other labor-intensive posts. Others transferred their former professional skills to the United States once they learned English. Bert Kirchheimer, for instance, recalled, "I started freelancing with cartoons. I sold to the leading magazines: *Colliers, Journal American*. To them I sold a whole Sunday page of cartoons in August or September 1936. They were German gags that my brother translated into English for me."[50] A former doctor resumed practicing medicine once he passed his English language exam and the New York Medical Exam, all of which he did within his first year of arrival.[51] Others were not so fortunate. For example, Walter Baum recalled that his father was unable to return to sales because his English was insufficient.[52]

European refugees, who served with the U.S. military during World War II were immediately exposed to American slang. They were integrated directly into the general U.S. Army, unlike most British refugees who were at first segregated to the Pioneer Corps. Ernest Stock remembered, "It was a very rough bunch in basic training. Many working as dockworkers in New Jersey . . . lots of obscenity, 'fuck'—which had been completely new to me. I had never had that kind of experience before, with what I would call this 'sub-culture'—but I learned a great deal."[53] Another soldier, called Rosenthal, who fought for the allies in Western Europe wrote, "A sergeant came up and posed the question, 'Any of youse guys talks the lingo of this G-- D--- country?!' We were a team of one lieutenant and four enlisted men, and we had to get information from the G-- D--- Krauts."⁵⁴ Rosenthal wrote down "youse," the grammatically incorrect form of the plural for "you," to help authenticate the request of his commander. His use of the word *Kraut* is telling. While he must have heard this word used quite frequently as a soldier in the army, one wonders whether he experienced any prejudice against himself as a German. That does not seem to be the case, though. His letter continues, "A few days later my hometown of Göppingen was our target and I went to see the company commander. Could I please be the first American GI in town, as this is the town of my birth? No problem, soldier! Take another buddy and a jeep."⁵⁵ Through his experience in the U.S. Army, he found his identity as an American, while his knowledge of German enabled him to assist his sergeant.

Another refugee private wrote to his girlfriend back in Washington Heights, "Thanks for the subscriptions to *Life* and *Reader's Digest*. Me and my buddies enjoyed the magazines very much. We exchange them and let them go around in the different sections."⁵⁶ This particular soldier seemed to feel quite comfortable with reading and speaking English, interspersing his letters with slang terms, such as *buddy, chow time,* and *jack-pot*. His letters were written completely in English in order to pass through the censors who read all U.S. Army mail. It seems some German refugee soldiers in the army were uninhibited about speaking and reading German. The soldier above wrote of a fellow refugee soldier, "He gets *Aufbau* regularly, so I will get a chance to read some news again. I didn't see it for almost two years. We got some fellows here who talk German but when I try to talk, I mix too much English in it and it sounds quite strange to me!"⁵⁷ German Jewish refugees in the United States, particularly those serving in the military, were part of the greater U.S. war effort. Yet, without the intensity of air raids and evacuations that jostled refugees in London up against their British neighbors, the war did not bring New York refugees much closer to "real" Americans. In addition, because of the housing shortage in New York during the war, refugees were significantly less mobile than their counterparts in London. This meant that German Jews who lived or worked alongside each other were more likely to speak German in their everyday lives during this time.

Adult refugees in New York spoke German at home, while their children, eager to become American, often replied in English. Max Frankel, who arrived as a child, recalled, "I had a thing about becoming American. . . . From the day I landed I wouldn't talk German to my mother. She talked German to me but I would reply in English."[58] Ernest Stock observed:

> These children quickly lost their German accents and became generally indistinguishable from their native-born classmates. . . . As a rule, the children speak German only at home, or they reply in English when their parents speak to them in German. Yet fundamental estrangement between the old and the younger generations, once the rule in immigrant families, seems to occur very rarely in this group. The parents encourage their offspring to imitate American customs and are proud to see them become such complete *Amerikaner*.[59]

Comparatively, because refugee children in Britain were frequently separated from their parents, they were more likely to become estranged from their German background and the German language, especially during the war. Parents whose children lived with them tended to learn English more quickly than those who lived only among adults. Saenger quoted a refugee doctor who lived in Washington Heights:

> My son has attended George Washington High School for two years, which has proved to be of great significance for our whole family. . . . He tells us which movies and theatres we should go to. Our English has improved tremendously since he began going to school. . . . My patients are amazed at my knowledge of baseball and football. My wife and I seriously contemplate nominating our son as general information publicity manager of the Kern family with a fixed salary for outstanding service![60]

Gerhard Saenger wrote himself:

> The refugee child, through his school, learns to speak English fluently and without an accent in the short time of one or, at most, two years. His parents are unable to follow at such a pace. . . . On the whole, the more rapid assimilation of the children is advantageous. The refugee family with young children who are attending school will usually adjust more rapidly and feel at home in America sooner than the childless couple. The quick Americanization of their children helps the parents to adapt themselves to the new life.[61]

There are indications that among refugee adults, women were more willing to attempt to speak English than men. Perhaps this was because many men, especially older ones, were depressed about having lost their earlier status. Work was typically the greatest indicator of self-worth for men at that time, compared to women who generally found their self-worth within the home and family. Therefore, some men may have lacked the confidence and optimism to take risks, even small ones such as speaking English. Women had opportunities to engage in all sorts of work and, as a result, learned English rather quickly. Davie referred to the case of a former stage conductor and his wife:

> He was 73 years old and unemployed here, and his wife, aged 65, who taught theatrical art abroad, is a factory worker here. [She] attends adult education classes for foreigners, and masters the language fairly well. [He] has not made the least attempt to study the language, and talks German at all times. [She] mixes well with people . . . she is sociable and talks readily to Americans.[62]

Peter Gay, a well-known historian and former refugee, observed, "While their husbands struggled to acquire or improve their English, the women forged forward in mastering the linguistic tools needed for a new life."[63] Davie further noted in his study, "The women appear to have acquired English and American customs more readily and have met with less prejudice at work, probably because they were regarded as temporary competitors."[64] While gender seemed to play an important role in the acquisition of English, age was also a factor. Elderly refugees living in New York, as in London, seemed to demonstrate the greatest resistance to learning a new language. Those who lived in refugee neighborhoods found less of a need to become fluent in English. Ernest Stock remembered that his grandfather "only spoke German—his life was now his family—he listened to German radio, read the *Staats Herald*, the daily German-language newspaper," and was quite satisfied living with his family, welcoming neighborly visits where they would reminisce, in German, about the old times.[65] Max Frankel said of refugees who settled in Washington Heights:

> They came with friends and/or relatives ready to receive them, with a neighborhood staked out, a place where they could feel comfortable, not learning the language for a year or two, with people to take them by the hand and if not, get them the same

kinds of jobs in business they were used to in the old country, at least show them the ropes of this new society.[66]

German Jewish refugees in New York were able to maintain close family ties. As a result, there was no immediate need to speak English in the home. Family members influenced each other in their language acquisition, and those with children learned English more quickly than young adults who lived and worked among fellow refugees. On the whole, however, most adult refugees were eager to learn English and often did so by attending evening classes. With the exception of refugee men serving in the U.S. military, most German Jews could adopt English at their own pace compared to their counterparts in London, who were continually separated from family and felt they had to disguise their German origins. As refugee families tended to remain intact in New York, cultural integration of adult refugees could proceed at a more "natural" rate than in London. German Jews in New York freely negotiated their native language with English, without external pressure to become invisible as Germans. The majority of adult refugees in the United States strove to master English. At the same time, there seemed to be less pressure placed on them by the outside community to speak English. There was no mention of becoming "English" in *While You Are in England*, its title serving as a reminder of their temporary status. This indicates significant differences in the way newly arrived German Jews were expected to behave in the two cities.[67]

Accent in London

Accent played a greater role for refugees in London than in New York. Across Britain, distinct English accents were signifiers of one's education, class, and region. In his 1945 comparison of British and American life, Crane Brinton, an American journalist, and not a refugee, acknowledged these differences and the difficulties faced while trying to transcend them. He wrote:

> You can tell a gentleman by his accent. We all know that it is impossible for an American to acquire even a moderately convincing English accent; it is just as nearly impossible for an ordinary Englishman not born a gentleman to acquire a gentleman's way of speaking. It is not a matter of pronouncing one's h's; it is a far more delicate matter of vowel quality, intonation,

and rhythm. And accent is, of course, but the beginning—though it is by far the simplest single sign of membership, so simple that a foreigner with any kind of ear can recognize, even though he cannot imitate it.[68]

German-speaking refugees faced several challenges in Britain in their quest to master English. The first was a stratified class system that was distinguishable to Britons by both social and regional accents. It was difficult for refugees to hear, let alone adopt, an English accent that was free from these associations.[69]

With German accents and a limited English vocabulary, refugee domestic servants were accepted neither by their mistresses, with whom they might once have shared social status, nor by fellow servants, who often resented them and their blatant lack of housekeeping experience. Working-class colleagues sometimes shunned their refugee co-workers. A refugee who arrived in her late teens wrote, "Working in the garment industry as a cutter, which was exacting and tedious but relatively well-paid, I felt like an outcast for whom there was no role to be had in England. I had not gone to the right schools and could not afford to attend university. Many of my co-workers used *ain't* and dropped their *aitches*."[70] Silvia Rodgers recalled, "With hindsight I can understand how threatened our working-class landlady must have felt by this strange woman and her children, with their strange clothes and manners, speaking a double-Dutch language and hardly a word of English."[71]

The growing middle class of 1930s Britain, made up of office workers, shop owners, doctors, lawyers, and government workers used a more neutral British accent. Brinton wrote that this cohort "neither drop their h's nor intone the so called Oxford manner."[72] This proved to be the easiest accent for German Jews living in London to emulate. Some refugees, such as Hanna Goddard, modeled their English accent on BBC newsreaders they heard on the radio, as that seemed to be acceptable without clearly indicating one's exact upbringing.[73] For many refugees, it was this neutral accent that was preferable, particularly because it did not disclose their origins.

In firsthand documents, refugee children commonly reported being embarrassed by their parents' German accented English, with the occasional Yiddish word thrown in. One former *Kindertransport* child wrote, "As I grew up I was paralyzed with shyness, petrified in case my parents should come to school and that my friends should hear them speak with their broken accents. Their speech and their ways were different and I suffered." Another recalled, "I went out more and more on my own and so did not have to put up with the loud foreign ways of my parents and relatives."[74] Charles Hannam, who attended an English boarding school, found that when he visited his family during holidays, his sense of alienation from them grew stronger. He wrote in the third person:

> Among them he felt a stranger. He detested their bad English; their mixture of German, Yiddish, and English words seemed to him alien. They talked with their hands and they wore continental clothes. Karl wanted to be like his teachers and friends at school whom he admired, whose manners and attitudes he was learning to respect and adopt; most of all he wanted to be accepted, and if the price was the rejection of the people to whom he had once belonged, it seemed well worth paying at that time.[75]

The escalation of anti-German feelings that exploded after the start of the war placed a heavy burden on the relationship between Anglicized children and their German-accented parents and caregivers. In Britain, it was typical for refugee children to live separately from their parents at some point. This could be due to evacuations, internment, boarding school, financial constraints, or because their parents remained in Germany. As a result, outside influences on their English acquisition were significantly stronger than parental ones. Additionally, once the war began, and especially during the Blitz, children were cognizant of the hostility Britons harbored toward Germany. Herbert Levy recalled, "We were there in the shelter with my Aunt Ellen. She used to talk to everyone in her heavily German-accented way, until someone asked where she came from. 'From across the road,' she quickly replied."[76] Refugees quickly recognized that it was in their best interest not to reveal their German origins, if possible, and they became eager to appear like any other typical English children. Some children, who arrived in their late teens, had trouble losing their German accents. Eric Sheldon, in an article in the 1951 anniversary publication of the Association of Jewish Refugees, wrote:

> As the years went by, my English improved, in fact it happened occasionally that my accent was not noticed at all, or at least not immediately. That was really what I had wanted. You see, I tried so very hard to get assimilated. But those who knew would continue to compliment me on my English, thereby putting

me into my place as to my origin and my chances concerning complete assimilation.[77]

Accent in New York

The American accent sounded more nasal to some refugees than a British accent. Elli Bickart, who worked in London as a maid, recalled upon hearing American English on the ship to New York, "It sounded like every American had a head-cold to me."[78] Julius Cohn wrote in a letter to his sister that the Americans "quack" more than the English.[79] In his study of the German Jewish community in 1946, Davie wrote, "Refugees who had studied English prior to coming to this country particularly stressed the difficulties presented by the peculiarities of American pronunciation and slang, the change from 'English-English' to 'American-English' and from academic knowledge of a language to conversational application of it."[80] Their "British" accent sounded charming to some New Yorkers. Walter Baum remembered that his Bronx relatives took him to visit their friends and family because "after all, showing off a newcomer, especially one who pronounced 'either' and 'afternoon' the British way, was an experience that only a few families had in those days."[81] Davie even wrote, "A number of refugees declare that they have found their accents to be an asset rather than a liability."[82] This could also be an effect of having learned British English prior to arrival.

A British accent did, and perhaps still does, sound appealing to American ears. New York was filled with many accents, but among the Jewish communities in New York's boroughs, a British accent was still noteworthy. Leo Grebler wrote that if the refugees' English betrays an accent, "this is so common in America that it gets little notice."[83] Although most refugees wanted to speak English with an American accent, they felt that in New York they could have a foreign accent and still identify as American. Most German Jewish refugees were under the impression that their accents were less likely to be an obstacle in the United States than in other places. After interviewing for a job, Leo Grebler recalled:

> The trip yielded no immediate results, but one of the visits served to boost my morale tremendously. This was an interview with E. A. Goldenweiser, Director of the Division of Research and Statistics of the Federal Reserve Board and economic adviser to

the Board. He turned out to be a Russian immigrant with a heavy accent although he had come to the U.S. as a young boy, as I later learned. If one can reach such a distinguished position with this much of an accent, I felt, my prospects are not too bad.[84]

In addition to many foreign accents, New York was unique in that one heard not only regional accents from the Bronx, Brooklyn, and Queens, but also different intonations and word usage among various ethnic groups. An American Southern accent and African American word usage sounded strange to the refugee ear. Baum recalled, "My first play was a social commentary . . . due to Harlem and Southern type speech patterns and pronunciations, I barely followed."[85] As all types of accents could be heard in New York, most German Jews felt it was acceptable to retain their German accent and still be American.

As discussed in the previous chapter on dress and appearance, class structures existed in the United States, but in a different form to those in Britain. Status was based almost entirely on individual wealth, and sometimes on ethnicity. Typical American accents varied according to region and ethnicity, but were not necessarily indicators of social or financial status. A nasal sounding "WASP" accent was used by the social elite of New York and Boston in the 1930s and 1940s. But it was the American English of their peers, tinged with the particular New York accent where they lived, that younger refugees generally tried to adopt. German Jewish children learned American English from their school friends and teachers. Stock recalled that by the time he joined the U.S. Army he no longer had a German accent, because, "I had a teacher earlier who taught me English and the first thing they did was try to get rid of the German accent."[86]

With an ocean separating them from the Nazis, most German Jews in New York experienced the early years of World War II through newspapers and radio. The lack of an immediate threat from Germany and the late entry of the United States into the war meant that anti-German sentiment was low in New York, particularly in comparison to Britain, as discussed in the previous section on dress and appearance. Refugees were designated "enemy aliens" in the United States, as in Britain, but they were not interned and their accounts do not seem to recall anti-German prejudice in New York City.[87] Leo Grebler was concerned about anti-German sentiment but found that:

[r]ight after Pearl Harbor, a member of the bipartisan Board, a man of very conservative opinions, asked me to replace him

for a speech at a business convention in Boston. I demurred; I was now an "enemy alien" and very conscious of my German accent. Would it not be in the Board's interest to send someone else? This arch-Republican "ordered" me to forget all that and go. I went; nothing happened.[88]

For refugees in London, the need to speak English, without a German accent, was made clear from the moment of their arrival. In New York, the pressure to learn English and speak it without an accent came mainly from the individual refugees themselves. In the community at large, they perceived greater acceptance in having a foreign accent. Children in both cities felt the need to fit in and rid themselves of their German accent. In New York, however, this seemed to be done at their own pace.

Manners and Mannerisms

Part of the pressure German Jews experienced in London to remain inconspicuous came from a British tradition of understatement and subtlety in speech and manner. The German-Jewish Committee's *While You Are in England* acknowledged this when it encouraged German refugees to moderate their volume level and any distinctive mannerisms that might draw attention to themselves.[89] In 1940, the German-Jewish Committee published *Mistress and Maid: General Information for the Use of Domestic Refugees and Their Employers*. It explained that "in this country it is good manners to speak and walk quietly, both in the house and in the street and public places."[90] Refugees were also sharply aware of the culture of politeness in Britain. Gabriele Tergit's article in the AJR's 1952 *Britain's New Citizens* included a section entitled *Land of Understatement*. In it she wrote:

> It is not by chance that "outsider" is an English word in many languages. The refugees found life in England a game dominated by rigid rules. "Manners maketh man," but it is not just manners that are different in different countries. Germany was the country of big words, England that of small talk in an inaudible voice. We said, "I am keen on doing so and so," when the correct thing to say would have been, "Unfortunately I am much too lazy to do this." Even when you were desperate you had to say, like your English neighbor who had lost a child in the war

or had been bombed out, "I'm fine, thank you," or perhaps, "Lovely day today."[91]

Niceties peppered British English, and some refugees incorporated these into their conversation. Eileen Erlund said of her landlady, "She was a marvelous person, but we were still so afraid that we never even tried to open our mouths. We just said 'sorry' to everything we did or did not!"[92] *While You Are in England* stated, "You will find that [the Englishman] says 'Thank you' for the smallest service—even for a penny bus ticket for which he has paid."[93]

Even if a refugee domestic servant gained a basic knowledge of English, the subtle manner in which her employers expressed commands and the cold treatment she sometimes received were disquieting. *Mistress and Maid* advised, "The mistress states orders as requests. Do not argue or grumble."[94] Alice Schwab was surprised by the tone of the policemen who collected her father for internment. She wrote, "The way they got hold of the refugees was quite strange. The police would come and say 'You'd better come with us, for if you don't, we'll have to arrest you.' In some cases they saw that their victim was a harmless old chap and they would let him pack up his few possessions to take with him before they carted him off."[95] The quiet manner of the average Briton intrigued German Jews. Dr. Furst, for instance, noted that during his initial journey to London, "people were not talking to one another in the train. It was still like a church. It was strange to us."[96]

German Jews were fascinated by the British proclivity to discuss the weather as a dependable topic of small talk. Marianne Walter recalled that the family friend who met her upon arrival in Britain "went on talking about the weather, which seemed strange to me, in Germany that was not done at the time. Then he talked about the time it would take us to get to his house in Coulsdon. He wanted to be pleasant, but I failed to understand that."[97] Unlike sports or politics, discussion of weather transcended class and gave refugees something to talk about. Julius Cohn began a letter to his sister, who also lived in England, "It is very important in England to say something about the weather."[98] Formal structures of British language and manners helped refugees adapt to everyday life in Britain. As Werner Rosenstock wrote in *Britain's New Citizens*, "The experience they had shared with the general population throughout the war years had accelerated the process of adaptation."[99]

German Jews in New York encountered other peculiarities about American mannerisms. They were surprised by the informality of dialogue between Americans of different social standing. One respondent in Davie's study wrote, "In Germany one could hear without seeing whether a person was talking to a *Vorgesetzten* (superior) or to somebody of his rank or to one below his rank. Here the janitor speaks to the director just as the director speaks to the janitor."[100] This discovery provided comfort to some refugees, as they knew that in the United States they would probably be working in more subordinate and low-level positions than they had in Germany. Saenger described how German class and prestige differed from U.S. social structures. He quoted a refugee university student who remarked, "Teachers in American schools are more friendly and helpful than European professors. I can see them whenever I wish and it is possible to talk with them almost on an equal footing. They are not the venerable and distinguished authorities you meet in so many European universities and high schools."[101] Because social boundaries were more fluid in the United States than in Britain, different classes could more easily engage in informal, off-the-cuff conversations with one another. Baseball and popular entertainment, rather than just the weather, provided fodder for such small talk. Leo Grebler, for example, realized that his lack of baseball knowledge might have hindered his ability to master the art of "small talk" with fellow Americans. He wrote:

> In my own case, I have never learned even the rudimentaries [*sic*] of baseball, my command of English stops short of appreciation of English poetry, and I admire but cannot emulate the ease with which American intellectuals can converse with filling station attendants, cab drivers or barbers. I recall how impressed I was when Professor Moulton, then head of the Brookings Institute in Washington, stepped out of the Brookings building with me and started talking to the street cleaner that happened to be working there. They discussed the baseball season and baseball history and gardening, areas of shared knowledge and interest from which I was barred. Besides, I was not used to conversations with street cleaners—how many German intellectuals were?—not so much because of conceit as for the reason that I did not know what to talk about.[102]

American sport, and particularly baseball, transcended class and ethnicity and acted as a common link among American men of all backgrounds. This was impossible in Britain due to the fact that the working classes had ties to entirely different sports than the upper classes. Weather seemed to be the only currency of conversation that spanned class lines.

In the *Aufbau Almanac*, Ernst Behrendt wrote an informative article in German (but translated by the author below) aimed at explaining American slang and idioms to refugees. He described different kinds of American terms heard on the street and in the military:

> One can simply not go in the street without hearing the word "guy" for a man, and "cute" for nice or "swell" for great. The more you immerse yourself in English, the more you realize that there are thousands of slang words and phrases to learn.[103]

In his 1947 study, Davie reported:

> Among the special difficulties cited by refugees in regard to language, colloquialisms, conversational language, and slang expressions recur most frequently. As one refugee expressed it, his greatest problem was in learning the "slanguage" in addition to the language. Some blamed their lack of knowledge of idiomatic language upon the fact that they had little opportunity to mix with Americans, and that their knowledge of English had been gained largely from reading.[104]

German Jews in New York commented on these difficulties more often than German Jews in London. British refugees, such as Eva Ehrenberg and Kenneth Ambrose, casually inserted words such as *digs* and *mates* into their writing without any further commentary, perhaps because there was no more novelty in their frequent use.

As in Britain, the refugees were struck by the use of euphemisms and niceties in American conversation. Davie found that "a language folkway which is strange, especially to the German immigrant, is the American's lack of definiteness in his answers." He continued quoting several respondents to his study, who reflected on this indirectness, "To save the newcomer some disappointment, instruct him that 'How do you do' means 'Hello' and that 'You must come and see us someday' is not usually an invitation." Another wrote, "It is hard to distinguish between a straightforward yes, a noncommittal remark, and a polite refusal." A third responded, "The American is always polite and does not wish to hurt your feelings, so he is not apt to tell you if he thinks differently, quite contrary to the German habit."[105] And lastly, "Newcomers should be instructed not to say 'yes' or 'no' but to say instead 'I think so' or 'I do not believe so.' "[106]

To the refugees, Americans appeared to use less apologetic language than the British. This was noted by Julius Cohn in a letter from New York to his sister in London:

> I like it here more than in London. . . . The Americans are overall more robust than the English, where you hear so often "I'm sorry" on the bus, or on the subway. Here I seldom hear this. To get an apology one must have done something that really hurts the other, like crushing someone's finger, and then in that case someone might say "pardon me." Still you won't get an apology . . . in the subway car one can only protect oneself with trained elbows. But, I don't want to say that the people here seem impolite.[107]

There was a consensus in refugee accounts that Americans were more forward and outgoing than the British. Leo Grebler in New York wrote of "an unfamiliar generosity in thought and deed. Even in large cities, people were friendlier in daily contacts than they had been in Germany or other European countries; neighbors were greeting each other as a matter of course instead of ignoring each other. While the amiability might have been only skin-deep, it struck us as a more civilized sort of behavior."[108] One respondent in Davie's *Refugees in America* wrote, "The Americans are so friendly. They ask you to their home and show affection. In England it takes years for a friend to ask you to her home. I have had more invitations here in one year than I had in five years in England."[109] Another refugee noted, "Here you can sit down in the streetcar, turn to your neighbor and say 'good morning,' and usually get an answer."[110] This perception was a distinct contrast to the descriptions of encounters on British trains.

Although they appreciated American friendliness, it seems that most refugees in New York did not develop close relationships with "real" Americans right away. Ernest Stock reported, "The Germans [German Jews] admire a great many traits in the 'typical' American: his energy, his lack of social inhibitions, his good humor, etc., but they feel themselves just a little too worldly-wise ever to be like that themselves."[111] The perceived friendliness and easygoing nature of Americans ran counter to the feeling experienced by German Jews, who continued to be plagued with worry about their friends and family in Europe. Some refugees felt that Americans, both Jews and Gentiles, did not understand or appreciate their traumatic experiences. Stock recalled his difficulty in maintaining close friendships with Americans in his early years in the United States, "They didn't have to go through anything. . . . Maybe I was jealous of their luck. Their outlook on life and preoccupations seemed frivolous and innocent. . . . They were more concerned with girls and shallow stuff. Conversations with German Jewish friends differed from those with Americans—there was a different sense of what was important."[112] Similarly, Saenger wrote:

> The recent arrival is often still too much disturbed by his previous experiences to seek new friends. In talking with Americans he has to concern himself with their problems, for which he is not yet ready. He needs to talk over all that he lived through with a sympathetic friend who knows from firsthand experience what the past meant to him. He is still too preoccupied with himself to feel for and with persons alien to himself. We have already seen that a period of recuperation for regaining emotional balance is necessary for most newcomers before they are able to look around and adjust themselves to their new environment. During this whole time, which rarely exceeds more than one or two years, they need to turn for advice and understanding to others who have suffered the same fate, believing that only those who have undergone the same experiences are able fully to understand their worries and fears.[113]

Most felt that the average American did not understand the seriousness of the situation in Europe. Across the Atlantic, however, the seriousness of war and the threat of Nazi invasion was all too real for Londoners.

Accounts from both London and New York have referred to a "German look," meaning a worried and almost paranoid countenance. In her memoirs, Marianne Walter described another refugee, "He stopped and looked round him to see if anyone was listening. The 'German Look' we used to call it. . . . I did it for years."[114] Ilse Kaufherr, who settled in New York, said, "I never spoke out loud, I whispered, because I was always afraid this could happen here too. You were timid. You were scared. But then, once I was here, and established myself a little bit, it was better. You know, you make ten dollars and you were a big shot."[115] Having experienced persecution under the Nazis, it is no wonder that German Jews brought their anxiety with them. It seems, however, that those in New York were able to lose their nervousness at a quicker rate than in London, due to differing circumstances.

There was a sense of informality among Americans, not just in language but also in manner, that many refugees found refreshing. Bert Kirchheimer recalled that in New York "it was a free life. Everybody was nice to me. Germans are stiffer in their behavior, and arrogant."[116] Saenger describes the typical refugee:

> His steps are stiff and heavy, instead of light and swinging as in the American manner of walking . . . when the refugee meets you on the street he may still click his heels and bow from his hips. It will take him a long time to forget to shake hands every time he says good-bye to you. The newcomer's habit of lifting his hat in a wide curve when meeting someone in the street may appear ridiculous.[117]

Walter Baum remembered, "I tried to fit in although my clothes and manners (the European handshake at every meeting) gave it away."[118]

In the United States, many refugees felt that they were finally permitted to speak freely. Haberman, an Austrian Jewish refugee, wrote:

> I brought with me [to the United States] the impression of the American as a gross, superficial and naive person who never learned to keep his voice down. It may be true that Americans speak somewhat louder than most others, in all likelihood because, being a free people, they aren't afraid to be overheard . . . one thing is sure, democracy is deeply rooted in the daily life of the American. Nowhere else is it as easy for the foreigner or newcomer to enter into the economic, social or political life of the nation and better his condition more rapidly than in America.[119]

Across the Atlantic, refugees in Britain were encouraged to be more inconspicuous than usual. Keeping a low voice and remaining subtle were values that Anglo-Jews and refugees perceived to be important to the English people.

Overall, German Jews in London found it necessary to master unaccented English at a significantly faster rate than their counterparts in New York. What refugees perceived to be Britain's homogeneous society and its preordained social hierarchy with unspoken rules regarding understatement, modesty, and gentility strongly influenced their desire to sound English.

Perhaps more important were the circumstances under which many refugees arrived. For example, many of the ten thousand *Kindertransport* children found themselves learning English once placed in British homes and schools. The twenty thousand refugees who arrived on domestic servant visas also acquired at least a rudimentary form of English at their place of employment. Yet by 1940, the very real threat of a Nazi invasion played the greatest role in the refugees' swift acquisition of English. With growing national mistrust of anything German, refugees in Britain felt an increasing need to speak English instead of German.

Refugees in New York experienced pressure to relinquish the German language. Acquisition of English was necessary in order to improve one's employment prospects and most German Jews were eager to master it. Yet, it was not a matter of survival as it was in London to lose one's German accent, particularly because the war seemed, for most so far away. To be heard speaking German in refugee neighborhoods, such as Washington Heights, was entirely acceptable and perceived to be compatible with becoming American. Those German Jews who chose to speak German and retain former ways could easily do so by opting to live or work among fellow refugees. Most German Jewish families and friendships in New York remained, on the whole, intact during this period. Comparatively, refugees in London faced air raids, evacuations, and internment, which separated refugee families. Refugees in New York adopted English at a slower pace, allowing each family to negotiate how German and English were used at home. While many New York German Jews chose not to live in refugee enclaves, close contact with fellow Europeans, whether through work or leisure, was the norm. Most refugees sought to speak English, but this pressure remained internal, rather than being a response to public hostility.

5

Organizational Life

As noted in the Introduction, Jewish organizational life in Germany flourished at the start of the twentieth century. It was no wonder, then, that in exile, German Jewish refugees formed a variety of social, professional, and cultural clubs, self-help organizations, and religious communities in London and New York. As with other aspects of immigrant life, distinct patterns of identity practices and cultural adaptation emerge in a comparative analysis of German Jewish organizational life in these two cities.[1]

Prior to emigration, German Jews were active members of a wide range of social, political, professional, and religious organizations that reflected this distinctively German Jewish culture. Regardless of their denomination, all Jews in Germany were officially represented at the national level by one organization, the Central Association of German Citizens of Jewish Faith (*Centralverein deutscher Staatsbürger jüdischen Glaubens* or *CV*). In Germany then, as now, religious groups were funded by taxpayers, and the *CV* distributed the money raised by Jewish citizens. When it became clear that the Jews were unsafe in Nazi Germany, it was the *CV* that coordinated efforts to assist them and to aid in emigration.

The organizational structure for the funding of religious communities in Britain was not organized through national agencies as it had been in Germany. An author in the *AJR Information* of September 1946 clearly explained this:

> Jews from Germany sometimes do not realize easily that there are in this country no "Jewish communities" of the kind they were accustomed to, i.e. corporate bodies to which every Jew belongs, recognized in public law, with rabbis and officials, recognized as public functionaries. The Jewish congregations in England are

private societies, of whom many have formed equally private associations such as the "United Synagogue," "The Federation of Synagogues," or the organizations of the Progressive and of the Liberal Synagogues, none of them having any official function. This principle also applies to the "Board of Deputies of British Jews" (originally "The London Committee of Deputies"), the representative body of the Jews in Great Britain, founded as early as 1760 and composed of delegates of every synagogue and of a number of other Jewish bodies.[2]

The same held true in the United States. Congregations in New York may have belonged to various sister organizations or been part of a larger denominational network, but the synagogues were and are still not centralized either in the United States or Great Britain, and rely solely on membership fees for funding, rather than on taxes.

British Jewish Aid Organizations

Upon arrival in Britain, German Jews quickly learned from one another that they needed to visit Woburn House on Upper Woburn Place in Central London. Woburn House was established by the German-Jewish Aid Committee, a group founded in 1933 by members of the Anglo-Jewish community intending to support Jews in Nazi Germany. The name "Woburn House" was familiar to every German Jewish adult refugee who arrived in London between 1933 and 1938. It was the first office they visited after finding a place to put their bags for the night. The German-Jewish Aid Committee's official aim was to rescue and support European Jews from Germany. Woburn House served as the headquarters for various refugee organizations, such as the Free Meal Service, the Academic Assistance Council, and later, the Society for the Protection of Science and Learning. It also housed a Clothing Department, a Retraining Department, and nationality-based assistance groups.[3] The programs there helped arrange housing, offered English classes, and provided visa advice. Woburn House also distributed financial assistance to refugees who were legally prohibited from seeking employment, from donations that were collected by the Central British Relief Fund beginning in 1933. In 1938, the German-Jewish Aid Committee was renamed the Jewish Refugee Committee and moved into new quarters at Bloomsbury House on Bloomsbury Street, also in Central London. With the exception of children who were part of the *Kindertransport*, every refugee who arrived in Britain was directed to Woburn House and later Bloomsbury House for all of their financial and legal concerns.

Refugee accounts frequently refer unenthusiastically to Woburn House (and later Bloomsbury House) as the place where they expected long waits in queues with fellow refugees for their weekly financial assistance. Despite the efforts of the Jewish Refugee Committee, Woburn House was inundated with refugees seeking their services. In *Children's Exodus, A History of the Kindertransport*, Vera Fast cites letters of complaint submitted to the Board of Deputies by refugees regarding their high level of frustration at the disorganization and understaffing of Woburn and later Bloomsbury House.[4] Yet she also provides evidence of the heavy caseloads of Woburn House staff. According to Fast, there were between six hundred and one thousand visitors a day to Woburn House requiring individual assistance. She cites a 1939 article in the *Jewish Chronicle* that reported that Bloomsbury House received twenty thousand letters per week regarding individual refugee issues.[5]

The Jewish Refugee Committee's other areas of focus included lobbying Parliament on behalf of refugees and raising funds to bring ten thousand children to Britain through the *Kindertransport* program. Judith Tydor Baumel-Schwartz's book *Never Look Back: The Jewish Refugee Children in Great Britain, 1938–1945* provides a thorough history of the establishment of Anglo-Jewish organizations for European refugees and addresses the continuing debate among historians regarding the motivations of Anglo-Jews. Baumel-Schwartz shows that the support they gave was undeniable in terms of their efforts in the *Kindertransport* program and the funds raised for a central organizational structure and allowances for refugees who were unable to work. However, what becomes clear in a comparative study with United States organizations was that the Woburn House/Bloomsbury House founders initially viewed the presence of German Jews as temporary and subtly encouraged refugees to "blend in" to British society while they were there. Woburn House and Bloomsbury House were established by British Jews. While many of the workers and volunteers there were German Jewish refugees, the board of directors and the people in power were not. From the start, the Jewish Refugee Committee had a prescribed mission to rescue and assist refugees until they could emigrate once more out of Britain. The original funding came from the British Jewish community and later the British government.

Despite the support of segments of the British Jewish community, there appears to have been an underlying concern that the unrestricted entrance of Jewish migrants would lead to an increase in antisemitism. It is difficult not to see that members of the British Jewish community, in their work through Woburn House, deliberately encouraged refugees to remain invisible as foreigners and as Jews in Britain. This was evident in the pamphlet given to every refugee who entered Woburn House, *While You Are in England: Helpful Information and Guidance for Every Refugee*, which directly addressed many of the behavioral expectations. Writing about refugee domestic servants who lived in designated hostels under strict conditions, historian Tony Kushner wrote, "By such monitoring the refugee bodies hoped to Anglicize their charges."[6] In another important work, *The Persistence of Prejudice: Antisemitism in British Society during the Second World War,* Kushner shows that by the end of 1935, British Jews were concerned about the fascist and anti-Jewish actions in the East End of London, such as the "Battle of Cable Street."[7] Louise London found solid evidence of this fear in her analysis of Jewish organizational documents.[8] Anglo-Jews advocated for the temporary, not permanent entrance of refugees into Britain. This was clear in their lobbying efforts before Parliament and their work in the German Jewish community. An earlier and perhaps more sympathetic account of Anglo-Jewry's work for refugees can be found in the 1956 publication by Norman Bentwich called *They Found Refuge: An Account of British Jewry's Work for Victims of Nazi Oppression.*[9] By the early spring of 1945, with the end of the war near, the Jewish Refugee Committee, through its work at Bloomsbury House, shifted its focus and began programs that assisted German Jews hoping to settle in Great Britain. It later provided lists of survivors from Nazi-occupied Europe and sought to reunite refugees with loved ones.

Refugee-formed Organizations in London

Articles on various refugee-formed organizations in the United Kingdom are provided in the collection *"I Didn't Want to Float; I Wanted to Belong to Something." Refugee Organizations in Britain 1933–1945*, edited by Anthony Grenville and Andrea Reiter.[10] In his own chapter, Grenville examines the largest refugee-formed organization in London, the Association of Jewish Refugees (AJR). Grenville has written extensively over the years about the AJR and has served as the *AJR Information*'s consultant editor since 2006. In this book, Grenville writes that the AJR "is recognizably heir to the communal organizations of German Jewry, especially to the *Centralverein* (the German-Jewish centralized umbrella organization)."[11] The AJR was founded in 1941 by German Jews recently released from British internment camps.

It served numerous functions between 1941 and 1945.[12] Initially, the AJR offered mainly legal and employment assistance. But soon it began to organize concerts and lectures for refugees, which were also attended by many nonmembers. One of the first refugee-formed assistance organizations, Self-Aid, was founded in 1938 on Finchley Road in Northwest London. It was later absorbed into the Association for Jewish Refugees, whose headquarters moved from Finchley Road to Fairfax Mansions in 1943.[13] By then, the AJR had become the umbrella organization for more than ten other refugee associations, including the Council of Jews from Germany and the AJR Employment Agency. At a time when their future naturalization was uncertain and work and movement restrictions remained in place, German Jews found a support network and a sense of belonging in the AJR. Until war's end, it was difficult to maintain a steady membership, particularly because so many refugees were evacuated out of London and young male refugees enlisted in the armed forces. However, it managed to retain a core group of members and by 1945, AJR membership had reached five thousand. Grenville points out that the bulk of AJR's members were secular liberal or nonobservant Jews with few Orthodox members or Zionists. As its name suggests, the Association of Jewish Refugees represented the needs of Jewish refugees from German-speaking countries, which differentiated it from earlier refugee groups, such as the Free German League of Culture (*FDKB*) and the Austrian Centre.[14] Because of this, the AJR "had an awareness that its members wouldn't return to Germany," and it therefore became a more established organization, lasting to the present day.[15]

Publicly, the AJR took great pains to present itself as a pro-British organization; its members resolutely avoided speaking German at public functions. Their publication, a newsletter called the *AJR Information*, established in 1946, was entirely in English.[16] Prior to this, the organization printed monthly circulars also in English. The *AJR Information* served as a means of connection for refugees, especially since few had permanent addresses and most were dispersed across London. Through its publications and pronouncements, the AJR also worked to inform the British public of the Jewish refugees' circumstances in the face of growing anti-German sentiment. It officially declared:

> We want to make it clear to the authorities and to the public that a Jewish refugee is unconditionally opposed to Nazi Germany. We shall press for the removal of restrictions which prevent full utilization of the services of those refugees in the common cause against Nazism.[17]

Kurt Alexander wrote in the ten-year anniversary publication of the AJR in 1951:

> The needs of the individual had to be explained and it also had to be pointed out that the arrival of this group—expelled from its own country—would not be the cause of any harm, but would rather be an asset for the United Kingdom. We went about to familiarize political and economic leaders of the country with the facts in question. Meetings were held in which members of both Houses of Parliament, as well as of the press, participated. This method proved to be the best medium for reaching the British public and our efforts in this direction were, therefore, crowned with success.[18]

The AJR played an advisory and supportive role for refugees, but also worked to create a favorable impression of German Jews and to declare their full support for the British war effort. From its inception through the end of the war, the AJR fought to end alien status, help dependents of refugee soldiers, and to get enlisted refugees naturalized as British citizens. By 1945, the AJR was pushing for permanent residency visas for its members who wished to settle in postwar Britain.[19]

From 1938 to 1945, the Free German League of Culture (*Freier Deutscher Kulturbund* or *FDKB*) provided an artistic and intellectual outlet for refugees who yearned to preserve a German identity and culture that opposed Nazism. Their newsletter, the *FDKB Nachrichten*, has been mentioned throughout previous chapters. Until recently, the *FDKB* and its seven-year existence was almost forgotten, arguably because some of its founding members were closely tied to the German Communist party, and many of its prominent members resettled in East Germany after the war. The history of the *FDKB* and its changing role in the refugee community was given a thorough analysis in 2010 by Charmain Brinson and Richard Dove in *Politics by Other Means: New German League 1939–46*.[20] This work shows how the *FDKB* created a space for politically minded and culturally aware German-speaking refugees. The group was founded in artist Fred Uhlman's Northwest London home at 47 Downshire Hill in response to the rapid influx of refugees in 1938 and 1939. According to Brinson and Dove, the *FDKB* was the first refugee-formed organization in Britain. In December 1939 its home was moved to Belsize Park, to a church-owned building at 36 Upper Park Road NW3. The *FDKB*'s original aims, as listed in the League's 1939 constitution, and reprinted in *Politics by Other Means*, were as follows:

1. To preserve and advance Free German Culture.
2. To further the mutual understanding between the refugees and the English people.
3. To emphasize and strengthen the solidarity of the refugees with all democratic, freedom-loving, progressive movements.
4. To look after the social interests of the refugees.
5. To cultivate and to develop relations with other friendly organizations and personalities.[21]

Brinson and Dove note that at its peak, the *FDKB* had 1,500 official members, although its wide range of activities reportedly attracted many more from the refugee community.

For this historian, the most useful remnant of the *FDKB*'s activities was its monthly newsletter, published from December 1939 to March 1945 and originally called *FDKB Nachrichten* (news). In April 1940, it was formally renamed *Freie Deutsche Kultur* (Free German Culture), but it was still generally referred to as the *Nachrichten*. The newsletter was intended as a monthly, for the most part, but with paper shortages during the war, it was published sporadically between March 1942 and October 1943. While the organization had fewer members than the AJR, its newsletter provided much needed information for a certain subset of refugees in London, namely, those interested in German art and culture. Throughout its existence, the *FDKB*'s newsletter reminded refugees about the offerings at its headquarters in Northwest London, such as its "Continental" restaurant and German-language library, with more than six thousand volumes.[22] It advertised exercise classes, children's puppet shows, and concerts.[23]

A review of the *Nachrichten* over the years of its existence reveals the extensive cultural and intellectual infrastructure that the *FDKB* provided for the refugee community. For example, the *FDKB* was home to the *Kleine Bühne*, the Little Stage, where members regularly produced plays and cabarets in German.[24] There were the Musicians' and Artists' Sections at the *FDKB* that met regularly to practice and further their work. The *FDKB* put on art exhibits and concerts throughout its existence. There was a writer's group that offered refugee authors a forum to present their work in German. It published fiction and poetry from 1942 through 1946.[25] In July 1942, the *FDKB* scholars' group established the *Freie Deutsche Hochschule*, the Free German Institute, which held lectures and discussion groups on a wide range of subjects. In these ways, the *FDKB* helped maintain the confidence and self-esteem of refugee authors, artists, actors, musicians, and scholars who had lost their standing in exile due to unemployment and language difficulties.

As stated in its goals, the *FDKB*'s mission went beyond preserving German culture. Its objective "to look after the social interests of the refugees," was evident in each issue of the *Nachrichten*.[26] This was particularly notable in the organization's devotion to helping interned refugees. In June 1940, the *FDKB* established a commission to advise distraught relatives of the interned. Over the next two years, the *Nachrichten* advertised *FDKB* concerts and refugee art exhibits organized to raise money and awareness of internment, including a London exhibit of art created by interned refugees.[27] It maintained close ties to interned refugees through letter-writing campaigns and care package programs that included hand-knit blankets made from donated yarn.[28] The *FDKB* offered advice to families of refugees applying for release from internment.[29] The *Nachrichten* began advertising meetings at the *FDKB* for ex-internees in March 1941.

The *FDKB* maintained close ties to British artists and intellectuals, some of whom were official members. In *Politics by Other Means*, Brinson and Dove wrote that the *FDKB* began "mobilizing British friends and supporters to campaign against internment, to improve conditions in the camps and, as time passed, to accelerate the process of release. . . . There were frequent contacts with friendly politicians, such as Sir Richard Acland and Labour MPs David Grenfell and Graham White."[30] Financial support for the *FDKB* also came from British individuals and from fundraisers, including a February 1940 show called "English Actors to their Friends," held at the Embassy Theater in Swiss Cottage.[31] During the London Blitz, the *FDKB* worked to assist refugees as well. In December 1941, the *Nachrichten* advertised that the *FDKB* was a source of advice regarding air raid procedures and a check-in point for missing refugees.[32]

The cultural and social programs of the *FDKB* might have appealed to a wider range of refugees than it did if it were not for its ties to the Communist Party and its lack of a Jewish identity. While the *FDKB* gave the pretense that it was a nonpolitical organization, there were tensions among its members regarding the degree to which it was actually aligned with communists and the Soviet Union. Three of its founding members were declared communists. In fact, Brinson and Dove found that MI5 was monitoring the activities of the *FDKB* for communist activity from its start.³³ What is particularly striking is that while it claimed no religious or political affiliation, there was a glaring absence of references to Jewish holidays or cultural traditions in the *FDKB Nachrichten*. At the same time, the December issues consistently covered the *FDKB*'s Christmas-related events, such as a fundraising Christmas Bazaar and pleas to send Christmas packages to interned refugees.³⁴ In its August and September issues, the High Jewish Holidays were ignored. This conscious or unconscious alignment with Christianity may have alienated refugees who identified culturally as Jews, regardless of their political or religious views. Brinson and Dove take it a step farther when they note:

> The greatest problem was the striking mismatch between the League's cultural and political aspirations, and the profile of its émigré constituency. There were an estimated 40,000 refugees from the German Reich living in Britain. . . . Of these 40,000, however, probably no more than 600 to 700 were genuine "political" refugees. The overwhelming majority (some 90 percent) were "racial refugees:" Jewish, middle class, and politically uncommitted. . . . Despite its impeccably liberal-democratic aims and principles, the League faced above all a question of credibility. The disparity between the refugee population and its own cultural-political agenda was a gulf which it never succeeded in bridging.³⁵

It was for this reason that many more refugees joined the AJR and considered Woburn House and Bloomsbury House their meeting point, rather than the *FDKB*. In the end, the *FDKB* retained a niche membership, which provided artistic and intellectual outlets for some refugees. Unlike the AJR and other groups, the *FDKB* was designed to be a temporary organization, whose main mission was to preserve German culture in exile.³⁶ In the last years of the war, the *FDKB* started to consider the options for German refugees in a postwar world. Brinson and Dove estimate that one-third of German refugees remained in Britain, one-third returned to Germany (mainly to the Soviet Zone which became East Germany), and one-third emigrated again to places such as Palestine and the United States. The *FDKB* officially disbanded in 1946.

In 1943, Club 43 was formed by disgruntled members of the *FDKB*, who felt that the communists were becoming too influential in running the league. Based in the Hampstead area of London, Club 43 organized public readings and lectures in German for the exile population. Its membership reached just two hundred at its peak.[37] The PEN Group of German Writers in England saw itself as an important branch of the International PEN and held close ties to the English PEN club.[38] The short-lived German-language *Kabarett*, cabaret, and PEN in London may have provided an outlet for frustrated and creative refugees, but did not significantly impact British society or refugee life in general.

In the Hampstead area of London, refugees formed their own branch of *B'nai B'rith*, a Jewish service organization founded in the United States in 1843. They named it Section 1943 (it was also formed in 1943) and consisted of two hundred German Jews who purportedly felt unwelcome in the Anglo-Jewish *B'nai B'rith* Lodge of England. Members of Section 1943 spoke German in the club's daily affairs, but English at all official and public events. After the war they officially changed its name to the Leo Baeck Lodge, in honor of the former Chief Rabbi of Germany.

German Jewish refugees in London faced many obstacles to establishing thriving organizations. Internment, enlistment, evacuations, and air raids all served to disrupt any attempt to establish regular meetings, set membership, and develop long-term vibrant organizations. The refugees had come from a place where clubs, organizations, and religious groups were a central part of the community, so in London they persevered in trying to create them. Such activities provided a temporary outlet for German Jews: a place where they could remain connected to their fellow refugees and, even briefly, feel less like an outsider. Yet some London refugees perceived their own experience as different from their New York City counterparts. In the September 1946 issue of the *AJR Information*, an author, K. A., wrote:

> During the war, when the Association approached the organizations of Jewish immigrants from Germany in the United States and Palestine with a view to furthering the mutual exchange of views, it seemed doubtful whether they would respond. At that time apprehension as to our own future was the main concern of the AJR. Our position then was uncertain; we did not know how the Government would decide on our fate. Our friends in America and Palestine were free from such anxieties because their future, at least with regard to their legal position, was secured. Therefore, while prepared to share our sorrows, would they be willing to work with us in solving impending problems? They

declared, without hesitation, their readiness to co-operate with us, and it soon became evident that, though the question of legal absorption did not exist for immigrants in America and Palestine, there remained the problems of psychological and material adaptation, beyond that many tasks emerged, only to be accomplished by united efforts. It became quite clear that people who were bred in the same atmosphere and had endured the same sufferings, had much in common.[39]

Even toward the end of the war, the legal status of refugees in Britain was uncertain and with that came anxiety for the future. Yet, as the quote reveals, refugees in the United States were not free from worry and distress either.

American Jewish Organizations for Refugees

There was no single New York equivalent to London's Woburn House or Bloomsbury House. As in the United Kingdom, there were many groups in the United States working to rescue and meet the immediate needs of refugees from Europe. Preexisting Jewish groups included the Hebrew Sheltering and Immigrant Aid Society (HIAS), founded in 1904, the National Council of Jewish Women, and the American Jewish Joint Distribution Committee, also known as "the Joint." The Joint offered financial and social assistance to refugees immediately upon arrival and lobbied Congress and President Roosevelt to issue more immigrant visas for European Jews in Nazi-occupied territory. The Joint acted as a public advocate for refugees, distributing pamphlets such as "The Contribution of German Immigrants" in 1939.[40] In Michael Dobkowski's book, *Jewish American Volunteer Organizations*, Sharon Lowenstein writes about the expansive efforts of the National Refuge Service or NRS. The NRS was founded in 1935 under the name National Coordinating Committee for the Aid to Refugees and Emigrants Coming from Germany (NCC).[41] The collection of NRS documents from 1935 to 1946 are currently archived at the American Jewish Historical Society at the Center for Jewish History in New York City. The NRS coordinated the work of more than twenty organizations, including the German Department of the Jewish Social Service Association; the National Coordinating Committee for Aid to Refugees and Emigrants coming from Germany; *Shomre Hadath*, an employment service for religious immigrants; German Jewish Children's Aid; American Friends Service Committee; Boston Committee on Medical

Émigrés; Placement Committee for German and Austrian Musicians; Federation for the Support of Jewish Philanthropic Societies of NYC; and the Emergency Committee in Aid of Displaced Foreign Scholars and Medical Scientists. Over the eleven years of its existence, the NCC (later the NRS) organized the work of many smaller groups to lobby Congress and provide support for refugee communities across the United States.

American Jewish organizations offered specialized programs throughout New York City, but maintained a broader focus on gaining ground in Washington, D.C. In a chapter of *Between Sorrow and Strength: Women Refugees of the Nazi Period,* historian Sybille Quack examines the role of refugee women in aid organizations.[42] She found that the longest-lasting support programs were formed by German Jewish refugees themselves and based mainly in refugee enclaves in Manhattan such as Washington Heights and the Upper West Side.

Refugee-formed Organizations in New York

Between 1935 and 1945, refugees formed more than one hundred German-Jewish organizations in New York. The U.S. equivalent to the London-based Association of Jewish Refugees was the New World Club. It was a community organization that included a job placement agency, lecture series, professional societies, sports clubs, literature groups, stamp collectors group, two kindergartens, tours of New York City, a choir, a bridge club, and numerous charity organizations. Initially formed in 1924 under the title German-Jewish Club by an earlier group of German Jewish immigrants, the New World Club became the largest refugee-formed organization in the city.

Perhaps the most significant contribution of the New World Club was its weekly publication, *Aufbau,* which loosely translates as "rebuild." With a circulation of fifty thousand at its peak, it was by far the most popular refugee publication in New York City.[43] Published almost entirely in German, *Aufbau*'s articles focused on a wide range of issues, from events in Germany to New York politics. It offered classifieds, advertisements, and organizational announcements that connected refugees across New York City and beyond. In its first issue, in December 1934, *Aufbau* served to inform refugees of the New World Club's services such as: help enrolling children in school, advice on immigration issues, assistance with illness, where to find furnished rooms, and a pamphlet called "How to Become an

American Citizen."[44] *Aufbau* advertised English classes offered through the New York State Education Department on weeknights at locations convenient for refugees, such as the YWHA (or the "Y") at West 100th St. and George Washington High School at 192nd St. in Washington Heights.[45] The first issue of *Aufbau*, also advertised various athletic activities available to refugees through the New World Club, including handball, soccer, ping pong, swimming at the Hotel Paris on the Upper West Side, ski trips, and excursions to Rockaway Beach.[46] Over the next few years, the New World Club continued to offer a range of cultural and athletic activities for German Jewish refugees in New York, such as a day trip to Ramapo Mountain, an evening ride on the Staten Island Ferry, a walk through Central Park, and "An Evening of Negro Music" (presumably jazz).[47] It continued to offer weekly listings for sports at the club and throughout New York, such as tennis, swimming, hiking, and ping pong. It announced summer night dances at Hotel Delano and sold advertisements for dancing lessons on 152nd St.[48] Driving lessons were also advertised regularly.[49] The *Aufbau* advertised the first meeting of the *Ärztegruppe,* doctors group, in the Sept 1, 1937, issue of *Aufbau*. A year later, the *Aufbau* announced a celebration of the *Ärztegruppe*'s first year at the Hospital for Joint Disease. They prided themselves on being the first *Berufsgruppe,* professional group, that provided work-related lectures to 100–150 colleagues.[50]

Aufbau's original editors formally defined it as a Jewish newspaper for German-speaking refugees of no specific Jewish denominational affiliation. This was in stark contrast to the *FDKB Nachrichten* in London, and more similar to the role of the *AJR Information*, which began printing in 1946.

From the start, *Aufbau* provided regular listings of religious services held in German in Washington Heights and the Upper West Side, especially around the High Holidays of Rosh Hashanah and Yom Kippur. Its advertisements reflected the religious needs of some of its readership, for example, emphasizing the Kosher kitchens of hotels in Florida and the Catskills. It also advertised lectures, such as "The Palestine Question" and "Jewish Fate in the Eyes of Poetry."[51]

To address the growing physical and psychological needs of the refugees, Selfhelp of Emigres from Germany was established in 1936. As a social service agency founded by refugees, it provided work networks, day care, and emotional and financial support. In 1945, Saenger wrote that Selfhelp "maintains its own loan fund, supported by the voluntary contributions of refugees. . . . It has been discovered that lack of sympathetic friends has

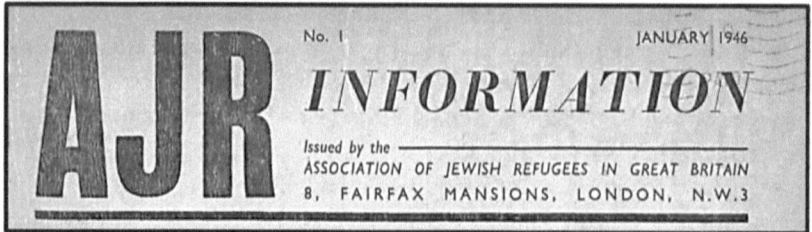

a. *AJR Information*, first issue, January 1946, Courtesy of Association of Jewish Refugees, London.

b. *FDKB Nachrichten*, February 1940, From the Exilpresse Digital—German Exile Journals 1933–1945, Deutsche National Bibliothek.

c. *Aufbau Reconstruction*, January 7, 1944, © JM Jüdische Medien AG / Serenade Verlag AG, Postfach 8027, Zürich, Switzerland.

Figure 5.1. Mastheads of refugee publications.

led, in some cases, to nervous breakdowns and suicides. This organization hopes to be able to prevent such unfortunate happenings by taking care of people in critical times."[52] Selfhelp also worked to assist refugees of all ages, young and old, such as providing summer placements in the country for émigré children.[53] Today, Selfhelp continues to meet the needs of elderly refugees and has caseloads of recent immigrants from around the world.[54] The American Federation of Jews from Central Europe, founded in 1941, became the centralized representative organization for Jewish refugees, par-

Unidentified couple seated on grass reading the *Aufbau* newspaper, undated, from the Herbert Buky Collection. Courtesy of Leo Baeck Institute, New York.

5.2. Couple reading *Aufbau*.

ticularly after the war.[55] It held annual meetings and published a monthly circular that provided updates on "communal and political issues." The organization was most widely known for its work on *Wiedergutmachung*, reparations from West Germany, into the 1960s.

The Prospect Unity Club was founded by Jews from Germany after World War I. Initially based in Yorkville on the Upper East Side, it moved its headquarters to Washington Heights in 1938. It boasted a sports field, kosher kitchen, dance hall, card evenings, and a cabaret as described in *Frankfurt on the Hudson*, by Steven Lowenstein. The Prospect Unity Club provided a place for refugees to socialize. Other refugee organizations included Maccabi Athletic Club, the Immigrant Jewish War Veterans, and the German American League for Culture Activities and Leisure. In comparison to London refugee organizations, German Jewish clubs in New York maintained high levels of membership and full activity calendars throughout the war. Except for the men who joined the armed services after 1941, most refugees lived in their apartments and neighborhoods for years at a time and their community life continued virtually undisrupted.

Synagogues and Organized Religious Life in London

It is estimated that in 1933, roughly 10 percent of the 525,000 registered Jews in Germany considered themselves to be Orthodox, while the majority were, as Marion Kaplan describes, liberals whose practice of Judaism was similar to the U.S. Jewish Conservative movement of today.[56] Kaplan also wrote that Jews in interwar Germany "preserved a sense of ethnic solidarity and religious cohesion. They did so by organizing religious or secular Jewish groups and creating new forms of German-Jewish culture in literature, music, fine arts, education, and scholarship. Most also maintained traditional holiday celebrations in the family."[57]

Unless they were descendants of Christian converts, or had converted themselves, most refugees in London identified as Jews. Refugee-formed organizations, such as the Association of Jewish Refugees and the Leo Baeck Lodge, provided a range of secular activities that included lectures on Jewish themes. Yet, these were not religious organizations per se. It was up to German Jews, who sought a religious community in London, to join an Anglo-Jewish congregation such as the English Liberal Synagogue in St. John's Wood formed in 1911, the Progressive Liberal West London Synagogue, or Alyth Gardens Synagogue, founded in May 1933 as the North Western Reform Synagogue and built in 1936 on the grounds of West London Synagogue off Finchley Road.[58] Anglo-Jewish synagogues tended to be more British in their practices, than the German *Liberale* movement was German, from which most refugees came.[59] Noticeable differences included the use of English in the services and the lack of classical music accompanying them.[60]

While individual refugees joined local Anglo-Jewish congregations, there was one synagogue founded entirely by and for refugees in 1939, the New Liberal Congregation, later renamed the Belsize Square Synagogue. In the first decade, sermons there were conducted in German, and its liturgy most closely resembled the practices of the German *Liberale* movement. Rabbi Ignaz Maybaum wrote in 1951, "Here in the Leo Baeck Lodge, and in the New Liberal Congregation of Rabbi Dr. Salzberger from Frankfurt am Main, are the only two instances in which German-speaking Jews have integrated themselves into Anglo-Jewry as separate bodies. Otherwise German Jews have joined the congregations, societies and organizations of Anglo-Jewry as individuals."[61] The Belsize Square Synagogue's website describes its own history as follows:

The first service held by what was to become Belsize Square Synagogue took place on 24 March 1939 in the continental *liberale* manner, organised by a group of refugees mainly from Berlin and Frankfurt-on-Main. Initially there was no formal congregational organization, and each service was conducted by a different rabbi and cantor recently arrived in the United Kingdom.

The group was supported by Lily Montagu, one of the founders of the English Liberal Movement and a lay minister in the Liberal Jewish Synagogue, who enabled them to use the Montefiore Hall for Friday evening services. However, despite her help, the founders of Belsize Square Synagogue could not simply integrate into an existing synagogue like their orthodox and reform refugee counterparts. Coming from the continental *Liberale* movement, English liberalism was too radical for them.

In June 1939 this ad hoc state of affairs was formalized by the foundation of the New Liberal Jewish Association, which became Belsize Square Synagogue in 1971. Lily Montagu was its first chairman and Rabbi Dr Georg Salzberger (formerly Frankfurt-on-Main) and Cantor Magnus Davidsohn (formerly Berlin) its first permanent ministers. Initially, the new organization occupied rented rooms in Swiss Cottage, until in 1951 when a former vicarage at Belsize Square was acquired and converted to accommodate a modest synagogue seating 80, communal offices, and a religion school.[62]

Bea Lewkowitz has studied the Belsize Square Synagogue and published a chapter on it in *We Thought We Could Float*. She writes that it was originally formed as a "friendship club" in late 1938 and met in St. John's Wood.[63] She writes that the founders believed they were creating a monument to the past, in order to preserve the *Liberale* Jewish tradition.[64] During air raids, sermons were held in the synagogue's basement, first at 20 Buckland Crescent in Northwest London and then down the street at number 30. Lewkowitz writes that attending services at the New Liberal Synagogue gave German Jewish refugees a sense of continuity and it became a kind of religious "home."[65] In 1940, they held Bible study groups on Thursday afternoons entirely in German and held Saturday services. Services remained in German until the late 1950s. It had a youth group that produced plays, such as *Esther* in 1944.[66] The inclusion of classical music, including Sunday afternoon concerts, free lectures, and a canteen helped the New Liberal Synagogue serve as an "important emotional anchor."[67]

For Orthodox refugees, there was also the smaller Orthodox Munk's Synagogue, formally known as Golders Green Beth Hamedrash, founded in 1934, whose first rabbi was Rabbi Elijah Munk of Berlin; Hampstead Adath Congregation; and Edgware Adath Yisroel founded in 1941. The extenuating conditions of war, internment, and displacement that interrupted refugee family life in London, affected the membership in clubs and synagogues in much the same way.

Synagogues and Religious Life in New York

In New York City, twelve German Jewish congregations had been formed around Washington Heights by 1945. These congregations reflected the wide range of Jewish denominations that had existed in Germany. The largest was the Conservative Congregation Beth Hillel. The Orthodox congregation Gates of Hope was founded in 1935. Most of these congregations maintained German sermons, songs, and rituals up through the 1950s. Congregation K'hal Adath Jeshurun was an Orthodox synagogue established by German refugees in Washington Heights and had its origins in Frankfurt am Main. Congregation Agudath Israel was also established in Washington Heights.[68] As mentioned previously, the *Aufbau* regularly published announcements of Jewish holiday celebrations for newly formed congregations, such as the "Sukkot Celebration and prayers in German at 'The Gates of Hope' Congregation held in the Royal Manor."[69] There were two existing American Jewish synagogues in Washington Heights that attracted individual refugee members. One, Hebrew Tabernacle, had hired a German cantor in the late 1920s, which meant that when refugees arrived, there was already a German feeling to services at this congregation. Congregation Habonim in midtown Manhattan identified itself as Conservative-Reform, and was founded in 1939 in the *Liberale* tradition, it served German Jewish refugees from all over New York City.[70] In 1946, Saenger wrote:

> Congregation Habonim in New York was formerly a centre of Jewish religious life in Germany. This congregation has its own community house here; it supports a Sunday school for children and gives lectures on religious subjects for adults. Apart from its religious functions, the congregation maintains a voluntary

social service headed by a "sisterhood." Refugee women volunteer to visit their sick countrymen and take care of them and their children. Once every two weeks the community center is opened for a social gathering.[71]

Other congregations such as *Kulturgemeinde,* cultural community, in Brooklyn and *Synagogengemeinde,* synagogue community, in the Bronx, were started by refugees and had members living in those boroughs. They too, retained a strong German tradition. Unlike in London, New York refugee congregations remained mostly intact for the duration of the war. As in London, though, synagogues acted as centers of support and community for German Jews across New York. Advertisements in *Aufbau* reveal that Jewish holidays were regularly observed in the refugee community.[72]

The evidence shows that in the communal sphere, refugees in New York and London differed in their processes of group identity practices and performance and cultural transformation. This is revealed in the German Jewish organizations' selected group names, language, and goals, which clearly show the perceptions they had of their place in British and American society.

6

Identities

Refugees, Immigrants, Émigrés, and Exiles

A CLOSE EXAMINATION OF REFUGEE LETTERS, diaries, memoirs, and organizational publications reveals striking differences between the self-identifying terms in the English language used by German Jews in London and New York. The most common self-descriptors among London refugees were, in order of frequency: "refugee," "exile," "*émigré*," "Continental," "Jew," and "German Jew." In New York they were: "immigrant," "*émigré*," "refugee," "German," and "European." In interviews, German Jews in London were more likely to use the term *refugee*, while those in New York preferred *immigrant*.[1] This was true in accounts both in English and in German.[2]

For refugees in Great Britain, the widely distributed booklet, *While You Are in England: Helpful Information and Guidance for Every Refugee*, discussed in chapter 1, introduced new arrivals to the term *refugee*, while reminding them of their temporary status in Britain.[3] Others encountered the term *refugee* from their British neighbors or other Europeans. Anne Koppel, who arrived on a *Kindertransport*, wrote of her first day with her foster family:

> Mrs. Wimborne told them who I was, and that was the first time I heard myself referred to as a refugee. It was a funny feeling, because I had never before considered myself as a refugee. It hurt, but when I thought it over, I knew that I was a refugee to these people who did not know me, to whom I was just a tired girl with a suitcase and a layer of dirt from the train and boat rides.[4]

English publications of the 1930s aimed at easing the apprehensions of the British public regarding German Jews also widely utilized the term *refugee*. Some examples were *The Refugee Problem: Report of a Survey*; *Humanity and the Refugees*; *The Refugees from Germany*; *You and the Refugee: the Morals and Economics of the Problem*; and *Refugees from Germany in English Literature and Art*.⁵ Perhaps the authors hoped the term *refugee* would elicit sympathy, or at least assure readers of the temporary nature of the newcomers' status. German Jewish organizations in London also used (and continue to use) *refugee* in titles and publications; the most prominent example is the Association of Jewish Refugees. There is no doubt that by 1940, German Jews in Britain knew they were considered refugees by both Anglo-Jewry and the British general public. As mentioned earlier, Britons were proud of their long heritage as a place of asylum for the persecuted. Calling German Jews refugees was, perhaps, a subconscious reminder of their own generosity. German Jews adopted this term as revealed in the ubiquitous usage of *refugee* in letters, diary entries, and memoirs. Refugees also drew from this romanticized narrative of exile to define their place in Britain. For example, Werner Rosenstock wrote in 1951, "Many of us still proudly describe ourselves as 'refugees;' we thus follow the example of other communities who, for several generations, have been integrated into their country of refuge, such as the Protestant *refugies* from France or the 'Spanish and Portuguese Jewish Community' in this country."⁶ In the same publication, Rabbi Ignaz Maybaum wrote, "We German Jews, utterly uprooted, are like the tribe of Levi who became the priestly tribe exactly because it was uprooted from the former historic soil of its past life and growth."⁷

Exile, émigré, and *Continental* were also favored terms among German Jews in London. By identifying as Continental, they could outwardly acknowledge that they were not British, while, at the same time, avoid disclosure of their German origins. "Continental" sounded, perhaps, more cosmopolitan and could imply that Paris, Rome, or Monte Carlo was their home. The title of Marion Berghahn's 1984 book, *Continental Britons*, also reflects the widespread use of Continental to describe German Jewish refugees.⁸ One can assume that, because Britain is considered part of Europe, it would be pointless to use the term *Europeans* in London, as refugees did in New York.

German Jews in New York generally called themselves immigrants immediately upon arrival in the United States. Many embraced the "melting pot" narrative in which they could instantly become American, while retaining their German Jewish ways. The refugees did not see any conflict in both calling themselves American and acting German Jewish. Unlike British organizational publications from the 1930s and 1940s, publications by New York groups mainly used *immigrant* or *émigré* in their titles. Manfred George, the editor of the *Aufbau Almanac: The Immigrant's Handbook*, stated explicitly in his 1941 introduction that *Aufbau* "is a newspaper by and for immigrants, not by and for refugees."[9] This was also true for some informational pamphlets and academic texts. Examples include: *The Contribution of the German Immigrants to American Life: Economic and Cultural Capacity of the Newcomers*; *The Immigrant in America, Vocational Adjustment of Jewish Immigrant Women and Girls*; *Immigrants and National Welfare*; "A Survey of Jewish Immigration to the US"; "Intellectual Émigrés Join American University Life"; and "The Émigré Physician in America,"[10] There were, however, circumstances in which *refugee* was the designated term for German Jews in the United States, mostly in publications geared toward the general public and academic texts. This was similar to the ones aimed at the British public. Such titles included: *The Refugees Are Now in America*; *Today's Refugees, Tomorrow's Citizens*; *Refugee Facts: A Study of the German Refugee in America*; *Refugees at Work*; and *You and the Refugee*. Sociological studies, often conducted by refugees themselves, used the term *refugee* in academic publications such as "Those German Refugees," "Experiences, Attitudes, and Problems of German-Jewish Refugees," "Refugee Social Workers," "The Problem of the Refugee Physician," and "The Meaning of the Day Nursery to the Refugee Parent."[11] Perhaps the use of the term *refugee* in scholarly writings reveals an academic tendency toward linguistic precision and a desire to demonstrate objectivity.[12]

There was certainly distaste for the term *refugee* within the New York German Jewish community that persisted for decades. Steven Lowenstein, author of *Frankfurt on the Hudson* and a child of German Jewish refugees in New York, wrote in the foreword to *We Were So Beloved* that the "refugees" (his quotation marks) hated the word "refugee." Throughout the book, however, he used the terms *refugee* (without quotation marks), *immigrant*, *German Jew*, and *German* (in relation to American Jews) to describe this population. Ernest Stock, a German Jew in New York, observed, "The word 'refugee' was not like in England where it stuck to you for many years. In England the German Jews were called 'refugees' for, I think, twenty or thirty years after their arrival. In America, you wanted to get rid of it."[13]

New York–based refugee memoirs used *refugee, immigrant, émigré, newcomer,* and *European* interchangeably. Leo Grebler wrote in 1976, "Identifications have become semantically indistinct. In common usage, the difference between 'immigrant,' 'refugee,' or '*émigré*' is not at all clear. I am unaware of any widespread discussion among us about 'proper' collective identification. Because the terms are so blurred, I am using throughout this document 'immigrant,' 'refugee,' '*émigré*' interchangeably."[14] Gerhart Saenger, himself a German Jew, also used a variety of words throughout his study *Today's Refugees, Tomorrow's Citizens*, a title that is particularly telling.[15]

Finding patterns in the terminology German Jews used to describe their status in London and New York should not imply that one or another essential identity prevailed. Rather, these patterns reveal the complex and nuanced processes of status renegotiation that German Jews experienced once they left Nazi Germany and entered Great Britain and the United States.[16]

Intersections of National Identity, Race, and Religion

As mentioned in the Introduction, there is growing interest among scholars to understand how perceptions of national belonging, race, and citizenship intersected with practices of "Jewishness" and "Germanness" throughout German Jewish history.[17] From the early nineteenth century through the end of World War II, there existed two competing and sometimes overlapping views in Europe on the meaning and role of nation. The first, which was idealized in the failed 1848 Liberal Revolutions, saw nation-states as citizen-led modern democracies. Citizenship in this liberal nation-state was not defined by one's race, religion, or "descent," but rather by one's participation as equal citizens in the *Bürgerschaft*, community of citizens. For many Germans, and Jews in particular, the Weimar Republic was meant to be the realization of this type of nation-state. Jews, Catholics, and Protestants could all identify as German under this construct.[18] The second meaning of nation was based on pseudo-scientific concepts of race, descent, empire, and so-called natural ties to the land, and dates back to the Franco-Prussian War and the unification of Germany in 1871. The most extreme form of this racially based *Volk* concept of nation was, of course, Nazi Germany, where only two categories could exist: German *Volk* and Jewish *Volk*. German Jews' legal status as German citizens was revoked in the 1935 Nuremburg Laws. Certainly the persecution and expulsion of Jews from Nazi Germany based on so-called inferior racial or *völkisch* origins affected the ways in which German Jews practiced national and religious identities in exile. Their national identities were formally rejected in Nazi Germany. In Great Britain and the United States, differences developed in the formation of national identity among German Jewish refugees.

In the UK, many younger refugees attempted to understand and adopt British culture, but faced resistance in identifying as British or English. For example, Marion Berghahn noted:

Like Mrs V., several respondents in this generation mentioned that, when they were younger, they "had tried to be very, very English," they had "made efforts to conform." But as with the older generation, there came the slow realization that the English did not consider them as being one of them. Thus Mr E. still feels "English; I am liberal, even a royalist. I want to say, 'we, the English,' and I must always stop myself, because it must sound too ridiculous to someone who knows I am from the Continent. But I have been here far longer than I was in Germany."[19]

Kenneth Ambrose wrote in his reply to a notice from the Home Office that stated his visa would not be renewed, "First, I am still a student, and secondly . . . I am one of the most Englishized [sic] refugees, and have the wish to settle in this country for good."[20] Around the same time he wrote in his diary:

> In the eyes of the English people I am still considered a German. . . . It is true that the Hitler government have [sic] deprived me—or better rid me—of my unwanted nationality . . . but Hitler's action is not recognized by the British Aliens Law . . . the vast majority of my fellow refugees are effectively debarred from taking any considerable part in the war effort. . . . The Jews, wherever they may happen to come from, are the natural allies of the British . . . and cannot be satisfied until they are recognized as such. We Jews from the countries that are now under Hitler do not generally refer to our duty to fight. We ask for our right to fight. Naturalization as British subjects would be welcome to many of us, but it is not essential. . . . It is as Jews that each one of us has an account to settle with the German gangsters.[21]

Kenneth Ambrose refers to himself as an "ally" of the British. His appreciation for British citizenship is noteworthy, but so is the fact that he felt the need to settle accounts with Hitler's Germany "as Jews." Refugee soldiers appreciated the kindness and even "tolerance" of their British counterparts. Gabriele Tergit wrote, for example, that young German Jews who joined the British armed forces after release from internment were, on the whole "suddenly happy in the army. They were equals, they enjoyed the good-humored kindly tolerance, and the patient cheerfulness of the simple Englishman, as their fathers had never enjoyed anything in the German army."[22]

Even after receiving British citizenship, most former refugees reconciled themselves with their Continental origins and the fact that they might never truly be considered British or English. In 1951, Eric Sheldon wrote that refugees who arrived as teenagers and young adults were "probably fated to remain 'foreigners.' "[23] In 1956, Herbert Freeden, a refugee in England, noted, "Many Jewish men and women have become citizens of a country which they respect and to which they are grateful, but who are blocked from full identification with their fellow countrymen. Their past lies buried on the continent and their future, as a group, lies in self-effacement."[24] The fact that their passports were stamped with temporary British transit visas and saw their stay as temporary most likely contributed to the reluctance of German Jews to adopt a British national identity in the early years upon arrival.

There are various circumstantial reasons why refugees in London did not consider themselves British, and perhaps internalized ones as well. Partially, there seemed to be a view of Britain on the part of the refugees as an ethnically homogenous population. Their being allowed to live in Britain was seen as an act of kindness or charity for which they should be grateful. There was a conflicted sense among refugees that in England one was born English, that this was an undisputable matter of descent. At the same time, Britain was perceived to be open to Jewish participation in British political and cultural life—Disraeli had been prime minister in the nineteenth century, and there were famous prominent Anglo-Jews who had made their way into the House of Lords and Commons. Yet, the feeling was that those were Anglo-Jews, who were perhaps British, but certainly not English.

In the United States, not only were refugees arriving on permanent immigrant visas, but they came to the country having bought into the idea of America as a land of immigrants and opportunity. The melting pot narrative appealed greatly to refugees. It was almost as if they saw the United States as a liberal democratic and modern nation-state, one made by and for the people, the antithesis of Nazi Germany. Of course, this was not the case for African Americans and Native Americans, nor any people of color. By the start of World War II, Jews were already being perceived as "white" by most of American society. Of course, antisemitism remained widespread in both the United States and Great Britain; however, Jews were no longer the primary victims of discrimination as they had been in Germany.[25] The generation of Americanization programs had been implemented for the masses of immigrants from all over Europe at the turn of the century through the 1920s. By the 1930s and 1940s, refugees believed that they could be "real" Americans. In some ways, especially in New York, refugees felt a freedom to be Jewish and American and even German. Many refugees placed their loyalties with America on par with Judaism. The complexity of this re-identification is reflected in the 1941 Statement of Policy of the German-Jewish Club's (now the New World Club's) newspaper, *Aufbau*:

> This paper is to serve the interests of all immigrants from Central Europe and their merging into life and society of the American democracy. It is written and published in America; it is an American paper in which American problems and the future in America are given first consideration. It is a Jewish paper, intended to preserve the traditions of Judaism and to nurture the ties of the individual to his Jewish heritage, Jewish history, culture and religion, without, however, wishing to forget or neglect the interests of the non-Jewish immigrant and his problems. . . . We are non-political, but liberal and true to the democratic traditions of the United States of America.[26]

German Jews in New York with permanent residency visas felt free to identify as American upon arrival on U.S. soil. In the meantime, most of their counterparts in Britain remained unsure of their residency status until 1945 and were, perhaps, more reluctant to identify themselves as British. Although some soldiers felt their service in the British armed forces might lead to naturalization, most considered themselves neither English nor British. For refugees in the U.S. armed forces, enlistment further accelerated their adoption of an American identity. In exile, divergent national identity practices among refugee soldiers in Britain and the United States were reflected in descriptions of their service. For example, a refugee soldier in the British military wrote, "While being in the army one has got to sacrifice some or rather a lot of this freedom . . . yet we have to carry on in order to help the country which has been so generous to us."[27] The next quote, from a refugee serving in the U.S. Army: "So it came that a Jew-boy who was chased in 1933, liberated the town as an American conqueror. . . . One thing this all taught me. I am proud to be an American. And even more proud to be an American soldier!"[28] The first soldier did not appear to fight as an Englishman but rather as a refugee returning the favor of asylum. The second swiftly identified as American, and his military service reinforced this.

Living in New York amid a mix of ethnicities and races was proof to many German Jews that there was no "one" way to be American. It also reinforced the idea that they were part of a heterogeneous nation-state. For instance, Bridget Stross Laky wrote about her first days in New York:

> I scrutinised the people of all races, black and white, yellow, and brown, who thronged the avenues. Many were well dressed, others in rags. Orthodox Jews in black garb mingled with youth in brightly coloured outfits. . . . Absorbing this jumble of sights and smells and sounds, it struck me that here I could remain an individual among individuals. There was not just one way to live. . . . I could be myself and still blend in.[29]

Harold Koppel, who had lived in Britain prior to arriving in America, wrote that on his first night in the United States, "I was very much surprised when I saw a colored man waiting on us. It was something new to me. I had never seen anybody who was not white."[30] His sister Anne, who had also lived in Britain, wrote, "I still could not get over the scores of Negroes in the streets, and nobody even turned his head to look at them."[31] In Britain, the massive migrations from former imperial colonies in South Asia and the West Indies would not occur for another decade.

In *Frankfurt on the Hudson*, Steven Lowenstein observed, "The German Jews of Washington Heights were in a fortunate position. They could retain their cultural distinctiveness, at least in the first generation, and they could still feel that they were Americans."[32] Many refugees felt that they would be accepted as German Jews in the United States, without having to try and become invisible. For instance, Leo Grebler wrote:

> Its openness and receptivity to newcomers, the diversity of people and the fluid class structure were in strong contrast to the Germany we had left behind—or to the other European countries where we had found temporary refuge. It was one thing to know these oft-described features in the abstract and an altogether different thing to experience them directly. For example, when I talked about my status as a fresh immigrant to Ormond Loomis, the official at the Federal Home Loan Bank Board who hired me in 1938, he responded by urging me to stop feeling self-conscious about it, "we all are immigrants except the Indians." I learned later that this was something of a cliché. At the time, it sounded highly original, was offered in a sincere spirit of encouragement and gave me a tremendous lift.[33]

The *Aufbau* declared itself an American paper, while publishing almost entirely in German. In fact, from November 1939, the only English included in the paper was the subtitle "Dedicated to the Americanization of the Immigrants." To "Americanize" while publishing a paper entirely in German may appear peculiar to some. Yet, the perception was that being an American citizen and retaining German Jewish culture was not mutually exclusive. *Aufbau*'s Statement of Policy included:

> Although we are firmly faced toward our American future, we are not ashamed of our European past but are prepared to save its values from destruction as far as it is possible for us. At the same time, we will uphold freedom and democracy; we will avoid politics and quarrels about political questions of the day.[34]

There were incidents of antisemitism and anti-German sentiment faced by German Jews in the United States. Yet, there seem to be fewer accounts of anti-German sentiment in New York than in London, perhaps because New York was not subjected to German air raids and a potential invasion. There are some reports from refugees outside New York City that describe anti-German attitudes and greater pressure to become invisible as Germans. However, these refugees usually lived in smaller towns where local populations tended to be more homogenous, and also more conservative.

While German Jews in America embraced the "Land of Immigrants" narrative, several examples of their own prejudice were evident in personal accounts. Rudolf Katz wrote after a day on Staten Island, "I had to learn that there are still much lower standards of people than the Coney Island visitors—most foreigners of Italy or some other south-eastern country."[35] Leo Grebler observed in his memoirs, "In our enthusiasm over the America we found, we ignored some deep-seated social issues, especially the race problem. The appealing idea of the 'melting pot,' whatever its validity, did not apply to Negroes and other 'non-whites.' But we shared this blind spot with the vast majority of the native population."[36] The mythology of this American "melting pot" was deeply embedded in the minds of many refugees. This is evident in the introduction to the *Aufbau Almanac* that states, "The diversity of the American population, which includes people from many lands and cultures, the prevalence of democratic principles in government and the presence of many religious denominations and sects, tend to bring about greater tolerance and mutual understanding."[37] Consequently, many German Jews believed they could become American while still retaining ethnic practices. They perceived the United States as a nation in the political/citizenship sense, as described earlier, rather than in the ethnic, racial sense of nation that was predominant in Europe. Therefore, refugees in New York, particularly those living in German Jewish neighborhoods, were less likely to try and hide their German origins than those in London, while still considering themselves new Americans.

It was uncommon for German Jews in Britain to refer to themselves as "German." With Britain preparing for a possible Nazi invasion, most German Jews felt pressure to remain invisible as Germans, even when distinguishing themselves from Anglo-Jews. This did not prevent others, however, from perceiving the refugees as Germans. Irene White recalled, "People did think of me as a German . . . that was the hardest thing in my life. . . . Yes I was very disappointed. I was actually more than disappointed. I was very upset about it but there was nothing you could do."[38]

In New York, refugees often called themselves *Deutsch*, German, but only to differentiate themselves from American Jews who were of East European descent. A few self-identified political refugees identified themselves as German, proud of their political struggles in Germany. Rudolf Katz, for example, called himself "an exiled German political man" in the introduction to his second volume of diaries. He then interchanged the words *European, exile, émigré,* and *German* throughout his daily entries, but rarely used *refugee*. Atina Grossman wrote in 2008 that she believed many refugees held onto their German identity, forming a kind of "hybrid" identity.[39]

Some refugees in London found solace in identifying foremost as Jews. Their persecution as Jews in Germany, in some cases, strengthened their Jewish identity. Berghahn wrote in *Continental Britons*, "In terms of ethnicity the large majority of the respondents had no problem of determining their identity: Jewish. And many, especially among the older generation, added that they are 'more aware of their Jewishness in Britain' than they had been in Germany."[40] Refugees who lived in the East End, which had a significant Jewish community in the 1930s, were immersed in the Anglo–Eastern European Jewish lifestyle. In Stevens's *The Dispossessed* he describes how Yiddish was spoken in the East End and Kosher food was widely available. German Jews experienced being Jewish more there than they had ever done in Germany.[41] Most German Jews lived only a short time in the East End, and by the war's end the established Eastern European Jewish community there had also left the neighborhood.

Herbert Strauss wrote in the introduction to the second volume of *Jewish Immigrants of the Nazi Period in the US* that the refugee in the United

States "had reacted to the culture shock of being denied his identity as a native German with an affirmation of his Jewish identity."[42] There was an implication in this that their "Jewishness" replaced their "Germanness." Leo Grebler wrote in 1976:

> There has been a greater change in the Jewish consciousness of refugees. More self-identification as a Jew, notoriously difficult for some of the more assimilated in Germany, now comes with greater ease and more often with a sense of pride than in a spirit of timidity. Quite a few émigrés who did not belong to Jewish organizations in Germany are now members of ethnic associations and are taking a more active interest in Jewish affairs.[43]

It seems from refugee accounts that this revived interest in Judaism occurred years after the discovery of the full extent of the Holocaust and the establishment of Israel. Some Orthodox Jews, however, had already formed strong Jewish identities in Germany, and transferred this into exile, particularly those communities that resettled in Washington Heights. In her research on the "One Thousand Children," Judith Tydor Baummel concludes that because the children rescued and placed in the United States were forced to be matched with Jewish families, they had an easier integration than *Kindertransport* children in Britain, whose foster families were generally not Jewish.[44]

Although German-speaking Jews found safety in the United States and Britain, there remained millions of Jews murdered by the Nazis and thousands whose applications for refuge were denied. This failure on the part of both nations should be remembered when examining the experiences of refugees who were able to escape. While appreciative of the granting of British and American visas, every refugee still dealt with the frustration of not being able to rescue family and friends left behind. This may have also affected the degree to which they embraced their new countries.

Conclusion

BETWEEN 1935 AND 1945, REFUGEES IN London experienced greater pressure to remain inconspicuous as German Jews than refugees in New York. Yet, despite their efforts to blend in, German Jews in London seldom identified as British or English. Meanwhile, refugees in New York more easily identified as American, while retaining much of their German Jewish way of life. Refugees' internalized views on religion, race, immigration, and nationality in the United States and Great Britain also contributed to this, but I argue that preconceived narratives of British and U.S. history played a less prominent part. This discrepancy between cultural adaptation and identity practice is due primarily to circumstantial or external factors, namely, differing British and American immigration visa policies and the proximity of each country to the events of World War II.

Role of British and U.S. Immigration Policies

Louise London concluded that the British government was willing to help refugees on a humanitarian basis, but only to the extent that it would not affect British self-interests. In Britain, this meant providing temporary refuge with severe restrictions on employment. London also concluded that Anglo-Jewish leaders resisted unrestricted Jewish immigration for fear of growing antisemitism. She found that the lack of an official policy on refugees aided the Home Office in curbing the number of visas allotted to European Jews during the critical years between 1938 and 1941, when Jews were eager and still able to leave Nazi-occupied Europe. Visa allotment was left to the discretion of individual passport control officers on the Continent. London argues that British immigration officers based in Germany and Austria felt immense pressure from the Home Office to limit the entry of Germans into the United Kingdom.[1] In the United States, immigration statistics are available, but they do not distinguish between Jewish and Christian German refugees, nor do they indicate where immigrants settled. In *Whitehall and the Jews*, Louise London examines the limited efforts of the British government to open its own doors and Palestine's to save European Jewry. In her work, London also acknowledges the many individual contributions Britons made to the rescue of European Jewry.[2]

The United States accepted a greater number of refugees from Nazi Germany than Great Britain. Yet, in proportion to the size and population of each country, Britain was significantly more generous. Altogether, more than 250,000 German-speaking Jews found refuge in these two countries. The differences in their entry visas also affected integration rates. The temporary and work-restrictive visas of Britain curbed initial enthusiasm among refugees in London, as discussed in chapter 1. The permanent immigrant visas that allowed full employment in the United States were a signal to refugees that they had found a new home. Most importantly, German Jewish impressions were tainted by Britain's proximity to Nazi-occupied territory. Enduring the Blitz, London refugees could feel that they were part of the broader British war effort and part of a community. There was no equivalent to this among refugee civilians in New York City. Instead, the circumstances around the United States' entry into the war led to a more cohesive, if somewhat scattered, German Jewish community. Refugee cultural integration and identity formation was tremendously affected by immigration restrictions, the threat of Nazi invasion, and early impressions of the United States and Great Britain as places of refuge.

Proximity to World War II

Of all the external factors affecting German Jewish integration in London, the outbreak of World War II was the most influential. Great Britain declared war against Germany in September 1939. This meant that refugees in London experienced war for two years longer than those in New York, as the United States did not enter into fighting until the attack on Pearl Harbor in December 1941.

The Nazis presented an immediate physical threat to refugees in Britain. Fear of a Nazi invasion of Britain was real, especially after the fall of Paris in June 1940. Widely distributed government pamphlets such as "If the Invader Comes: What to Do and How to Do It" and "Personal Protection against Gas," further fueled their anxiety.[3] Anti-German sentiment flourished and repeatedly refugee accounts express the intense pressure placed on German Jews to disguise their German background. This was realized in the enactment of laws classifying German Jews as enemy aliens, and the subsequent internment policy. Anthony Grenville wrote in an issue of the *AJR Information* called "Remembering Internment," "Worst of all was the psychological blow of being unjustly imprisoned; the deprivation of liberty, the confinement and humiliation were made more wounding by the apparent willingness of the authorities to identify Jewish refugees with the agents of Nazism."[4] Many former refugees in Britain retained mixed feelings about the long-term effects of their internment. They emphasized the cultural and educational activities of the camps and the eagerness of German Jews to serve in the British armed forces upon release. Nevertheless, the evidence will prove that internment severely disrupted family life and the integration and identity transformation of German Jews in Great Britain.

From September 1940 to May 1941, London and Southern England were under Nazi air attack. More than forty thousand civilians were killed during the Blitz and approximately one million buildings were destroyed. This had several important implications for German Jewish life. First, there

Image C.3. Hampstead street scene. © reserved; Collection of Burgh House and Hampstead Museum.

was the daily fear of death or injury and the anticipation of a likely Nazi invasion. The deportations of German Jews, who had escaped to Holland, Italy, and France, were not lost on the refugees in Britain. Second, one can see that families were continually separated due to the evacuation of thousands of children and some women into the countryside. Third, during the bombings, cultural and communal life was severely disrupted. Nevertheless refugee accounts also showed that for many refugees who remained in London, the air raids and constant vigil on the home front allowed for a camaraderie to develop with so-called typical Londoners. They lived on the same wartime rations as their neighbors.[5]

Some of the particularly unique stressors faced by the *Kindertransport* children in Britain included "change of language, change of country, loss of (or limited) communication with parents, change of name, disrupted education, change of national allegiance."[6] Employment restrictions on refugees in Britain were lifted once the war began. This meant that they could then find any type of work, and were not limited to handouts from refugee agencies and domestic service salaries. They found work alongside Britons of all classes and backgrounds. Refugee entrepreneurs could start war-related businesses. A sense of belonging to the greater war effort and growing intimacy with the local population seems to have accelerated integration into British life. Upon release from internment in 1941, more than nine thousand refugee men enlisted in the British armed forces, mainly into the Pioneer Corps. This was a noncombatant army unit and one of the only service options for former "enemy aliens." By the end of 1942, they were permitted to transfer to fighting units, and many did. Others used their German fluency and knowledge of German life and geography to work in the Intelligence Corps.[7]

With America's late entry into World War II at the end of 1941 and New York's distance from either front, war did not affect German Jews in New York the way it had in London. While German nationals were also labeled "enemy aliens" in the United States, they were not interned like those in Britain. Instead, because of the Japanese bombing of Pearl Harbor, Japanese Americans bore the brunt of American hostility and were interned en masse. As enemy aliens, however, German Jews were required to register with the FBI and needed written permission to leave New York State.

As the evidence proves, New York refugees felt less societal pressure to disguise their German origins than their counterparts in London. This may be due to the fact that many New York refugees lived and worked within their own communities during the war. In New York, German Jews experienced greater stability in their daily lives than their counterparts in London, due to the absence of internment, air raids, and evacuations. The housing shortage in New York City during World War II meant that German Jews tended to remain in the same apartments and neighborhoods from 1941 to 1945. Refugee organizations and social networks thrived. War rations in the United States were neither as severe, nor as long-lasting as in Great Britain. With the exception of military-aged men enlisting in the U.S. armed forces, most refugee families remained intact. This led to a greater retention of German Jewish culture in the home. Approximately 9,500 German Jewish refugees served in the U.S. armed forces.[8] From December 1941 to the middle of 1943, they could only enlist in the medical or ordinance corps. After that period, they were permitted to serve in infantry and combat units. As in Britain, a small number served in military intelligence capacities. German Jewish refugees in the United States, particularly those serving in the military, were part of the American war effort. Yet, without the intensity of air raids and evacuations that refugees in London lived through alongside their British neighbors, the war did not bring New York refugees close to "real" Americans. It also meant that they lacked the camaraderie that refugees in London experienced with native Londoners during the Blitz. Like refugee soldiers in Britain, those in the United States felt that their integration into the dominant culture was expedited by army service. Ernest Stock, a former refugee said, "I joined the army two and a half years after my arrival in America. The army was a big sort of leveler and I learned a lot there. When I came out of the army I felt much more American."[9] There are accounts of antisemitism in the army, but fewer reports of anti-German sentiment. In fact, a German background could be advantageous, particularly for those stationed in Europe, where there were opportunities to translate and provide tactical information.

The close examination of refugee home and family life in chapter 3 reveals discrepancies in the rates of cultural adaptation and integration. In London, refugee families experienced separation and upheaval until 1945. They had greater difficulty maintaining German Jewish décor, food traditions, and family rituals. Refugee domestics and fostered children experienced British home life first hand. As a result, they adopted English customs and practices at a quicker rate than unemployed counterparts and most German Jewish refugees in New York. Compared to German Jewish youth in New York, the London *Kindertransport* children and war evacuees had more opportunities to adopt local living and eating conditions with British foster families.

In New York, the American entry into war in 1941 had the opposite effect. The resultant housing shortage in New York meant that refugees remained in the same apartments throughout the war. Refugees owned their own businesses in refugee enclaves that catered to the needs of the community. German housewares, furniture, and food were widely accessible. German Jews in New York had many opportunities to live and work among one another where they could find sympathy and encouragement. Comparatively, the constant upheaval of German Jews in London did not allow for the development of an extensive and steady refugee support network. Nevertheless, London refugees developed a much stronger sense of solidarity with native Britons due to the immediate threat of invasion and the Blitz. Changes in parent/child and male/female dynamics also illuminate these differences. Family and social networks were interrupted in Britain, while in New York they were strengthened during the war; this directly affected the role of family and friendship on migration processes. As seen in chapters 3 and 4, refugee use of dress, manners, titles, names, language, and accent reveal significant differences in rates of integration at the individual level between German Jews in London and New York. The formal styles of dress, manner, and language in Britain more closely resembled German culture. The casual dress and language of Americans and informal use of first names were greater obstacles to overcome.

What are the reasons for these divergent patterns in cultural adaptation and identity formation? It has become clear that the broader historical and sociological contexts of German Jewish settlement in London and New York must be considered. First, when comparing the immigration policies of Britain and the United States, neither appears to have been more generous to German Jews seeking refuge. Both countries craftily limited the number of refugees through visa restrictions from the British Home Office, or through quotas and halved quotas initiated by the U.S. State Department. Admittedly, most German Jews arriving in Britain held transit visas, while most in the United States immediately received permanent immigrant visas. Yet, in proportion to the general population, Britain allowed more entry to European refugees and by 1945 had begun granting permanent status to German Jews who chose to remain there. The United States had a strong tradition of immigration, but by the 1920s, American nativists forced the enactment of restrictive immigration laws that directly affected German Jews in the 1930s and 1940s.

Second, the conditions under which refugees arrived in both countries strongly influenced the degree to which German Jews integrated into British and American life. In Britain, the twenty thousand domestic service visas meant that many individuals arrived alone. By nature of their employment, most refugee domestics were separated from the German Jewish community and were immersed in British culture. In addition, many of the ten thousand refugee children who arrived on *Kindertransports* were integrated into mainstream British society while living with foster families or in boarding schools. Had the Wagner-Rogers Bill for a U.S. *Kindertransport* program succeeded, there would have been twenty thousand refugee children directly immersed in American life, as well. The failure of this bill is a reminder that German Jewish immigrants were not welcomed into the United States with open arms. Because family members often lived separately in London, they were less likely to retain German Jewish practices in their everyday lives. In the United States, families often arrived intact, which made it easier to maintain German Jewish culture. While immigration restrictions and the types of American and British entry visas granted affected refugee rates of acculturation, the greatest factor in their divergent rates of integration was, undoubtedly, World War II.

Third, had Britain not suffered from the threat of a Nazi invasion, the German Jewish experience in London would probably have more closely resembled the experience of refugees in New York. Evidence of this can be found upon a close examination of the German Jewish community in the years prior to and after the war. Beginning in 1935, the roots of a German Jewish community in Northwest London were being planted with the formation of refugee clubs and organizations, and significant numbers of German Jews moving to bedsits and flats in the neighborhood. The German language was audible in local cafés until around 1938, when talk of war began to circulate. Once the Nazi threat became real and German Jews were labeled enemy aliens, the German Jewish community in Northwest London began to lose its foothold. Internment was an indication to native Britons that all Germans were to be mistrusted, regardless of religious faith. Air raids and evacuations further disrupted the community. In these unstable times, refugees who remained in London felt intense pressure to disguise their German origins. However, this hostility toward German Jews appears to have been less anti-immigrant and more anti-German.

In New York, German Jews narrowly escaped being the targets of hostility due to the fact that the Japanese, instead of the Germans, attacked the United States on December 7, 1941. Anti-German sentiment grew once the United States entered the war, but refugees in New York were less susceptible to it because of the close ties they had with each other there. Rather, Japanese Americans were interned in vast numbers and many lost their homes and businesses in the process. This again reiterates the fact that the United States was not necessarily more accepting of ethnic diversity than Britain during this time. If the German Jews in New York had been interned en masse in the United States, rather than the Japanese Americans, and if Germany had been directly attacking American territory, the refugee experience in New York would have more closely mirrored the London refugee experience.

Refugee families in London were separated due to the nature of their initial entry visas. It was not until the entry of Britain into war with Germany in 1939, however, that pressure to conform became most intense. Air raids, evacuations, internment, and enlistment all contributed to the refugees' attempts to disguise their German origins. Had they been able to remain settled in German Jewish neighborhoods in Northwest London without the disruptions of war, this process might have proceeded at a rate similar to New York. Further evidence that the war was the dominant factor in the acceleration of refugee integration into British life can be found in the years after the war. During the 1950s and 1960s, the German Jewish community of Northwest London flourished, looking more similar to the German Jewish neighborhoods in New York. Refugees were reunited with families and friends and quickly settled in Northwest London. Berghahn wrote, "These moves took place mainly during the 1940s and early 1950s. . . . In fact, the relative stability of the residential pattern, once it had established itself after the first years of instability, is quite remarkable. The majority of the respondents were still living in the house or flat they had acquired some twenty or thirty years ago."[10] An examination of the *AJR Information*, begun in 1946, reveals the types of German Jewish activities and organizations that developed in the postwar period.

The reasons for a swifter acculturation in Britain were largely circumstantial, rather than an innate British hostility to foreigners. Britain prided itself on its tradition of liberty and as a place of refuge for persecuted people, and the United States was certainly racist in its immigration policies, particularly in the 1920s. Steven Lowenstein similarly found:

> Our respondents in Washington Heights did not express similar feelings of alienation to German Jews in England . . . few seem to have had any doubt about their right to call themselves Americans or American Jews. This is not because their daily life or cultural preferences are similar to those of the average American. Far from it! The residents of Washington Heights, in their language, religious practices, customs, and social patterns, exhibit immigrant traits that distinguish them from their non-German-Jewish neighbors. One could argue that, in their

overt cultural traits, they are more German-Jewish than most of those interviewed in Israel and England.[11]

It is difficult to determine whether native Londoners or native New Yorkers were more open to immigrants and their German ways. It seems however, that from the first minutes of arrival, refugees perceived New York to be more welcoming than London, as is evident in the section on arrivals in the first chapter of this book. German Jews in New York wholeheartedly embraced the melting pot narrative, and, as revealed in their accounts, felt they could easily become American while retaining some of their German ways. Another important factor was the granting of immigrant visas by the United States and, at the same time, transit visas by Great Britain. The temporary nature of UK visas may have contributed to their hesitancy in identifying themselves as British. This calls for the reexamination of the assumption that the United States was inherently more open to immigrants than Britain.

Final Thoughts

Current migration discourse in the United Kingdom and across the European Union focuses on "incorporation" and "absorption." It was not until the influx of West Indian immigration from 1948 to 1962 that Britain formalized a policy of "incorporation" that included intensive language instruction and citizenship proceedings. Terms such as *absorption* and *reception* reflect the efforts of Britain, the receiving country, to direct immigrant behavior. In the 1930s, the Anglo-Jewish community encouraged newly arrived German-speaking refugees to be less conspicuous as Jews and Germans. There were no official government policies aimed at refugee "absorption" and "incorporation." Rather, the goal of the government appears to have been to emphasize the temporary nature of their stay in Britain prior to the outbreak of war.

Through researching and writing this book, numerous avenues for future study have arisen. Possible studies include a comparison of the *AJR Information* and *Aufbau*, in order to compare German Jewish identity practices in Britain and the United States in the post-1945 period. In chapter 2, I only briefly touched on friendships between refugees and "real" Britons and Americans. I hope in a future project to examine the development of such romantic relations and friendships across the first and second generation of German Jewish immigrants.[12] There should also be more work that considers the intergenerational transmission of identity practices among German Jewish refugees that focuses on the second and third generation of this population in both cities and the degree to which they maintained identities as German Jews, Judaism, Americans, or Britons.[13] A study of German Jewish experience in rural United States and Britain would also be of interest. Moreover, a study that would include a comparison of refugee experiences in other cities such as Tel Aviv, Buenos Aires, Shanghai, Cape Town, and Los Angeles, would also be extremely useful in creating a more complete picture of the German Jewish diaspora. On that note, if the materials could be uncovered, I would like to study the recommendations of pre-emigration Jewish agencies as well as foreign consulates in Germany prior to the outbreak of war.

In a careful application of the divergent migration design espoused by Nancy Green, *Cities of Refuge* challenges the widely held notion that immigrants wholly assimilated into American society because they were the recipients of a greater tradition of tolerance and diversity, compared to their counterparts in Great Britain. Drawing on a wide range of published and unpublished sources, this work analyzes why Jewish refugees in London adopted local ways more quickly than in New York, yet identified less as British during this period, than those in the United States identified as American. This discrepancy between rates of identity formation and cultural adaptation is due to several historical factors that are explored in every chapter. These include the timing and proximity of World War II, the internment of German Jews in British camps, and refugee perceptions of the dominant cultures' attitudes toward foreigners. Given that both groups of refugees derived from similar origins, the conclusions reached in this specific historical investigation have implications for the more general understanding of processes of migration and cultural transfer, not only for the Jewish Diaspora but also for other displaced ethnic groups. The findings in *Cities of Refuge* differ from equivalent divergent design studies. The discrepancies in identity formation and cultural adaptation in London and New York are due more to broader national policies around immigration and war, rather than to preconceived notions of British or American diversity and openness to foreigners. External contexts for refugee settlement had a greater influence than their internalized perceptions of their host societies. Hindsight and historical analysis provide a unique perspective for understanding more recent immigrant experiences. This study's results have implications for a stronger understanding of the culture and identity formation for refugee and immigrant groups around the world today.

Notes

Preface

1. Steven M. Lowenstein, *Frankfurt on the Hudson: The German-Jewish Community of Washington Heights, 1933–1983: Its Structure and Culture* (Detroit: Wayne State University Press, 1989), 251.

2. Marion Berghahn, "Women Émigrés in England," in *Between Sorrow and Strength: Women Refugees of the Nazi Period*, ed. Sibylle Quack (Cambridge: Cambridge University Press, 1995), 74. In the late 1960s, Perry Anderson described England as formal and unyielding. He wrote, "The wave of emigrants who came to England in this century were by and large fleeing the permanent instability of their own societies—that is, their proneness to violent, fundamental change. England epitomised the opposite of all this: tradition, continuity, and an orderly empire. Its culture was consonant with its special history. A process of natural selection occurred, in which those intellectuals with an elective affinity to English modes of thought and political outlook gravitated here. Those refugees who did not went elsewhere." Perry Anderson, "Components of National Culture," *New Left Review* 50 (1969): 18.

3. Samuel Baily, *Immigrants in the Lands of Promise: Italians in Buenos Aires and New York City, 1870 to 1914* (Ithaca: Cornell University Press, 1999).

4. Debórah Dwork and Robert Jan van Pelt, *Flight from the Reich: Refugee Jews, 1933–1946* (New York: W. W. Norton, 2009).

5. Nancy Foner, *In a New Land: A Comparative View of Immigration* (New York: New York University Press, 2005); and Nancy Foner, "How Exceptional Is New York? Migration and Multi-culturalism in the Empire City," *Ethnic and Racial Studies* 30, no. 6 (2007): 999–1023.

6. Judith Gerson, "In Between States: National Identity Practices among German Jewish Immigrants," *Political Psychology* 22, no. 1 (2001): 195; and Lisa Silverman, *Becoming Austrians: Jews and Culture between the World Wars* (New York: Oxford University Press, 2012).

Introduction

1. See Judith Gerson, "Family Matters: German Jewish Masculinities among Nazi Era Refugees," in *Jewish Masculinities: German Jews, Gender, and History*, eds. Benjamin Maria Baader, Sharon Gillerman, and Paul Lerner (Bloomington: Indiana University Press, 2012); and Peter Gay, *My German Question: Growing Up in Nazi Berlin* (New Haven: Yale University Press, 1998).

2. See Gershom Scholem, "Jews and Germans," *Commentary* 42 (November 1966): 31–40; and Paul Lawrence Rose, *German Question—Jewish Question* (Princeton: Princeton University Press, 1992). Thomas Pegelow writes of the field's strongly debated "liberal-cultural" and "Zionist master narratives" in "'German Jews,' 'National Jews,' 'Jewish Volk' or 'Racial Jews'? The Constitution and Contestation of 'Jewishness' in Newspapers of Nazi Germany, 1933–1938," *Central European History* 35, no. 2 (2002): 196–97. Pegelow credits Evyatar Friesel for the term *liberal-cultural* and argues that George L. Mosse and Michael A. Meyer also follow the liberal-culturalist narrative. See Thomas Pegelow and Evyatar Friesel, "'Jewish and German-Jewish Historical Views: Problems of a New Synthesis," *Leo Baeck Institute Year Book* 43 (1998): 323, George L. Mosse, *German Jews beyond Judaism* (Bloomington: Indiana University Press, 1985), and Michael A. Meyer et al., eds., *German-Jewish History in Modern Times, Vols. 1–4* (New York: Columbia University Press, 1996–98).

3. Scott Spector, "Forget Assimilation: Introducing Subjectivity to German-Jewish History," *Jewish History* 20, no. 3/4 (2006): 349–61; and Paul Lerner, introduction to *Jewish Masculinities*, eds. Baader et al.

4. Andreas Gotzmann, Rainer Liedtke, and Till van Rahden, eds., *Juden, Bürger, Deutsche: Zur Geschichte von Vielfalt und Differenz, 1800–1933* (Tübingen: Mohr Siebeck, 2001); Rainer Liedtke and David Rechter, eds., *Towards Normality? Acculturation and Modern German Jewry* (Tübingen: Mohr Siebeck, 2003); and Till Van Rahden, "Germans of the Jewish *Stamm*: Visions of Community between Nationalism and Particularism, 1850 to 1933," in *German History from the Margins, 1800 to the Present*, eds. Mark Roseman, Nils Roemer, and Neil Gregoreds (Bloomington: Indiana University Press, 2006).

5. See, for example, Michael Brenner, *The Renaissance of Jewish Culture in Weimar Germany* (New Haven: Yale University Press, 1996), Paul Mendes-Flohr, *German Jews: A Dual Identity* (New Haven and London: Yale University Press, 1999), Sharon Gillerman, *Germans into Jews: Remaking the Jewish Social Body in the Weimar Republic* (Stanford: Stanford University Press, 2009), Marion Kaplan, *The Making of the Jewish Middle Class: Women, Family and Identity in Imperial Germany* (New York: Oxford University Press, 1991) and "Friendship on the Margins: Jewish Social Relations in Imperial Germany," *Central European History* 34, no. 4 (2001): 471–501.

6. It should be acknowledged that this book focuses on Jews from Germany proper (circa 1933) and not Austria or German-speaking regions of Czechoslovakia and Poland. Occasionally, however, I draw on the testimony of German-speaking

refugees from Austria who had lived in Germany or who retained close ties to Germany. These are indicated within the text. The decision to focus mainly on German Jewish refugees derives from an appreciation of the unique cultures and identity formation of Jews in other German-speaking lands. It would be a disservice to assume that Austrian or other German-speaking refugees from outside of Germany had the same experience as those from Germany. This becomes particularly clear later in the book when national identity formation is more closely examined.

7. Ludwig Berger, Bruno W. Häuptli, Thomas Hufschmid, Franziska Lengsfeld, Urs Müller, Kurt Paulus, and Verena Vogel Müller, *Der Menora-Ring von Kaiseraugst. Jüdische Zeugnisse römischer Zeit zwischen Britannien und Pannonien*, August, Swiss Museum of Augusta Raurica, 36 (2005). This is a research paper published on the finding of a Jewish ring in 2001 at an Ancient Roman site on the Rhine River. The ring dates back to the first century CE.

8. See Michael Toch, *The Economic History of European Jews: Late Antiquity and Early Middle Ages* (Boston: Brill, 2012).

9. The historiography of medieval Jewry is vast. Particularly useful is Michael Toch's *Peasants and Jews in Medieval Germany* (Aldershot: Ashgate, 2003). Also see the publications of conference proceedings such as Christoph Cluse, ed., *The Jews of Europe in the Middle Ages (Tenth to Fifteenth Centuries): Proceedings of the International Symposium Held at Speyer, 20–25 October 2002* (Turnhout: Brepols, 2004); and Michael A. Signer and John Van Engen, eds., *Jews and Christians in Twelfth-Century Europe, Notre Dame Conferences in Medieval Studies* (South Bend: University of Notre Dame Press, 2001).

10. See David B. Ruderman, *Early Modern Jewry: A New Cultural History* (Princeton: Princeton University Press, 2010); and Jonathan Israel, *European Jewry in the Age of Mercantilism, 1550–1750* (Oxford: Clarendon Press, 1985).

11. See Amos Elon, *Founder: A Portrait of the First Rothschild and His Time* (New York: Penguin, 1996); and Fritz Backhaus, Gisela Engel, Robert Liberles, and Margarete Schlueter, eds., *The Frankfurt Judengasse: Jewish Life in an Early Modern German City* (London: Vallentine Mitchell, 2010).

12. See Maria Diemling and Guiseppe Veltri, eds., *The Jewish Body: Corporeality, Society, and Identity in Renaissance and Early Modern Period* (London: Brill, 2009); and Meyer et al., *German-Jewish History in Modern Times, Volume 1*. Monika Richarz, ed., *Jüdisches Leben in Deutschland: Volume 2 Selbstzeugnisse zur Sozialgeschichte im Kaiserreich* (Stuttgart: Deutsche Verlags-Anstalt, 1979) has firsthand accounts of Jewish tradespeople in Germany during this period. Also see Jacob Katz, *Out of the Ghetto: The Social Background of Jewish Emancipation, 1770–1870* (Cambridge: Harvard University Press, 1973).

13. In "Jews and the Ambivalences of Civil Society in Germany, 1800–1933: Assessment and Reassessment," *Journal of Modern History* 77, no. 4 (December 2005): 1031, Till van Rahden cites Mordechai Breuer, "*Frühe Neuzeit und Beginn der Moderne*," in *German-Jewish History, Volume 1*, eds. Michael A. Meyer et al.

14. In "Jews and the Ambivalences of German Civil Society," Till van Rahden explores the various arguments on the role of middle-class Jews in developing German liberal middle-class society in nineteenth-century cities such as Bremen, Hamburg, and Frankfurt. He draws from the work of Rainer Liedtke, Andrea Hopp, and Shulamit S. Magnus. He also cites the local histories done by Richard Mehler, Ulrich Baumann, Ulrich Sieg and Stefanie Schueler-Springorum on Jews across Germany in the eighteenth and nineteenth centuries.

15. Shmuel Feiner and Natalie Naimark-Goldberg, *Cultural Revolution in Berlin: Jews in the Age of Enlightenment* (Chicago: University of Chicago Press, 2011) focuses on the *Haskalah* movement (or the "Jewish Enlightenment") of Moses Mendelsohn et al. See Shmuel Feiner, *The Jewish Enlightenment*, trans. Chaya Naor (Philadelphia: University of Pennsylvania Press, 2004) for a thorough analysis of the ways in which the *Haskalah* thinkers sought to balance Jewish religious beliefs with a growing sense of secularism through the late eighteenth and nineteenth centuries.

16. See Benjamin Maria Baader, *Gender, Judaism, and Bourgeois Culture in Germany, 1800–1870* (Bloomington: Indiana University Press, 2006) for a closer look at the ways the nineteenth-century Reform Movement players such as Gotthold Solomon and Eduard Kley addressed issues around motherhood and family in this period and reflect the envelopment of bourgeois middle-class values into Jewish liturgy and practice. See also Michael A. Meyer, *Response to Modernity: A History of the Reform Movement in Judaism* (New York: Oxford University Press, 1988).

17. For more on 1871 and the years leading up to World War I, see Michael A. Meyer et al., *German-Jewish History in Modern Times, Volume 3*, Kaplan, *Making of the Jewish Middle Class*, Jehuda Reinharz, *Fatherland or Promised Land: The Dilemma of the German Jew, 1893–1914* (Ann Arbor: University of Michigan Press, 1975), and Gotzmann et al., *Juden, Bürger, Deutsche*.

18. Robin Judd, "Moral, Clean Men of the Jewish Faith: Jewish Rituals and Their Male Practitioners, 1843–1914" in *Jewish Masculinities*, eds. Baader et al., 78.

19. Kaplan, *Making of the Jewish Middle Class*.

20. Ibid., 9.

21. For more on this topic see Uwe Westphal, *Berliner Konfektion und Mode: Die Zerstörung einer Tradition, 1836–1939* (Berlin: Edition Hentrich, 1986).

22. German Jewish surnames were created under the edicts of individual principalities. Many Jews took the name of the village they lived in as a last name, such as Ettlinginer or Pforzheimer. Others chose biblical names or typical Jewish first names like Joseph or Isaacs or priestly Jewish names such as Kohn. "Rothschild" derived from the red shield hanging outside their house in Frankfurt's *Judengasse*. For more on the development of German Jewish surnames see Leopold Zunz, *Namen der Juden. Eine geschichtliche Untersuchung* (reprint of 1837 Leipzig edition, Hildesheim, 1971) and Georg Meyer-Erlach, "Die 60 häufigsten jüdischen Familiennamen," *Jüdische Familienforschung-Mitteilungen* (Berlin) 8 (December 1932): 500–503.

23. Peter C. Appelbaum, *Loyal Sons: Jews in the German Army in the Great War* (London: Vallentine Mitchell, 2015). Also see Tim Grady, *The German-Jewish Soldiers*

of the First World War in History and Memory (Liverpool: Liverpool University Press, 2012) for a focus on the fate of veterans and the memorialization of their service.

24. Sharon Gillerman, *Germans into Jews*; Brenner, *Renaissance of Jewish Culture*; Steven Aschheim, "German Jews Beyond Bildung and Liberalism: The Radical Jewish Revival in the Weimar Republic," in *The German-Jewish Dialogue Reconsidered: A Symposium in Honor of George L. Mosse*, ed. Klaus Berghahn (New York: Peter Lang, 1996).

25. The number 37,000 originates with Herbert Strauss in "Jewish Emigration from Germany: Nazi Policies and Jewish Responses (1)," in *Leo Baeck Institute Yearbook* 25 (1980): 326 and is cited in Dwork and van Pelt, *Flight from the Reich: Refugee Jews*, 388. Dwork and van Pelt actually estimate the number to be slightly higher, between 40,000 and 45,000.

26. See Marion Kaplan, *Between Dignity and Despair: Jewish Life in Nazi Germany* (Oxford: Oxford University Press, 1998).

27. For a summary of international refugee policy at the time see Susanne Heim's chapter in *Refugees from Nazi Germany and the Liberal European States*, eds. Frank Caestecker and Bob Moore (New York: Berghahn Books, 2010). The chapters written by Caestecker and Moore offer a comparative analysis of various nations' visas policies throughout the 1930s.

28. Nevertheless, a small number of Jews somehow managed to escape the Nazis.

29. See Zucker, Bat-Ami, *In Search of Refuge: Jews and U.S. Consuls in Nazi Germany, 1933–1941* (London: Vallentine Mitchell, 2001).

30. Louise London, *Whitehall and the Jews, 1933–1948: British Immigration Policy, Jewish Refugees and the Holocaust* (Cambridge: Cambridge University Press, 2000), 12, 237.

31. Of the six million Jews killed at the hands of the Nazis, approximately three million came from Poland, two million from the Soviet Union, and the remaining Jews from all parts of Nazi-occupied Europe.

32. Association of Jewish Refugees, *Britain's New Citizens: The Story of the Refugees from Germany and Austria* (London: Association of Jewish Refugees, 1951), 10.

33. As cited by Ronald Stent, *A Bespattered Page? The Internment of His Majesty's "Most Loyal Enemy Aliens"* (London: Deutsch, 1980), 581. Thus far, we can only estimate the actual number of German Jews who entered Britain and the United States. The precise number of refugees in Britain is particularly elusive due to the paucity of official records. Louise London wrote, "The Home Office studiously avoided keeping its own statistics on the highly sensitive issue of Jewish immigration to Britain. This saved it from having to give precise answers to embarrassing questions asked in parliament and the press about the numbers of Jewish refugees in the country." London, *Whitehall and the Jews*, 237; Ruth Gay, *The Jews of Germany: A Historical Portrait* (New Haven: Yale University Press, 1992), 270, 281; David Wyman, *Paper Walls: America and the Refugee Crisis, 1938–1941* (Amherst: University of Massachusetts Press, 1968), 36.

34. London, *Whitehall and the Jews*, 11–12.

35. Herbert Strauss, "The Immigration and Acculturation of the German Jews in the United States of America," *Leo Baeck Institute Yearbook* 16 (1971), as cited by Lowenstein in *Frankfurt on the Hudson*, 47. This number does not include nonquota immigrants, or those born in Austria.

36. See Marion Kentworthy Papers, 1938–1952, at the American Jewish Historical Society, Center for Jewish History for a complete record of the U.S. *Kindertransport* initiative.

37. Lowenstein, *Frankfurt on the Hudson*, 47.

38. Colin Pooley and Ian Whyte, eds., *Migrants, Emigrants, and Immigrants: A Social History of Migration* (London: Routledge, 1991).

39. See, for example, Robert Zecker, " 'Where Everyone Goes to Meet Everyone Else': The Translocal Creation of a Slovak Immigrant Community," *Journal of Social History* 2, no. 38 (Winter 2004): 423–53; and Kenneth Scherzer, *The Unbounded Community* (Durham: Duke University Press, 1992).

40. Lowenstein, *Frankfurt on the Hudson*; Marion Berghahn, *Continental Britons* (Oxford: Berg, 1984). A more recent work, *Crossing Broadway: Washington Heights and the Promise of New York City*, by Robert Snyder, examines the intersectionality of multiple immigrant populations in Washington Heights from the 1930s into the twenty-first century, including German Jews. His work provides a useful followup to *Cities of Refuge* in that it examines how German Jewish refugees experienced this diverse urban space through the 1970s and 1980s. Robert W. Snyder, *Crossing Broadway: Washington Heights and the Promise of New York City* (Ithaca: Cornell University Press, 2014).

41. Andrew C. Godley, *Jewish Immigrant Entrepreneurship in London and New York, 1881–1914: Enterprise and Culture* (London: Palgrave, 2001); Andrew S. Reutlinger, "Reflections on Anglo-American Jewish Experience: Immigrants, Workers, and Entrepreneurs in New York and London, 1870–1914," *American Jewish Historical Quarterly* 66 (1977): 472–84; Nancy Foner, "West Indians in New York City and London," *International Migration Review* 13 (1979): 248–97; Selma Berrol, *East Side/East End: East European Jews in London and New York, 1870–1920* (Westport, CT: Praeger, 1994). Lloyd Gartner, *American and British Jews in the Age of Great Migration* (London: Vallentine Mitchell, 2009) is not a direct comparative study, but it provides an overview of Gartner's sixty years as a historian of East European Jewish immigration to the United States and Britain. Another work, Sebastian Rejak, *Jewish Identities in Poland and America: The Impact of the Shoah on Religion and Ethnicity* (London: Vallentine Mitchell, 2011) is useful as a post-Holocaust comparison.

42. The exact number of German Jews, in either London or New York, at any particular time is especially difficult to approximate. Steven Lowenstein, in *Frankfurt on the Hudson*, provided some numbers regarding the New York area but focuses primarily on Washington Heights. With wartime evacuations of London,

the fluctuating number of refugees there is impossible to maintain. Additionally, much of the literature does not distinguish between German, Austrian, and Czech Jews. Many organizations catered to all German-speaking Jews and, after the annexation of Austria, most were just referred to as "German," particularly in U.S. government records.

43. In 1933, almost 68 percent of Jews in Germany lived in cities with populations over one hundred thousand, including Berlin, Frankfurt am Main, Breslau, Hamburg, Cologne, and Leipzig. Figures from London, *Whitehall and the Jews*; and Herbert Strauss, "Jewish Emigration from Germany," 323.

44. Nancy L. Green, "The Comparative Method," in *Migration, Migration History, History: Old Paradigms and New Perspectives*, eds. Jan Lucassen and Leo Lucassen (New York: Peter Lang, 1997), 58.

45. Foner, *In a New Land*.

46. Baily, *Immigrants in the Lands of Promise*; Berrol, *East Side/East End*.

47. More common are edited collections that derive from academic conferences. In the introductions, the editors engage in comparative analysis in setting up the individual case studies. Useful examples are Dirk Hoerder and Jörg Nagler, eds., *People in Transit: German Migrations in Comparative Perspective, 1820–1930* (Cambridge: Cambridge University Press, 1995); Michael Brenner, Rainer Liedtke, and David Rechter, eds., *Two Nations: British and German Jews in Comparative Perspective* (Tübingen: Mohr Siebeck, 1999); Daniel Elazar and Morton Weinfeld, eds., *Still Moving: Recent Jewish Migration in Comparative Perspective* (New Brunswick, NJ: Transaction Publishers, 2000); Ava F. Kahn and Adam D. Mendelsohn, eds., *Transnational Traditions: New Perspectives on American Jewish History* (Detroit: Wayne State University Press, 2014); Richard Alba and Mary C. Waters, eds., *The Next Generation, Immigrant Youth in a Comparative Perspective* (New York: New York University Press 2011).

48. Nancy Green, "The Comparative Method and Poststructural Structuralism: New Perspectives for Migration Studies," *Journal of American Ethnic History* 13, no. 4 (1994): 3–22.

49. Werner Mosse, introduction to *Two Nations*, eds. Michael Brenner et al., 13.

50. Rainer Liedtke, *Jewish Welfare in Hamburg and Manchester, 1850–1914* (New York: Oxford University Press, 1998).

51. Donna R. Gabaccia, *Italy's Many Diasporas* (Abingdon: Routledge, 2003).

52. Silverman, *Becoming Austrians*; and Baader et al., *Jewish Masculinities*.

53. Ruth Vogel, "The Meaning of the Day Nursery to the Refugee Parent," Masters Thesis, New York School of Social Work, Columbia University, June 1941; Ariel Tartakower, "The Jewish Refugees: A Sociological Study," *Jewish Social Studies* 4 (1942): 311–48. Others include Joanna Colcord, "Refugee Social Workers," *Social Work Today* 7 (December 1939): 37–38 and Anne Langman, "The Problems of the Refugee Physician," Masters Thesis, New York School of Social Work, Columbia University, June 1940.

54. Maurice Davie, *Refugees in America: Report of the Committee for the Study of Recent Immigration from Europe* (New York: Harper and Brothers, 1947); Gerhart Saenger, *Today's Refugees, Tomorrow's Citizens: A Story of Americanization* (New York: Harper and Brothers, 1941). Other valuable works include Sophia Robison, *Refugees at Work*, The Committee on Selected Social Studies (New York: King's Crown Press, 1942); Freda Heilberg, "Experiences, Attitudes, and Problems of German-Jewish Refugees," Federation Employment Services, NY, *Jewish Social Services Quarterly* 15, no. 3 (March 1939): 322–27; Maurice Davie and Samuel Koenig, *The Refugees Are Now in America*, New York Public Affairs Committee: Committee for the Study of Recent Immigration from Europe (New York: 1945), Ernest Stock, "Washington Heights' 'Fourth Reich,'" *Commentary* 11 (June 1951): 581–88, and AJR, *Britain's New Citizens*.

55. Laura Fermi, *Illustrious Immigrants: The Intellectual Migration from Europe* (Chicago: University of Chicago Press, 1968); Anthony Heilbut, *Exiled in Paradise: German Refugee Artists and Intellectuals in America from the 1930s* (New York: Viking, 1983); Jean Medawar and David Pyke, *Hitler's Gift: Scientists Who Fled Nazi Germany* (London: Richard Cohen Books, 2000); Jack Beatson and Reinhard Zimmerman, eds., *Jurists Uprooted: German-speaking Émigré Lawyers in Twentieth-Century Britain* (Oxford: Oxford University Press, 2004). A more expansive list includes Norman Bentwich, *The Rescue and Achievement of Refugee Scholars: The Story of Displaced Scholars and Scientists, 1933–1952* (The Hague: Martinus Nijhoff: Studies in Social Life, 1953); D. Peterson Kent, *The Refugee Intellectual: The Americanization of the Immigrants of 1933–1941* (New York: Columbia University Press, 1953); Jarrell Jackman and Carla Borden, eds., *The Muses Flee Hitler: Cultural Transfer and Adaptation, 1930–1945* (Washington, DC: Smithsonian, 1983); Helmut Pfanner, ed., *Exile in New York: German and Austrian Writers after 1933* (Detroit: Wayne State University Press, 1983); Lewis Coser, *Refugee Scholars in America: Their Cultural Impact and their Experiences* (New Haven: Yale University Press, 1984); Claus-Dieter Krohn, *Wissenschaft im Exil: deutsche Sozial- und Wirtschaftswissenschaftler in den USA und die New School for Social Research* (Frankfurt am Main: Campus, 1987); Mitchell Ash and Alfons Söllner, eds., *Forced Migration and Scientific Change: Émigré German-speaking Scientists and Scholars after 1933* (Cambridge: Cambridge University Press, 1996); Edward Timms and Jon Hughes, eds., *Intellectual Migration and Cultural Transformation: Refugees from National Socialism in the English-speaking World* (Vienna: Springer, 2003); Ehrhard Bahr, *Weimar on the Pacific: German Exile Culture in Los Angeles and the Crisis of Modernism* (Berkeley: University of California Press, 2007); Dorothy Lamb Crawford, *A Windfall of Musicians: Hitler's Emigres and Exiles in Southern California* (New Haven: Yale University Press, 2011); and Richard Bodek and Simon Lewis, *The Fruits of Exile: Central European Intellectual Immigration to America in the Age of Fascism* (Columbia: University of South Carolina Press, 2010).

56. Sibylle Quack, *Zuflucht Amerika: Zur Sozialgeschichte der Emigration deutsch-jüdischer Frauen in die USA 1933–1945* (Bonn: Dietz, 1995); Berghahn, *Continental Britons*.

57. Walter Laqueur, *Generation Exodus: The Fate of Young Jewish Refugees from Nazi Germany* (Hanover, NH: University Press of New England, 2001); Gerhard Sonnert and Gerald J. Holton, *What Happened to the Children Who Fled Nazi Persecution?* (New York: Palgrave Macmillan, 2008); Philip K. Jason and Iris Posner, eds., *Don't Wave Goodbye: The Children's Flight from Nazi Persecution to American Freedom* (Westport, CT: Praeger, 2004). See Muriel Emanuel and Vera Gissing, *Nicholas Winton and the Rescued Generation: The Story of "Britain's Schindler"* (London: Vallentine Mitchell, 2002); and Barbara Wolfenden, *Little Holocaust Survivors and the English School that Saved Them* (Westport, CT: Greenwood, 2008). On the *Kindertransport* program, see Iris Guske, *Trauma and Attachment in the Kindertransport Context: German-Jewish Child Refugees' Accounts of Displacement and Acculturation in Britain* (Newcastle: Cambridge Scholars, 2009); Wolfgang Benz, Andrea Hammel et al., eds., *Die Kindertransporte 1938/39* (Frankfurt am Main: Fischer Taschenbuch Verlag, 2003); Vera Fast, *Children's Exodus: A History of the Kindertransport* (Lanham, MD: Lexington Books, 2011); and Judith Tydor Baumel-Schwartz, *Never Look Back: The Jewish Refugee Children in Great Britain, 1938–1945* (West Lafayette, IN: Purdue University Press, 2012).

58. See Marion Kaplan, *Dominican Haven: The Jewish Refugee Settlement in Sosúa, 1940–1945* (New York: Museum of Jewish Heritage, 2008); Leo Spitzer, *Hotel Bolivia: The Culture of Memory in a Refuge from Nazism* (New York: Hill and Wang, 1998); Katherine Morris, ed., *Odyssey of Exile: Jewish Women Flee the Nazis for Brazil* (Detroit: Wayne State University Press, 1996); David Kranzler, *Japanese, Nazis, and Jews: The Jewish Refugee Community of Shanghai, 1938–45* (New York: Yeshiva University Press, 1976); James Rodman Ross, *Escape to Shanghai: A Jewish Community in China* (New York: Maxwell Macmillan, 1994); Frank Shapiro, *Haven in Africa* (Jerusalem: Gefen Publishers, 2002); Anil Bhatti and Johannes H. Voight, eds., *Jewish Exile in India* (New Delhi: Manohar, 1999); Konrad Kwiet, "The Second Time Around: Re-Acculturation of German-Jewish Refugees in Australia," *The Journal of Holocaust Education* 10, no. 1 (June 2001): 34–49; Lowenstein, *Frankfurt on the Hudson*; and Rhonda F. Levine, *Class, Networks, and Identity: Replanting Jewish Lives from Nazi Germany to Rural New York* (Lanham, MD: Rowan and Littlefield, 2001).

59. Alfred Hässler, *The Lifeboat is Full: Switzerland and the Refugees, 1933–1945* (New York: Funk and Wagnalls, 1969); Irving Abella and Harold M. Troper, *None Is Too Many: Canada and the Jews of Europe, 1933–1948* (New York: Random House, 1983); Michael Blakeney, *Australia and the Jewish Refugees, 1933–1948* (Sydney: Croom Helm Australia, 1985); Kwiet, "The Second Time Around"; Vicki Caron, *Uneasy Asylum: France and the Jewish Refugee Crisis, 1933–1942* (Stanford: Stanford University Press, 1999); Stanford J. Shaw, *Turkey and the Holocaust: Turkey's Role in*

Rescuing Turkish and European Jewry from Nazi Persecution, 1933–1945 (New York: New York University Press, 1993); Dermot Keogh, *Jews in Twentieth-Century Ireland: Refugees, Anti-Semitism, and the Holocaust* (Cork: Cork University Press, 1998). See also Gisela M. B. Holfter, ed., *German-speaking Exiles in Ireland, 1933–1945* (Amsterdam: Rodopi, 2006).

60. Tony Kushner, *Remembering Refugees: Then and Now* (Manchester: Manchester University Press, 2007).

61. See Tony Kushner, *The Persistence of Prejudice: Anti-Semitism in British Society during the Second World War* (Manchester: Manchester University Press, 1989); Tony Kushner, *The Holocaust and the Liberal Imagination: A Social and Cultural History* (Oxford: Blackwell, 1994); Tony Kushner and Katharine Knox, *Refugees in an Age of Genocide: Global, National, and Local Perspectives during the Twentieth Century* (London: Frank Cass, 1999); and Tony Kushner and Nadia Valman, eds., *Remembering Cable Street: Fascism and Anti-Fascism in British Society* (London: Vallentine Mitchell, 2000).

62. Anthony Grenville and Marian Malet, eds., *Changing Countries: The Experience and Achievement of German-speaking Exiles from Hitler in Britain, 1933 to Today: A Study Based on Thirty-Four Interviews* (London: Libris, 2002); and Anthony Grenville, *Jewish Refugees from Nazi Germany and Austria in Britain, 1933–1970: Their Image in AJR Information* (London: Vallentine Mitchell, 2010).

63. Anthony Grenville, "Researching AJR Information," in Anthony Grenville, ed., *Refugees from the Third Reich in Britain*, Yearbook of the Research Centre for German and Austrian Exile Studies (Amsterdam: Rodopi, 2002), 202.

64. Dwork and van Pelt, *Flight from the Reich*.

65. Atina Grossman, "Versions of Home: German-Jewish Refugee Papers: Out of the Closet and into the Archives," *New German Critique* 90 (Fall 2003): 95–122. See Andrea Hammel and Anthony Grenville, eds., *Refugee Archives: Theory and Practice*, Yearbook of the Research Centre for German and Austrian Exile Studies (Amsterdam: Rodopi, 2007) for an examination of the scope of archives worldwide established to preserve German-speaking Jewish history.

66. See Henry Greenspan, *On Listening to Holocaust Survivors: Recounting and Life History* (Westport, CT: Praeger, 1998), and his most recent updated edition entitled *On Listening to Holocaust Survivors: Beyond Testimony* (Minneapolis: Paragon House, 2010), which says this should be done, not to preserve memories or to make a moral statement, but instead to allow for a type of catharsis of traumatic memory for the survivor. See also Dominick LaCapra, *Representing the Holocaust: History, Theory, Trauma* (Ithaca: Cornell University Press, 1994); Lawrence L. Langer, *Holocaust Testimonies: The Ruins of Memory* (New Haven: Yale University Press, 1991); and Christopher Browning, *Remembering Survival: Inside a Nazi Slave-Labor Camp* (New York: W. W. Norton, 2011).

67. Judith M. Gerson, "'In Cuba I was a German Shepard': Questions of Comparison and Generalizability in Holocaust Memoirs," in *Sociology Confronts the*

Holocaust: Memories and Identities in Jewish Diasporas, eds. Judith M. Gerson and Diane L. Wolf (Durham: Duke University Press, 2007), 120–21.

68. David Biale, ed., *Cultures of the Jews: A New History* (New York: Schocken, 2002); David Cesarani, Tony Kushner, and Milton Shain, eds., *Place and Displacement in Jewish History and Memory Zakor v'Makor* (London: Vallentine Mitchell, 2009).

Chapter 1. Arrival and Settlement

1. C. C. Aronsfeld, *Wanderer from My Birth* (London: Janus, 1997), 74.

2. Unnamed author, *Kitchener Camp Review* (April 1939) in Kitchener Camp Collection, Wiener Library, London, 6.

3. Susanne Samson, interview for *London Voices*, Museum of London (2000).

4. Marianne Maxwell, unpublished diaries at Centre for German-Jewish Studies, University of Sussex (London, 1940).

5. Liselotte Kahn, memoirs, LBI NY, 1.

6. Lilly Friedmann, *Hard Times—Life as a Refugee! Experiences by a Newcomer to a Foreign Land*, LBI NY (1991), 5; Harold Koppel, *My Autobiography*, LBI NY (1943), 28.

7. Koppel, *My Autobiography*, 28; and Henry Kramer, memoirs, "How Rich Was Rich" and Other Topics such as "How Mother Got Us Out of Germany," LBI NY (1941).

8. Kahn, memoirs, 1.

9. Saenger, *Today's Refugees, Tomorrow's Citizens*, 67.

10. Walter Baum, *A Personal History*, memoirs, LBI NY (1990), 17.

11. Kahn, memoirs, 1.

12. Friedmann, *Hard Times*, 4.

13. Rabbi Manfred Swarensky, transcript of speech, Swarensky Family Collection, LBI NY (July 1939).

14. Laqueur, *Generation Exodus*, 132.

15. This may be because African Americans, Native Americans, and Japanese Americans were at the receiving end of racist United States policies and laws. Racism and refugee perceptions of this in the United States are explored in the Conclusion.

16. Alice Schwab, *Thank You for Everything: The Memoirs of Alice (Liesel) Schwab* CGJS (1990), 11. The Mrs. Rathbone she refers to on page 78 was Eleanor Rathbone, a national figure who fought at the parliamentary and grassroots level for refugees from Nazi Germany.

17. Judith Kerr, *The Other Way Round* (London: Putnam, 1975).

18. Unnamed respondent, in Karen Gershon, *We Came as Children: A Collective Autobiography of Refugees* (London: Gollancz, 1966), 52.

19. London's Liverpool Street Station has a memorial to the *Kindertransport* children that was dedicated in September 2006.

20. For books focused on the *Kindertransport* see Andrea Hammel and Bea Lewkowitz, eds., *Kindertransport to Britain, New Perspectives* (Amsterdam/New York: Rodopi, 2012); Tydor Baumel-Schwartz, *Never Look Back*; Gerson, *We Came as Children*; and Fast, *Children's Exodus*. See also Barry Turner, . . . *And the Policeman Smiled: 10,000 Children Escape from Nazi Europe* (London: Bloomsbury, 1990); Mark Jonathan Harris and Deborah Oppenheimer, *Into the Arms of Strangers: Stories of the Kindertransport* (London: Bloomsbury, 2000); and Bertha Leverton and Shmuel Lowensohn, eds., *I Came Alone: The Stories of the Kindertransports* (Lewes: Book Guild, 1990).

21. Saenger, *Today's Refugees, Tomorrow's Citizens*, 67.

22. Goldwein and Birnbrey, in *Don't Wave Goodbye*, eds. Jason and Posner, 122, 154.

23. Judith Tydor Baumel, introduction to *Don't Wave Goodbye*, eds. Jason and Posner, 12–14.

24. Julius Cohn, letter to Uncle Eddi, March 26, 1940, Bertha Cohn Collection, Exilarchiv, Deutsche Bibliothek and Rudolf Katz, diaries 1933–1939, LBI NY (December 3, 1939).

25. Inge Heiman and Joseph Heiman, *Joseph and His Daughter*, LBI NY (1996), 85.

26. Baum, *A Personal History*, 1.

27. Ilse Gutman, interview with author, July 2002.

28. Werner Rosenstock, "The Jewish Refugees: Some Facts," in *Britain's New Citizens*, AJR, 19.

29. Miri Freud-Kandel, *Orthodox Judaism in Britain since 1913: An Ideology Foresaken* (London: Vallentine Mitchell, 2006).

30. FDKB (*Freie Deutsche Kulturbund*) *Nachrichten*, March 1940, Exilpresse, Deutsche Nationale Bibliothek, 4.

31. Ilse Jacoby, *My Life's History*, memoirs LBI NY (1994), 9.

32. Bridget Stross Laky, *On Being Jewish*, LBI NY, 65.

33. Unnamed respondent, in Gershon, *We Came as Children*, 52.

34. Gabrielle Tergit, "How They Resettled," in *Britain's New Citizens*, AJR, 62.

35. Tony Kushner, "An Alien Occupation—Jewish Refugees and Domestic Service in Britain, 1933–1948," in *Second Chance: Two Centuries of German-speaking Jews in the United Kingdom*, eds. Werner Mosse and Julius Carlebach et al. (Tübingen: J. C. B. Mohr, 1991), 567.

36. Elli Bickart, interview with author, Connecticut, June 1992.

37. Kushner, "An Alien Occupation," 565.

38. Kushner and Knox, *Refugees in an Age of Genocide*, 158.

39. Charles Leigh, *The Autobiography of a Jewish Refugee, 1921–1998*, LBI NY (London: 1990), 35–36, 40.

40. Samson, interview for *London Voices*.

41. Laqueur, *Generation Exodus*, 194.

42. Unnamed respondent, in Gershon, *We Came as Children*, 62.

43. See Kushner and Valman, *Remembering Cable Street*.

44. The British fascist movement's activities and their effects on the Jewish community in the East End are also explored in the first chapter of Tony Kushner's *Persistence of Prejudice*.

45. Kushner, *Persistence of Prejudice*, 118.

46. Laqueur, *Generation Exodus*, 204.

47. Bea Lewkowitz, "Belsize Square Synagogue: Community, Belonging, and Religion among German-Jewish Refugees" in *"I didn't want to float,"* eds. Grenville and Reiter, 126.

48. Kushner, *Persistence of Prejudice*, 118. Dan Stone also explores antisemitism and British responses to the refugees in Dan Stone, *Responses to Nazism in Britain 1933–1939: Before War and Holocaust* (Basingstoke: Palgrave Macmillan, 2003).

49. Richard Dove, ed., *"Totally un-English?" Britain's Internment of "Enemy Aliens" in Two World Wars* (Amsterdam/New York: Rodopi, 2005).

50. Anthony Grenville, "Remembering Internment," *AJR Journal*, July 2007. http://www.ajr.org.uk/index.cfm/section.journal/issue.Jul07/article=875.

51. Books on Britain's internment program include Maxine Seller, *We Built Up Our Lives: Education and Community among Jewish Refugees Interned by Britain in WWII* (London: Greenwood, 2001); David Cesarani and Tony Kushner, *The Internment of Aliens in Twentieth-Century Britain* (London: Frank Cass, 1993); Connery Chappell, *Island of Barbed Wire: Internment on the Isle of Man in World War II* (London: Robert Hale, 1984); Francois Lafitte *The Interment of Aliens* (Harmondsworth: Penguin, 1940); Stent, *A Bespattered Page?*; and Peter and Leni Gillman, *"Collar the Lot!" How Britain Interned and Expelled Its Wartime Refugees* (London: Quartet Books, 1980).

52. Edward Timms, "Ordeals of Kinder and Evacuees in Comparative Perspective," in *Kindertransport to Britain*, eds. Hammel and Lewkowitz, 130.

53. *FDKB Nachrichten*, April 1940, 4.

54. British Ministry of Information in cooperation with the War Office and Ministry of Home Security, "If the Invader Comes: What to Do and How to Do It" (1940); "Personal Protection against Gas," *Air Raid Precautions 1* (London, 1938).

55. *FDKB Nachrichten*, October 1941, 8.

56. Grenville, "Remembering Internment."

57. *FDKB Nachrichten*, November 1941, 8.

58. For a detailed personal account of a refugee soldier in the British army see Norman Bentwich, *I Understand the Risks* (London: 1950). See also Martin Sugarman, *Fighting Back: British Jewry's Military Contribution in the Second World War* (London: Vallentine Mitchell, 2010); and Peter Leighton-Langer, *The King's Own Loyal Enemy Aliens: German and Austrian Refugees in Britain's Armed Forces, 1939–1945* (London: Vallentine Mitchell, 2006).

59. Austin Stevens, *The Dispossessed: German Refugees in Britain* (London: Barrie and Jenkins, 1975), 229.

60. *FDKB Nachrichten*, December 1940, 10.
61. Stevens, *The Dispossessed*, 157.
62. Kushner, "An Alien Occupation," 567.
63. *FDKB Nachrichten*, August 1940, 5.
64. Jane Dorner, *Fashion in the Twenties and Thirties* (London: Arlington House, 1975), iv.
65. Ulrike Walton-Jordan, "Designs for the Future: Gaby Schreiber as an Exponent of Bauhaus Principles in Britain," in *Intellectual Migration*, eds. Edward Timms and Jon Hughes.
66. Schwab, *Thank You for Everything*, 18.
67. Anthony Grenville, ed., *Refugees from the Third Reich*, Yearbook of Exile Studies (2002), 114.
68. Ulrike Walton-Jordan, "'Although he is Jewish, he is M & S': Jewish Refugees from Nazism and Marks & Spencer from the 1930s to the 1960s" in *Refugees from the Third Reich*, Grenville, 120–28.
69. *FDKB Nachrichten*, January 1941, 1.
70. *FDKB Nachrichten*, February 1941, 7.
71. *FDKB Nachrichten*, March 1941, 7.
72. *FDKB Nachrichten*, April 1941, 9.
73. *FDKB Nachrichten*, August 1941, 10.
74. Charmian Brinson and Richard Dove, "The Continuation of Politics by Other Means: The *Freie Deutsche Kulturbund* in London, 1939–1946," in *"I didn't want to float,"* eds. Grenville and Reiter, 11.
75. The degree to which this avoidance of the Lower East Side could have been due to long-standing prejudices of German Jews against *Ostjuden*, is purely speculative. I have not found any explicit mention of this in refugee interviews or writings.
76. Bert Kirchheimer, in *We Were So Beloved: Autobiography of a German Jewish Community*, eds. Manfred Kirchheimer and Gloria DeVidas Kirchheimer (Pittsburgh: University of Pittsburgh Press, 1997), 2.
77. The limitations of this analysis include the unknown number of refugee deaths and their origins that were not announced in the *Aufbau*.
78. I chose to calculate the number of rooms for rent by looking at the Rosh Hashanah issue of each year. There were no rooms advertised in this issue for 1935, and only three rooms advertised in October and November of 1935. Looking at the September issues also gave me the opportunity to pore through announcements and articles relating to the Jewish High Holidays. This informed my findings on religion in chapter 5.
79. Kramer, "*How Rich Was Rich.*"
80. Katz, diaries (August 6, 1934; August 8, 1934; April 19, 1938).
81. Jacoby, *My Life's History*, 12.
82. Joshua Franklin, "Victim Soldiers: German-Jewish Refugees in the American Armed Forces during World War II," Honors Thesis, Clark University, 2006, 9.

83. Davie and Koenig, *The Refugees Are Now in America*, 192–94.
84. Stock, "Washington Heights' 'Fourth Reich,'" 584–85.
85. Kahn, memoirs.
86. Davie, *Refugees in America*, 51.
87. *Aufbau,* September 1, 1936.
88. *Aufbau,* September 1, 1938.
89. Melitta Hess, in *We Were So Beloved*, eds. Kirchheimer and Kirchheimer, 101.
90. *Aufbau,* September 1, 1936.
91. Robison, *Refugees at Work*, 38.
92. Kahn, memoirs.
93. Walter Baum, interview with author, March 14, 2001.
94. Kirchheimer, in *We Were So Beloved*, eds. Kirchheimer and Kirchheimer, 95.
95. Kahn, memoirs.

Chapter 2. Family, Friendship, and Food

1. Gerson, "Family Matters"; and Gay, *My German Question,* 214.
2. Nancy Foner, ed., *Across Generations: Immigrant Families in America* (New York: New York University Press, 2009), 127–46; Donna Gabaccia, *From the Other Side: Women, Gender and Immigrant Life in the U.S., 1820–1990* (Bloomington: Indiana Univ. Press, 1994); Susan A. Glenn, *Daughters of the Shtetl: Life and Labor in the Immigrant Generation* (Ithaca: Cornell University Press, 1991); Pyong Gap Min, *Changes and Conflicts: Korean Immigrant Families in New York* (Boston: Allyn and Bacon; 1998).
3. See Kaplan, *Making of the Jewish Middle Class*; and Atina Grossman, "German Women Doctors from Berlin in New York: Maternity and Modernity in Weimar and in Exile," *Feminist Studies* 19 (1993): 65–88.
4. See Kaplan, *Between Dignity and Despair.*
5. Tergit, "How they Resettled," 62.
6. Joseph Adler, *The Family of Joseph and Marie Adler: Jews in Germany, German Jews in America* (1992), LBI NY, 93–94.
7. Jacoby, *My Life's History,* 9.
8. See Jillian Davidson, "German-Jewish Women in England," in *Second Chance,* eds. Mosse et al., 533–51.
9. Eva Reichmann, *The Years Before*, LBI NY (1964), 3.
10. Gerson, "Family Matters."
11. Charmian Brinson, "'In the Exile of Internment' or '*Von Versuchen aus einer Not eine Tugend zu machen*': German-speaking Women Interned by the British during the Second World War," in *Politics and Culture in Twentieth-Century Germany,* eds. William Niven and James Jordan (Rochester: Camden House, 2003), 63–87.
12. Davie, *Refugees in America*, 125.

13. See Part III of *Between Sorrow and Strength*, Quack.
14. Davie, *Refugees in America*, 145.
15. Linda Camino and Ruth M. Krufeld, eds., *Reconstructing Lives, Recapturing Meaning: Refugee Identity, Gender, and Cultural Change* (Washington, DC: Gordon and Breach, 1994).
16. Peter Gay, Epilogue: "The First Sex," in *Between Sorrow and Strength*, Quack, 357.
17. Leo Grebler, *German-Jewish Immigrants to the United States during the Hitler Period: Personal Reminiscences and General Observations*, YIVO (1976), 84.
18. Gerson, "Family Matters," 213.
19. Ibid.
20. Ibid., 213–17. For more on constructs of masculinity for German Jewish men see Gregory Caplan, "Militärische Männlichkeit in der deutsch-jüdischen Geschichte," *Die Philosophin* 22 (2000): 85–100.
21. Based on 1933 census data and *Reichsvereinigung* statistics of 1939 as cited in Herbert Strauss, "Jewish Emigration from Germany," 318, Table IIIa.
22. Marianne Kröger and Andrea Hammel, "Child Exiles: A New Research Area?" *SHOFAR* 23, no. 1 (Fall 2004): 8–20.
23. Ruben G. Rumbaut and Alejandro Portes, eds., *Ethnicities: Children of Immigrants in America* (Berkeley: University of California Press, 2001).
24. See Foner, *Across Generations*; Seungsook Moon, "Immigration and Mothering: Case Studies from Two Generations of Korean Immigrant Women," *Gender and Society* 17 (December 2003): 854–56; Denise A. Segura, "Ambivalence or Continuity? Motherhood and Employment among Chicanas and Mexican Immigrant Women Workers," *Aztlan* 20 (1991): 119–50; Carola Suarez-Orozco and Marcelo M. Suarez-Orozco, *Children of Immigration* (Cambridge: Harvard University Press, 2001); Selma S. Berrol, *Growing Up American: Immigrant Children in America Then and Now* (New York: Twayne, 1996).
25. Kenneth Ambrose, *The Suitcase in the Garage: Letters and Photographs of a German-Jewish Family, 1800–1950* (London: Kenneth Ambrose, 1996).
26. See Gillian Lathey, "From Emil to Alice: The Hiatus in the Childhood Reading of Exiles from Germany and Austria, 1933–45," in *German-Speaking Exiles in Great Britain*, ed. Anthony Grenville (Amsterdam/Atlanta: Rodopi, 2000).
27. Kerr, *Other Way Round*.
28. See Marjorie Faulstich Orellana, Lisa Dorner, and Lucila Pulido, "Accessing Assets: Immigrant Youth's Work as Family Translators or Para-phrasers," *Social Problems* 50, no. 4 (2003): 505–24.
29. Had the Wagner-Rogers Bill passed, then potentially there would have been at least twenty thousand German Jewish children arriving alone in the United States.
30. Robison, *Refugees at Work*, 68.
31. Saenger, *Today's Refugees, Tomorrow's Citizens*, 165.

32. Ibid., 180. Benjamin Maria Baader cites Rebekka Habermas and Anne-Charlott Trepp's research on parenting in nineteenth-century Germany, which finds that the expectation in the middle classes was that both mothers and fathers were responsible for raising their children with love and affection. There seems to be an expectation of Jewish men to play a central role in the raising of their children, as Baader explores in "Jewish Difference and the Feminine Spirit of Judaism in Mid-Nineteenth-Century Germany," in *Jewish Masculinities*, eds. Benjamin Maria Baader et al., 50–71.

33. Davie, *Refugees in America*, 147.

34. Ibid., 53.

35. Saenger, *Today's Refugees, Tomorrow's Citizens*, 137.

36. Baum, *A Personal History*; Gutman, interview with author, July 2002.

37. See, for example, Loretta Baldassar, Cora Baldock, Raelene Wilding, *Families Caring across Borders: Migration Aging and Transnational Caregiving* (New York: Palgrave McMillan, 2007); Daniel W. L. Lai et al., "Relationships between Culture and Health Status: A Multi-Site Study of the Older Chinese in Canada," *Canadian Journal on Aging* 3, no. 26 (Fall 2007): 171–83; and Lori Gemeiner Bihler, "Omis and Grandmas: A Community of German-Jewish Women in Washington Heights, New York," in *Beyond Camps and Forced Labour: Current International Research on Survivors of Nazi Persecution*, eds. Johannes-Dieter Steinert and Inge Weber-Newth (Osnabrück: Secolo, 2005).

38. As reported by Bob Moore in *Second Chance*, eds. Mosse et al., 73.

39. He found out in 1945 that she had not survived, but he was unsure of her actual fate at the time. Otto Bickart, family papers.

40. Hasia Diner, *Hungering for America: Italian, Irish, and Jewish Foodways in the Age of Migration* (Cambridge: Harvard University Press, 2001); Donna Gabaccia, *We Are What We Eat: Ethnic Food and the Making of Americans* (Cambridge: Harvard University Press, 1998).

41. See Marion Kaplan, "Friendship on the Margins."

42. Schwab, *Thank You for Everything*, 8.

43. Charmian Brinson, "A Woman's Place . . . ? German-speaking Women in Exile in Britain, 1933–1945," *German Life & Letters* 51, no. 2 (1998): 204–24.

44. Jacoby, *My Life's History*, 9.

45. Tergit, "How They Resettled," 69.

46. *FDKB Nachrichten*, February 1940, 4, and April 1940, 4.

47. *FDKB Nachrichten*, February 1941, 7, and repeatedly throughout 1941.

48. *FDKB Nachrichten*, March 1941, 8.

49. Leo Bettelheim, letter to Clementine Zernik, *Clementine Zernik Collection*, Exilarchiv, Deutsche Bibliothek (November 6, 1941).

50. *FDKB Nachrichten*, March 1940, 2.

51. Ibid., 4.

52. *FDKB Nachrichten*, January 1941, 4.
53. *FDKB Nachrichten*, June 1941, 7.
54. *Your Food in Wartime*, Public Information Leaflet 14 (London, July 1939); British Ministry of Food, *Food Facts for the Kitchen Front: A Book of Wartime Recipes and Hints* (London, 1941); *Daily Express War Time Cookery Book: Practical Advice and Recipes Specially Prepared for War Time Conditions* (London, 1939).
55. Rudolf Apt, *My Life*, LBI NY (1978), 25.
56. *FDKB Nachrichten*, October 1941, 10.
57. Anne Koppel, *Citizenship None*, LBI NY (1942), 10.
58. Unnamed respondent, in Gershon, *We Came as Children*, 59.
59. Unnamed respondent, in ibid., 63.
60. Leigh, *Autobiography*, 43.
61. Ibid., 41.
62. Unnamed respondent, in Gershon, *We Came as Children*, 54.
63. Unnamed respondent, in ibid., 60.
64. Dr. F. Brodnitz, "*Kleiner Gesundheitsführer*" (little health tips) in *Aufbau Almanac: The Immigrant's Handbook* (New York: Verlag German-Jewish Club, 1941).
65. Grebler, *German-Jewish Immigrants*, 44.
66. According to Hasia Diner in *Hungering for America*, early-twentieth-century Eastern European Jews in New York ate the cold cuts sold by German Jewish immigrants of the nineteenth century and adapted them into their diets. These delicatessens of the Lower East Side became temples of "typical" Jewish food.
67. *Aufbau*, Sept 1, 1938.
68. For example, see *Aufbau*, July 26, 1940.
69. Stock, "Washington Heights' 'Fourth Reich,'" 584.
70. *Aufbau*, Sept 1, 1936, for an advertisement for "Mayers E 87th Beer and Wein 1st class kitchen."
71. Elsa Heineman, "Your Household," in *Aufbau Almanac*.
72. Katz, diaries, November 26, 1939.
73. Kahn, memoirs.
74. J. Heiman, *Joseph and His Daughter*, 85.
75. Kahn, memoirs.
76. Ibid.
77. Koppel, *Citizenship None*, 12–13.
78. Jacoby, *My Life's History*, 12.
79. Katz, diaries, April 25, 1938.
80. Ibid., September 5, 1938.
81. An analysis of the psychological stress for refugees from Nazi Germany is best left in the hands of someone more qualified. This book will remain focused on understanding the complexities of culture and identity transformation.
82. *Aufbau* advertised *Tanztees* (dance teas) on Sundays at 3:30pm at Hotel Empire West 63rd Street and Broadway, for example, September 1, 1938.

83. It bears mentioning again that there is currently no way to track precisely the patterns of familial cohabitation in both cities. Refugees in both cities found temporary housing with siblings, aunts and uncles, distant cousins, and strangers. I do believe, however, that it will be possible to do this in the relatively near future. In this vein, I have begun working with digital historians to devise a geo-temporal database and interactive map that would be able to capture the paths of the 500,000+ Jews from pre-1933 Germany and plot where they ended up. While the task is gargantuan, the information is out there and I don't think it is impossible, even if it will take years to complete. I plan to cull immigration records, census data, and the archives at ITS Bad Arolsen, Yad Vashem, and the Leo Baeck Institute as a start. I am currently applying for a range of grants and working on developing partnerships to get this off the ground.

84. Gerson, "Family Matters," 213.

Chapter 3. Dress and Names

1. Barbara Schreier, *Becoming American Women: Clothing and the Jewish Immigrant Experience, 1880–1920* (Chicago: Chicago Historical Society, 1994), 4–5. Another related comparative study is Nancy Green's *Ready to Wear, Ready to Work: A Century of Industry and Immigrants in Paris and New York* (Durham: Duke University Press, 1997).

2. Kaplan, *Making of the Jewish Middle Class*, 31.

3. *Baer-Oppenheimer Family Collection*, LBI NY.

4. Herbert Jonas, Herbert Jonas Papers, LBI NY; Marianne Berel, *Memoirs and Translations of My Family's Writings*, LBI NY.

5. Tergit, "How They Resettled," 69.

6. Ambrose, *The Suitcase in the Garage*, 240.

7. German-Jewish Aid Committee and the Jewish Board of Deputies, *While You Are in England: Helpful Information and Guidance for Every Refugee* (Essex: Anchor, 1938), 12–14.

8. Clarence Crane Brinton, *The United States and Britain* (Cambridge: Harvard University Press, 1945), 77–78.

9. Friedmann, *Hard Times*, 2.

10. Tergit, "How They Resettled," 65.

11. Eileen Erlund, *The Early Days in Europe*, LBI NY, 18.

12. Jacoby, *My Life's History*, 11.

13. Victor Ehrenberg, letter to Ludwig (no date), Lewis Elton Papers, CGJS, University of Sussex.

14. "Letter from London," *Aufbau*, September 1, 1944. A refugee soldier describes anti-alien sentiment he read in the newspaper, *Hampstead-Harrow Express*.

15. Leigh, *Autobiography*, 44.

16. Ibid., 46.
17. Ambrose, *The Suitcase in the Garage*, 183.
18. Ibid., 214.
19. Eva Ehrenberg, letter to sons, November 24, 1942, Lewis Elton Papers.
20. Unnamed respondent, in Gershon, *We Came as Children*, 55.
21. Marianne Walter, *An Exile in England*, private collection, 6.
22. Phineas May, *Kitchener Camp Diary* (February 18, 1939).
23. Koppel, *Citizenship None*, 10.
24. Anne Marie Grebler, letter to friend, September 19, 1937, in Grebler, *German-Jewish Immigrants*.
25. Davie, *Refugees in America*, 53.
26. Kramer, "How Rich Was Rich."
27. E. Ehrenreich, "*Kosmetik in Amerika*," in *Aufbau Almanac*.
28. *Aufbau* September 1, 1936.
29. Alice Oppenheimer in *We Were So Beloved*, eds. Kirchheimer and Kirchheimer, 89.
30. Caroline Rennolds Milbank, *New York Fashion: The Evolution of American Style* (New York: Harry N. Abrams, 1989), 134.
31. Laky, *On Being Jewish*, 94.
32. Ambrose, *The Suitcase in the Garage*, 324.
33. Ernest Stock, interview with author, London, November 27, 2000.
34. Gerda Sabor, *My First Thirty Years*, LBI NY (1994), 3.
35. Baum, interview with author, March 14, 2001.
36. Yvonne Gemeiner, interview with author, June 2001. The term *Jeckes* or *Jekkes*, is slang for German Jews who wear jackets at all times.
37. This is still true today. The top American designers such as Donna Karan, Calvin Klein, and Ralph Lauren have all made their name in creating expensive casual wear. Interestingly, all three are Jewish and have a strong "WASP" quality to their clothes. There also seems to be a greater acceptance and appreciation for casual clothes in the United States that has only in the last ten years made its way to Europe.
38. *Aufbau*, January 1936, 9, 12.
39. *Aufbau*, September 1936.
40. Kahn, memoirs.
41. Lowenstein, *Frankfurt on the Hudson*, 179.
42. Ibid.
43. *Aufbau*, September 6, 1940, 10. Translated from "*Hutsalon Madame Hermy früher Wien I Kohlmarkt Feinste Indivduelle Arbeit.*"
44. Davie and Koenig, *The Refugees Are Now in America*, 13.
45. Lowenstein, *Frankfurt on the Hudson*, 141.
46. Grebler, *German-Jewish Immigrants*, 44.
47. Sabor, *My First Thirty Years*, 3.

48. Baum, *A Personal History*, 2.
49. Katz, diaries.
50. F. Brodnitz, "*Kleiner Gesundheitsführer*" (Little Health Guide) in *Aufbau Almanac*.
51. Reichmann, *The Years Before*, 1–2. She used their social and professional titles rather than Mr. or Mrs.
52. Schwab, *Thank You for Everything*, 3–8.
53. Walter, *An Exile in England*, 6–8.
54. Resi Kohen, memoirs, CGJS, 16–18.
55. Leigh, *Autobiography*, 36.
56. V. Ehrenberg, letter to Gottfried and Ludwig Ehrenberg (October 17, 1942).
57. Julius Cohn, letter to his parents (December 20, 1938), Bertha Cohn Papers.
58. Grebler, *German-Jewish Immigrants*, 89.
59. See, for example, Otto "Robert" Bickart, personal collection, and Katz, diaries.
60. Stock, interview with author, November 27, 2000. His first name was originally "Ernst" but after living in France prior to his arrival in New York he added the second "e" to make it less German.
61. Bickart, personal papers.
62. Ernst Maass, "Integration and Name Changing among Jewish Refugees from Central Europe in the United States," *Names* 6, no. 3 (September 1958): 156.
63. Baby announcements in *Aufbau* in 1935 show a predominance of American Jewish naming patterns among German Jews.
64. Lowenstein, *Frankfurt on the Hudson*, 194–95.
65. Anne-Marie Fortier, *Migrant Belongings: Memory, Space, Identity* (London: Berg, 2000), 11.
66. Ambrose, *The Suitcase in the Garage*, 354.
67. Royal Air Force, Air Ministry name change document in Ambrose, *The Suitcase in the Garage*, 355.
68. Ibid., 354.
69. Schwab, *Thank You for Everything*, 18.
70. Maass, "Integration and Name Changing," 141–42.
71. Rudolf Glanz describes this further in his article "German-Jewish Names in America," *Jewish Social Studies* 23, no. 3 (July 1961): 143–69. Here he examined the significance of nineteenth-century German Jewish merchants who helped pioneer the American West and their role in creating an "image of success" for future German Jewish immigrants.
72. J. A. Kugelmass, "Name-Changing and What It Gets You: Twenty-Five Who Did It," *Commentary* 14 (August 1952): 145.
73. Maass, "Integration and Name Changing," 159.

180   Notes to Chapter 4

74. Ibid., 152.

75. Ibid., 159. Perhaps his boss feared that a Jewish name would not appeal to small-town customers.

76. Kugelmass, "Name Changing and What It Gets You," 147–48.

77. Louis Adamic, *What's Your Name?* (New York: Harper, 1942), 108.

78. Maass, "Integration and Name Changing," 162.

79. Birth announcement in Clementine Zernik Collection, Exilarchiv, Deutsche Bibliothek.

80. Some aristocratic families in England, including the King's, were directly related to those in Germany.

81. Saenger, *Today's Refugees, Tomorrow's Citizens*, 94.

82. Postcards to Oskar Bern, Clementine Zernik Collection.

83. Saenger, *Today's Refugees, Tomorrow's Citizens*, 149.

84. Gabrielle Schiff in *We Were So Beloved*, eds. Kirchheimer and Kirchheimer, 207.

85. Business card included in Clementine Zernik Collection.

86. *Aufbau Almanac*.

87. Saenger, *Today's Refugees, Tomorrow's Citizens*, 123.

88. Katz, diaries, November 17, 1938.

89. Davie and Koenig, *Refugees Are Now in America*, 58.

Chapter 4. Language and Mannerisms

1. Polish Jewish immigrants lived in Germany in the 1920s and 1930s, and they spoke Yiddish. They considered themselves to be Germans of Jewish descent and thereby, spoke German. Yiddish words or accents were perceived to be for the uncultured and unassimilated Jews.

2. Monika S. Schmid, "'I Always Thought I Was a German—It Was Hitler Who Taught Me I was a Jew': National-Socialist Persecution, Identity, and the German Language," in *German-Jewish Identities in America*, eds. Christof Mauch and Joe Salmons (Madison: University of Wisconsin Press, 2003), 133–53. Schmid's monograph, *First Language Attrition, Use and Maintenance: The Case of German Jews in Anglophone Countries* (Amsterdam: John Benjamins, 2002) further explores the linguistic attrition of German by refugees in the United States and Great Britain. Her results again prove that the degree of persecution experienced by the refugees in Germany determined the degree of language attrition sixty years later. While she looks at refugees sixty years after their arrival, she does not compare how language usage differed in their first ten years in either country.

3. Samson, Interview for *London Voices*.

4. Schwab, *Thank You for Everything*, 8.

5. Kerr, *The Other Way Round*.
6. The italics were from the original document. German-Jewish Aid Committee, *While You Are in England*, 12.
7. Berghahn, *Continental Britons*, 145–46.
8. Eileen Erlund, *Early Days in Europe*, 19.
9. Herbert Levy, *Voices from the Past* (Lewes: Temple House, 1995), 52.
10. Reichmann, *The Years Before*, 2.
11. For more on English lessons and educational opportunities for interned men and the limitations for women's learning see the related books in Sellers, *We Built Up Our Lives*.
12. Charles Hannam, *Almost an Englishman* (London: Deutsch, 1979), 12.
13. Oliver Pond, letter to wife, Oliver Pond Collection, Imperial War Museum.
14. Leigh, *Autobiography*, 49. Songs and music were a way that many refugees used to improve their language skills in exile. Ruth Westheimer wrote extensively of how music influenced her refugee experience in her memoir, *Musically Speaking: A Life Through Song* (Philadelphia: University of Pennsylvania Press, 2003).
15. Peter William Johnson, letter to his father, A. Joseph, May 11, 1940, Imperial War Museum.
16. Leigh, *Autobiography*, 59.
17. Schwab, *Thank You for Everything*, 15.
18. Ambrose, *The Suitcase in the Garage*. There were still English lessons being offered on Tuesdays and Thursdays through the *FDKB* as advertised in their newsletter in March 1940.
19. Victor Eisler, postcard, November 26, 1939, Imperial War Museum; Julius Cohn, letter to Bertha Cohn, July 18,1937, Bertha Cohn Papers.
20. Koppel, *Citizenship None*, 10.
21. Unnamed respondent, in Gershon, *We Came as Children*, 60.
22. Unnamed respondent, in ibid., 51.
23. Levy, *Voices from the Past*, 52.
24. Eric Sheldon, "The Younger Generation," in *Britain's New Citizens*, AJR, 70.
25. Kerr, *Other Way Round*, 13–14.
26. Tergit, "How they Resettled," 69.
27. Dr. Furst, Furst Papers, at Parkes Institute, University of Southampton.
28. Apt, *My Life*, 26.
29. Unnamed respondent, in Gershon, *We Came as Children*, 54.
30. Inge's diary, in ibid., 57.
31. Unnamed respondent, in ibid., 54.
32. Unnamed respondent, in ibid., 53.
33. Kerr, *Other Way Round*, 299.
34. Ambrose, *The Suitcase in the Garage*, 270.
35. As quoted in Berghahn, *Continental Britons*, 140.

36. This fear of harassment was not always justified. In most cases their British neighbors and colleagues accepted their accents. It was the occasional stinging anti-German remark that produced anxiety and apprehension.
37. Inge Heiman, *Joseph and His Daughter*, 86.
38. Cohn, letter to his parents, December 20, 1938, Bertha Cohn Collection.
39. *Aufbau* advertised "English for Doctors" through the German-Jewish Club (New World Club), July 26, 1940.
40. E. K. Schwartz, "How to Become an American," in *Aufbau Almanac*.
41. Ilse Kaufherr, in *We Were So Beloved*, eds. Kirchheimer and Kirchheimer, 188.
42. Ambrose, *The Suitcase in the Garage*, 319.
43. Davie, *Refugees in America*, 89.
44. Stock, interview with author, November 27, 2000.
45. Sabor, *My First Thirty Years*, 37.
46. Hans Steinitz, in *We Were So Beloved*, eds. Kirchheimer and Kirchheimer, 125.
47. The Rosh Hashanah issues of *Aufbau* for 1934 through 1936 advertised *Moderne Deutsche Buchhandlung* (Modern German Bookstore): "Books for immigrants and modern readers" on 250 East 84th Street in Yorkville, Upper East Side.
48. Unnamed respondent, in Davie, *Refugees in America*, 82.
49. Felix Pollak, "Felix Pollak: An Autobiographical Sketch," *Northeast Series* 5, no. 5 (Winter 1991–92): 16.
50. Bert Kirchheimer, in *We Were So Beloved*, eds. Kirchheimer and Kirchheimer, 95.
51. Kahn, memoirs.
52. Baum, interview with author, March 14, 2001.
53. Stock, interview with author, November 27, 2000.
54. Siegfried Rosenthal, memoirs, LBI NY, 6.
55. Ibid.
56. Otto Bickart, letter to Elli Eckhaus. August 18, 1942, private collection.
57. Bickart, letter to Eckhaus, August 18, 1943.
58. Max Frankel, in *We Were So Beloved*, eds. Kirchheimer and Kirchheimer, 110.
59. Stock, "Washington Heights' 'Fourth Reich,'" 585.
60. Walter Kern, in *Today's Refugees, Tomorrow's Citizens*, Saenger, 181.
61. Ibid.
62. Davie, *Refugees in America*, 144.
63. Gay, Epilogue, "The First Sex," in Quack, 356. Other refugees, such as Walter Baum, also recalled that his mother mastered English much more quickly than his father.
64. Davie, *Refugees in America*, 125.
65. Stock, interview with author, November 27, 2000.
66. Frankel, in *We Were So Beloved*, eds. Kirchheimer and Kirchheimer, 113.

67. The majority of articles in the *Aufbau Almanac* were written in German, although the *Aufbau*'s official "Statement of Policy" was printed in English. This may have been because the booklet was geared toward newly arrived refugees whose grasp of English may not have been very strong. The use of English by refugee organizations is more closely examined in chapter 5.

68. Brinton, *United States and Britain*, 78.

69. The poignant article by Arnold Paucker published in 1996 entitled "Speaking English with an Accent" gives an interesting look back on this experience. Arnold Paucker, "Speaking English with an Accent," in *"England? Aber wo liegt es?" Deutsche und österreichische Emigranten in Großbritannien 1933–1945*, eds. Charmian Brinson and Richard Dove et al. (London: Institute for Germanic Studies, University of London, 1996), 21–31.

70. Laky, *On Being Jewish*, 70.

71. Sylvia Rodgers, *Red Saint, Pink Daughter: A Communist Childhood in Berlin and London* (Manchester: Carcanet, 1996), 218, as cited in "A Woman's Place . . . ?" Brinson, 204–24.

72. Brinton, *United States and Britain*, 68.

73. Hanna Goddard, interview with author, January 2001.

74. Both quotes from unnamed respondents in Gershon, *We Came as Children*, 54.

75. Hannam, *Almost an Englishman*, 10. He wrote this book in the third person, although the experiences are his own.

76. Levy, *Voices from the Past*, 52.

77. Sheldon, "The Younger Generation," 70.

78. Bickart, interview with author, Connecticut, June 1992.

79. Cohn, letter to Bertha Cohn (February 14, 1938), Bertha Cohn Collection.

80. Davie, *Refugees in America*, 90.

81. Baum, *A Personal History*, 6.

82. Davie, *Refugees in America*, 90.

83. Grebler, *German-Jewish Immigrants*, 120.

84. Ibid., 45.

85. Baum, *A Personal History*, 7.

86. Stock, interview with author, November 27, 2000.

87. The Japanese experienced the brunt of hostility. Germans in more provincial areas of the United States experienced more anti-German prejudice than in the cities.

88. Grebler, *German-Jewish Immigrants*, 49.

89. It stated, "Do not make yourself conspicuous by speaking loudly. . . . The Englishman attaches very great importance to modesty, under-statement in speech rather than over-statement . . . he values good manners far more than he values the evidence of wealth," German-Jewish Aid Committee, *While You Are in England*, 12–14.

90. Bloomsbury House, *Mistress and Maid: General Information for the Use of Domestic Refugees and Their Employers* (London, 1940).

91. Tergit, "How They Resettled," 63.
92. Erlund, *Early Days in Europe*, 18.
93. German-Jewish Aid Committee, *While You Are in England*, 14.
94. Bloomsbury House, *Mistress and Maid*.
95. Schwab, *Thank You for Everything*, 13.
96. Furst, personal papers.
97. Walter, *An Exile in England*, 7.
98. Cohn, letter to Bertha Cohn, July 19, 1937, Bertha Cohn Collection.
99. Rosenstock, "The Jewish Refugees," 17.
100. Davie, *Refugees in America*, 55.
101. Saenger, *Today's Refugees, Tomorrow's Citizens*, 94.
102. Grebler, *German-Jewish Immigrants*, 88–89.
103. E. Behrendt, "Was nicht im Lexikon steht," ("What Is Not in the Dictionary"), in *Aufbau Almanac*.
104. Davie, *Refugees in America*, 90.
105. Ibid., 57–58.
106. Ibid.
107. Cohn, letter to Bertha Cohn, February 14, 1938, Bertha Cohn Collection.
108. Grebler, *German-Jewish Immigrants*, 70.
109. Unnamed respondent, in Davie, *Refugees in America*, 57.
110. Ibid.
111. Stock, "Washington Heights' 'Fourth Reich,'" 587.
112. Stock, interview with author, November 27, 2000.
113. Saenger, *Today's Refugees, Tomorrow's Citizens*, 146.
114. Walter, *An Exile in England*, 37.
115. Kaufherr, in *We Were So Beloved*, eds. Kirchheimer and Kirchheimer, 60.
116. Bert Kirchheimer, in ibid., 94.
117. Saenger, *Today's Refugees, Tomorrow's Citizens*, 83.
118. Baum, *A Personal History*, 6.
119. Joshua Haberman, *Born in Vienna*, LBI NY (1993).

Chapter 5. Organizational Life

1. See Floris Vermeiden, "Organizational Patterns: Surinamese and Turkish Associations in Amsterdam, 1960–1990," *Journal of Ethnic and Migration Studies* 31 (2005): 951–97; Irene Bloemraad, "The Limits of de Tocqueville: How Government Facilitates Organizational Capacity in Newcomer Communities," *Journal of Ethnic and Migration Studies* 31 (2005): 865–88; Peggy Levitt, "Redefining the Boundaries of Belonging: The Institutional Character of Transnational Religious Life," *Sociology of Religion* 65, no. 1 (2004): 1–18; Marlou Schrover and Floris Vermeulen, "Immigrant Organizations," *Journal of Ethnic and Migration Studies* 31 (2005): 823–32;

and Him Mark Lai, *Becoming Chinese American: A History of Communities and Institutions* (Walnut Creek, CA: Alta Mira Press, 2004).

2. Unnamed Author, "Law and Land," *AJR Information* (September 1946), 68.

3. Tydor Baumel-Schwartz, *Never Look Back*, 35.

4. Fast, *Children's Exodus*, 87–88.

5. Ibid., 88.

6. Kushner, "An Alien Occupation," 565.

7. Kushner, *Persistence of Prejudice*. Also see Kushner and Valman, *Remembering Cable Street*.

8. London, *Whitehall and the Jews*.

9. Norman Bentwich, *They Found Refugee: An Account of British Jewry's Work for Victims of Nazi Oppression* (London: Cresset, 1956).

10. Grenville and Reiter, "*I Didn't Want to Float*," 89–91.

11. Ibid., 89.

12. Ibid., 91.

13. Ibid.

14. Ibid., 93.

15. Ibid., 91.

16. Ibid., 96.

17. Ronald Stent, "Jewish Refugee Organizations," in *Second Chance*, eds. Mosse et al., 596.

18. Kurt Alexander, "From Here to the Future," in *Britain's New Citizens*, AJR, 12.

19. Grenville and Reiter, "*I Didn't Want to Float*," 96.

20. Charmian Brinson, Richard Dove, and Anna Mueller-Haerlin, *Politics by Other Means: The Free German League of Culture in London, 1939–1946* (London: Vallentine Mitchell, 2010). There is a chapter in Grenville and Reiter's *Float* by Brinson and Dove called "The Continuation of Politics by Other Means: The Freie Deutsche Kulturbund in London, 1939–1946," 1–25. Another chapter in *Float*, by Marian Malet, looks at the artist Oskar Kokoschka and his role in the FDKB.

21. Brinson, *Politics by Other Means*, 16. The file they reference is SAPMO-BArch, SgY13/V239/1/1.

22. *FDKB Nachrichten*, December 1941, 5 and Brinson, *Politics by Other Means*, 35.

23. *FDKB Nachrichten*, March 1941; August 1940, 3; December 1941, 5.

24. The Cabaret closed during parts of the war, but it was announced open again in June 1944. *FDKB Nachrichten*, June 1944, 18.

25. In May 1942 the *FDKB* published *Verbannte und Verbrannte* (Banned and Burned), and in August 1942 they published a Jewish-themed booklet of poems and prose in German. In 1944 the *FDKB* printed, in English, Rita Hausdorff's *Silesian Story: The Story of a Jewish family in Germany*. See Brinson, *Politics by Other Means*, 45–47.

26. Advertisements for English and Spanish language courses and help with professional training skills such as stenography were just two examples. *FDKB Nachrichten*, March 1941.

27. *FDKB Nachrichten*, August 1940, 3; *FDKB Nachrichten*, April 1941, 3 for a showing of Internment Camp art in London April 9, to raise awareness.

28. *FDKB Nachrichten*, October 1940, 7; *FDKB Nachrichten*, February 1941.

29. *FDKB Nachrichten*, March 1941, 7.

30. Brinson, *Politics by Other Means*, 33.

31. The show of British actors is described in Brinson, *Politics by Other Means*, 28–29.

32. *FDKB Nachrichten*, October 1940; and December 1941, 5.

33. Brinson, *Politics by Other Means*, 30–31.

34. *FDKB Nachrichten*, December 1940.

35. Brinson, *Politics by Other Means*, 17.

36. It held a housewarming party on January 7, 1940, for the opening of the *FDKB* clubhouse at 36a Upper Park Rd London. At this event Mr. H. Field Chief speaker said, "adapt here but remain German and you will go back to Germany." *FDKB Nachrichten*, February 1940, 2.

37. See Jens Bruening in Grenville and Reiter, "*I Didn't Want to Float*," 67.

38. The first PEN Centre was formed in the UK in 1921 as an organization for writers that promoted the freedom of expression and literature. The name originally stood for Poets, Essayists, and Novelists.

39. Kurt Alexander, *AJR Information*, 9 (September 1946), 65.

40. Kurt Grossman, *The Contributions of German Immigrants to American Life: Economic and Cultural Capacity of the Newcomers*, for the American Jewish Joint Distribution Committee (New York: 1939).

41. Sharon Lowenstein, "Jewish Refugee Service," in *Jewish American Volunteer Organizations*, ed. Michael Dobkowski (Westport, CT: Greeenwood, 1986), 364–72.

42. See Quack, *Between Sorrow and Strength*. This edited collection offers a look at the experiences of German-speaking refugee women and organizations around the world. Herbert Strauss, ed., *Jewish Immigrants of the Nazi Period in the USA*, 2 (New York: K. G. Saur, 1981), also provides a thorough list of refugee organizations in the United States.

43. The next largest press was *Jewish Way*, which began publication in 1940 and had between six and seven thousand subscribers. Steven Lowenstein provides a brief history of the rivalry between *Aufbau* and *Jewish Way* in *Frankfurt on the Hudson*, 126. According to Lowenstein, the *Jewish Way* was published in Washington Heights by Max Oppenheimer and considered itself more Jewish in its focus than the *Aufbau*. It remained in print from 1940 until 1965.

44. *Aufbau*, December 1934; August 1935.

45. *Aufbau*, December 1934.

46. Ibid.

47. *Aufbau*, September 1, 1936.

48. Ibid.
49. *Aufbau*, July 26, 1940.
50. *Aufbau*, September 1, 1938.
51. *Aufbau*, September 1, 1937.
52. Saenger, *Today's Refugees, Tomorrow's Citizens*, 161.
53. See Selfhelp of Emigres from Central Europe, Inc., "Summer Placement for Émigré Children: Report for 1943, New York," cited in *Jewish Immigrants*, ed. Strauss, 210.
54. It is still called Selfhelp.
55. See titles cited in *Jewish Immigrants*, ed. Strauss, 206. American Federation of Jews from Central Europe published *Circular* between December 23, 1941, and May 4, 1945. The *Circular* provided news and activities of its member organizations, and after the war, its efforts in *Wiedergutmachung*, getting reparations from West Germany. The American Federation continued to publish its annual meetings proceedings and reports through the 1950s and 1960s.
56. Kaplan, *Between Dignity and Despair*, 12; and Nancy Foner and Richard Alba, "Immigrant Religion in the U.S. and Western Europe: Bridge or Barrier to Inclusion?" *International Migration Review* 42 (2008): 360–92.
57. Kaplan, *Between Dignity and Despair*, 12.
58. Its second rabbi was Rabbi Dr. Werner van der Zyl, a German refugee who studied under Leo Baeck in Berlin. His start as rabbi had to be postponed in 1942, while he was interned on the Isle of Man for a year. See Alyth Garden's current website, which provides the synagogue's history from a 2008 speech by its president, Jeffrey Rose, on the 75th anniversary of the congregation, at http://www.alyth.org.uk/.
59. On the Reform Movement in Britain, see Anne Kershen and Jonathan A. Romain, *Tradition and Change: A History of Reform Judaism in Britain, 1840–1995* (London: Vallentine Mitchell, 1995); and Miri Freud-Kandel, *Orthodox Judaism in Britain since 1913: An Ideology Forsaken* (London: Vallentine Mitchell, 2006).
60. Derek Taylor, *Chief Rabbi Hertz: The Wars of the Lord* (London: Vallentine Mitchell, 2014).
61. Inge Maybaum in *Britain's New Citizens*, AJR, 22.
62. http://www.synagogue.org.uk/about-us/.
63. Lewkowitz, "Belsize Square Synagogue," 119.
64. Ibid., 116. The *Liberale* movement was more conservative than British liberals or the American Reform movement and incorporated more classical music into its services as well.
65. Ibid., 121.
66. Ibid., 128.
67. Ibid., 126.
68. See Max Braunfeld, "A Short History of Agudath Israel in Washington Heights," presented at the occasion of the annual dinner of Agudath Israel of Upper Manhattan, March 19, 1972, as cited in *Jewish Immigrants*, ed. Strauss, 208.

69. *Aufbau*, Sept 1, 1936. See Lowenstein "Sisterhoods and Females in Choirs," in *Between Sorrow and Strength*, ed. Quack.
70. See Congregation Habonim, *Anniversary Yearbook, 1939–1949* (New York: 1949).
71. Saenger, *Today's Refugees, Tomorrow's Citizens*, 156–57.
72. See the Rosh Hashanah issues of *Aufbau*, September 1, 1933–1945. In the September 1, 1938, issue, for example, there are announcements for Rabbi Max Koppel, A Holiday Prayer (fr. Berlin) (earlier from Berlin); There is also "Happy New Year" services across the Upper West Side and Washington Heights such as the German-Jewish Club's service at Royal Manor 157th Street and Broadway and another at a synagogue on West 183rd Street.

Chapter 6. Identities

1. Books published in Germany prior to emigration in the 1930s used the term *Auswanderung* (emigration) almost exclusively. It is rare to find *Flüchtling* (refugee) in any of these titles. See, for example, Ernst F. Lowenthal, ed., *Philo-Atlas: Handbuch für die jüdische Auswanderung* (Berlin: Philo-Verlag, 1938); Michael Traub, *Die jüdische Auswanderung aus Deutschland: Westeuropa, Übersee, Palästina* (Berlin: Jüdische Rundschau, 1936); and Hans Martin Schwarz, *USA als Einwanderungsland, Jüdische Wirklichkeit Heute, eine Schriftenreihe*, 5 (Berlin: 1938).
2. In German, the equivalent words were used. In Britain it was *Flüchtlinge* or *Exil* and in the United States it was *Deutsche, Europaischer*, or *Immigranten*.
3. German-Jewish Aid Committee, *While You Are in England*.
4. Koppel, *Citizenship None*, 10.
5. John Hope Simpson, *The Refugee Problem: Report of a Survey* (London: 1939); G. George Kennedy and Allen Bell, *Humanity and the Refugees* (London: Jewish Historical Society of England, 1939); Norman Bentwich, *The Refugees from Germany: April 1933 to December 1935* (London: G. Allen & Unwin 1936); Norman Angell and Dorothy Buxton, *You and the Refugee: The Morals and Economics of the Problem* (London: Penguin, 1939); Sophie Engel, "Refugees from Germany in English Literature and Art," *Jewish Forum* 22 (March 1939): 20.
6. Rosenstock, "The Jewish Refugees," 15.
7. Rabbi Ignaz Maybaum, "German Jews and Anglo-Jewry," in *Britain's New Citizens*, AJR, 20.
8. Berghahn, *Continental Britons*. One could argue that it was easier for refugees to call themselves "Continental Britons" in postwar, postcolonial Britain, especially with the influx of immigrants from former colonies of the British Empire.
9. Manfred George, "Über den 'Aufbau'" (about the *Aufbau*), in *Aufbau Almanac*, 8.

10. Kurt Grossman, *The Contribution of the German Immigrants to American Life: Economic and Cultural Capacity of the Newcomers* (New York: American Jewish Joint Distribution Committee, 1939); Judith Lowenstein, "Vocational Adjustment of Jewish Immigrant Women and Girls Assisted by the New York Section of the National Council for Jewish Women," Master's Thesis, New York School of Social Work, Columbia University, 1938; Felix S. Cohen, *Immigrants and National Welfare* (New York: League for Industrial Democracy, 1940); Samuel Joseph, "Survey of Jewish Immigration to the United States," *Jewish Social Services Quarterly* (March 15, 1939), 299–304; Alfred Cohn, "Exiled Physicians in the United States," *American Scholar* (July 12, 1943): 352–61; David Edsall and Tracy Putnam, "The Émigré Physician in America," *Journal of the American Medical Association* 117 (Nov 29, 1941): 1881–88.

11. Davie and Koenig, *Refugees are Now in America*; Saenger, *Today's Refugees, Tomorrow's Citizens*; American Friends Service Committee, *Refugee Facts: A Study of the German Refugee in America*; Robison, *Refugees at Work*; Angell and Buxton, *You and the Refugee*; Henry Smith Leiper, "Those German Refugees," *Current History* 50 (May 1939): 19–22; Freda Heilberg, "Experiences, Attitudes, and Problems of German-Jewish Refugees," *Jewish Social Services Quarterly* XV, no. 3 (March 1939): 322–27; Joanna Colcord, "Refugee Social Workers," *Social Work Today* 7 (December 1939): 37–38; Anne Langman, "The Problem of the Refugee Physician," Master's thesis, New York School of Social Work, Columbia University, June 1940; Ruth Vogel, "The Meaning of the Day Nursery to the Refugee Parent," Master's thesis, New York School of Social Work, Columbia University, June 1941.

12. On hybrid identities see Atina Grossman, "German Jews as Provincial Cosmopolitans: Reflections from the Upper West Side," *LBI YB* (2008): 161–62.

13. Stock, interview with author, November 27, 2000.

14. Grebler, *German–Jewish Immigrants*, 68–69.

15. Saenger, *Today's Refugees, Tomorrow's Citizens*.

16. Pegelow writes of German Jewish journalists in Germany who shifted between 1933 and 1938 from defining themselves and their community as Germans of Jewish descent to Jewish Volk. Under the Nazi regime, "they used language to resist discursively imposed identities and reformulated their own and their communities' sense of self." Pegelow, " 'German Jews,' 200.

17. See for example, Andreas Gotzmann et al., *Juden, Bürger, Deutsche*; Liedtke and Rechter, *Towards Normality?*; and Van Rahden, "Germans of the Jewish *Stamm*."

18. Judith Gerson has done some interesting work on this topic. She finds that in her analysis of the memoirs of refugee men in the United States, there is a consistent emphasis on how German they were prior to emigration. Gerson uncovers two patterns of expressions of "Germanness" in their memoirs. First, the refugees stressed long-standing genealogical ties to specific regions in Germany. Second, the refugee men proved their "Germanness" through descriptions of their own or family

members' service in the German military between the Franco-Prussian War through World War I. Upon reflection, I realized that these common narratives were woven into the refugee memoirs and interviews of a wide range of women and men in both Great Britain and the United States. Gerson, "Family Matters."

19. Berghahn, *Continental Britons*, 182.

20. Ambrose, *The Suitcase in the Garage*, 281.

21. Ibid., 351, from his diary dated April 5, 1942.

22. Tergit, "How They Resettled," 55.

23. Sheldon, "The Younger Generation," in *Britain's New Citizens*, AJR, 71.

24. Herbert Freeden, "Britain's New Citizens," *Congress Weekly*, 23 (November 19, 1956), 9.

25. Future research might explore the degree to which German Jews' "whiteness" served as a kind of capital that aided in their ability to blend in in the United States and the UK, especially after the influx into Britain of "Imperial" immigrants from the West Indies and India in the late 1940s and 1950s. Another area of future study could be the connections between German Jewish refugees and the U.S. civil rights movement. Martin Luther King Jr. frequently made references to the plight of Jews in Nazi Germany in his early speeches. Gabrielle Simon Edgcomb's *From Swastika to Jim Crow: Refugee Scholars at Black Colleges* (Malabar, FL: Krieger, 1993) touches on this.

26. "Statement of Policy," *Aufbau Almanac*, 9.

27. Aronsohn, letter to Bertha Cohn, Bertha Cohn Papers.

28. Rosenthal, letter.

29. Laky, *On Being Jewish*, 94.

30. Koppel, *My Autobiography*, 27.

31. Koppel, *Citizenship None*, 13.

32. Lowenstein, *Frankfurt on the Hudson*, 251–52.

33. Grebler, *German-Jewish Immigrants*, 70.

34. *Aufbau Almanac*, 1.

35. Katz, diaries, July 5, 1936.

36. Grebler, *German-Jewish Immigrants*, 72.

37. Introduction, *Aufbau Almanac*, 18.

38. Irene White, Interview for *London Voices*, Museum of London.

39. Grossman, "German Jews as Provincial," 163.

40. Berghahn, *Continental Britons*, 216.

41. Stevens, *The Dispossessed*, 145.

42. Herbert Strauss, introduction, *Jewish Immigrants of the Nazi Period in the USA*, xiii.

43. Grebler, *German-Jewish Immigrants*, 103.

44. Baumel, Introduction, in *Don't Wave Goodbye*, eds. Jason and Posner, 16–17.

Conclusion

1. London, *Whitehall and the Jews*, 19.

2. Recent publications that also do so include Susan Cohen, *Rescue the Perishing: Eleanor Rathbone and the Refugees* (London: Vallentine Mitchell, 2010). More critical works include Pamela Shatzkes, *Holocaust and Rescue: Impotent or Indifferent? Anglo-Jewry, 1938–1945* (London: Palgrave Macmillan, 2002); and Frank Caestecker and Bob Moore's edited collection of comparative essays on European policy called *Refugees from Nazi Germany and the Liberal European States* (New York: Berghahn Books, 2010).

3. British Ministry of Information in cooperation with the War Office and Ministry of Home Security, "If the Invader Comes: What to Do and How to Do It," (1940) and "Personal Protection against Gas," *Air Raid Precautions 1* (London, 1938).

4. Anthony Grenville, AJR Journal (July 2007).

5. See Sonya O. Rose, *Which People's War? National Identity and Citizenship in Wartime Britain, 1939–1945* (Oxford: Oxford University Press, 2003).

6. Edward Timms, in *Kindertransport to Britain*, eds. Hammel and Lewkowitz, 129.

7. For a detailed personal account of a refugee soldier in the British army see Bentwich, *I Understand the Risks*.

8. Franklin, "Victim Soldiers." This does not include the number of Austrians and other German speakers serving in the military. See the film *Ritchie Boys* about refugee soldiers at Camp Ritchie.

9. Ernest Stock, interview with author, November 27, 2000.

10. Berghahn, *Continental Britons*, 127.

11. Lowenstein, *Frankfurt on the Hudson*, 249.

12. I am impressed with the approach of Marion Kaplan's article, "Friendship on the Margins" and am considering a similar project on relationships between individual refugees and American and Anglo-Jews, as well as refugee personal relationships with non-Jewish Americans and Britons. It would be interesting to extend it to the second and, perhaps, third generations as well.

13. Research that examines aspects of this include Esther Jilovsky, Jordana Silverstein, and David Slucki, eds., *In the Shadows of Memory: The Holocaust and the Third Generation* (London: Vallentine Mitchell, 2015); Richard Alba et al., eds., "Only English by the Third Generation? Loss and Preservation of the Mother Tongue among the Grandchildren of Contemporary Immigrants," *Demography* 3, no. 39 (August 2002): 467–84; and Rebecca L. Clark, Jennifer E. Glick, and Regina M. Bures, "Immigrant Families over the Life Course: Research Directions and Needs," *Journal of Family Issues* 30 (2009): 852–72.

Bibliography

Abbey, William, Charmian Brinson, Richard Dove, Marian Malet, and Jennifer Taylor, eds. *Between Two Languages: German-speaking Exiles in Great Britain, 1933–1945.* Stuttgart: Hans-Dieter Heinz, 1995.
Abella, Irving M., and Harold Martin Troper. *None Is Too Many: Canada and the Jews of Europe, 1933–1948.* New York: Random House, 1983.
Adamic, Louis. *What's Your Name?* New York: Harper and Brothers, 1942.
Alba, Richard, John Logan, Amy Lutz, and Brian Stults. "Only English by the Third Generation? Loss and Preservation of the Mother Tongue among the Grandchildren of Contemporary Immigrants." *Demography* 39, no. 3 (August 2002): 467–84.
Alba, Richard, and Mary C. Waters, eds. *The Next Generation, Immigrant Youth in a Comparative Perspective.* New York: New York University Press, 2011.
Ambrose, Kenneth. *The Suitcase in the Garage: Letters and Photographs of a German-Jewish Family, 1800–1950.* London: Self-Published Memoir, 1996.
American Friends Service Committee. *Refugee Facts: A Study of German Refugees in America.* Philadelphia: American Friends Service Committee, 1939.
Anderson, Perry. "Components of National Culture." *New Left Review* 50 (1969): 3–58.
Angell, Norman, and Dorothy Buxton. *You and the Refugee: The Morals and Economics of the Problem.* London: Penguin, 1939.
Appelbaum, Peter C. *Loyal Sons: Jews in the German Army in the Great War.* London: Vallentine Mitchell, 2015.
Aronsfeld, Caesar C. *Wanderer from My Birth.* London: Janus, 1997.
Ash, Mitchell, and Alfons Söllner, eds. *Forced Migration and Scientific Change: Émigré German-speaking Scientists and Scholars after 1933.* Cambridge: Cambridge University Press, 1996.
Association of Jewish Refugees in Great Britain. *Britain's New Citizens: The Story of the Refugees from Germany and Austria.* London: Association of Jewish Refugees in Great Britain, 1951.
Baader, Benjamin Maria. *Gender, Judaism, and Bourgeois Culture in Germany, 1800–1870.* Bloomington: Indiana University Press, 2006.

———, Sharon Gillerman, and Paul Lerner, eds. *Jewish Masculinities: German Jews, Gender, and History*. Bloomington: Indiana University Press, 2012.

Backhaus, Fritz, Gisela Engel, Robert Liberles, and Margarete Schlueter, eds. *The Frankfurt Judengasse: Jewish Life in an Early Modern German City*. London: Vallentine Mitchell, 2010.

Bahr, Ehrhard. *Weimar on the Pacific: German Exile Culture in Los Angeles and the Crisis of Modernism*. Berkeley: University of California Press, 2007.

Baily, Samuel L. *Immigrants in the Lands of Promise: Italians in Buenos Aires and New York City, 1870–1914*. Ithaca: Cornell University Press, 1999.

Baldassar, Loretta, Cora Baldock, and Raelene Wilding. *Families Caring across Borders: Migration Aging and Transnational Caregiving*. New York: Palgrave McMillan, 2007.

Barkai, Avraham. *Branching Out: German-Jewish Immigration to the United States, 1820–1914*. New York: Holmes and Meier, 1994.

Baumel-Schwartz, Judith Tydor. *Never Look Back: The Jewish Refugee Children in Great Britain, 1938–1945*. West Lafayette, IN: Purdue University Press, 2012.

Beatson, J., and Reinhard Zimmermann, eds. *Jurists Uprooted: German-Speaking Émigré Lawyers in Twentieth-Century Britain*. Oxford: Oxford University Press, 2004.

Bentwich, Norman. *The Refugees from Germany: April 1933 to December 1935*. London: G. Allen and Unwin, 1936.

———. *Jewish Youth Comes Home: The Story of the Youth Aliyah, 1933–1943*. London: Victor Gollancz, 1944.

———. *I Understand the Risks: The Story of the Refugees from Nazi Oppression Who Fought in the British Forces in the World War*. London: Victor Gollancz, 1950.

———. *The Rescue and Achievement of Refugee Scholars: The Story of Displaced Scholars and Scientists, 1933–1952*. The Hague: Martinus Nijhoff, 1953.

———. *They Found Refuge: An Account of British Jewry's Work for Victims of Nazi Oppression*. London: Cresset Press, 1956.

Benz, Wolfgang, Claudia Curio, and Andrea Hammel, eds. *Die Kindertransporte 1938/39: Rettung und Integration*. Frankfurt: Fischer Taschenbuch Verlag, 2003.

Berghahn, Klaus, ed. *The German-Jewish Dialogue Reconsidered: A Symposium in Honor of George L. Mosse*. New York: Peter Lang, 1996.

Berghahn, Marion. *Continental Britons: German-Jewish Refugees from Nazi Germany*. Oxford: Berg, 1984.

Berrol, Selma S. *East Side / East End: East European Jews in London and New York, 1870–1920*. Westport, CT: Praeger, 1994.

———. *Growing Up American: Immigrant Children in America Then and Now*. New York: Twayne, 1996.

Bhatti, Anil, and Johannes H. Voight, eds. *Jewish Exile in India*. New Delhi: Manohar, 1999.

Biale, David, ed. *Cultures of the Jews: A New History*. New York: Schocken, 2002.

Bihler, Lori Gemeiner. "Omis and Grandmas: A Community of German-Jewish Women in Washington Heights, New York," in *Beyond Camps and Forced*

Labour: Current International Research on Survivors of Nazi Persecution, eds. Johannes-Dieter Steinert and Inge Wever-Newth. Osnabrück: Secolo, 2005.

Blakeney, Michael. *Australia and the Jewish Refugees, 1933–1948*. Sydney, NSW: Croom Helm Australia, 1985.

Bloomsbury House. *Mistress and Maid: General Information for the Use of Domestic Refugees and Their Employers*. London: Bloomsbury House, 1940.

Bodek, Richard, and Simon Lewis. *The Fruits of Exile: Central European Intellectual Immigration to America in the Age of Fascism*. Columbia: University of South Carolina Press, 2011.

Breitman, Richard, and Alan M. Kraut. *American Refugee Policy and European Jewry, 1933–1945*. Bloomington: Indiana University Press, 1987.

Brenner, Michael. *The Renaissance of Jewish Culture in Weimar Germany*. New Haven: Yale University Press, 1996.

———, Rainer Liedtke, and David Rechter, eds. *Two Nations: British and German Jews in Comparative Perspective*. Tübingen: Mohr Siebeck, 1999.

Brinson, Charmian. "A Woman's Place . . . ? German-speaking Women in Exile in Britain, 1933–1945." *German Life and Letters* LI, no. 2 (April 1998): 204–24.

Brinson, Charmian, Richard Dove, Marian Malet, and Jennifer Taylor, eds. *"England? Aber, wo liegt es?" Deutsche und österreichische Emigranten in Großritannien 1933–1945*. London: Institute of Germanic Studies, 1996.

Brinson, Charmian, Anna Muller-Harlin, and Julia Winckler. *His Majesty's Loyal Internee: Fred Uhlman in Captivity*. London: Vallentine Mitchell, 2009.

Brinson, Charmian, and Richard Dove. *Politics by Other Means: The Free German League of Culture in London, 1939–1946*. London: Vallentine Mitchell, 2010.

Brinton, Clarence Crane. *The United States and Britain*. Cambridge: Harvard University Press, 1945.

British Ministry of Food. *Food Facts for the Kitchen Front: A Book of Wartime Recipes and Hints*. London, 1941.

———. "Your Food in Wartime." *Public Information Leaflet* 14. London, 1939.

British Ministry of Information with the War Office and Ministry of Home Security. *If the Invader Comes: What to Do and How to Do It*. London, 1940.

———. "Personal Protection against Gas." *Air Raid Precautions Handbook* 1. London: H.M. Stationer's Office, 1938.

Bronner, Simon J. *Jews at Home: The Domestication of Identity*. Oxford: The Littman Library of Jewish Civilization, 2010.

Browning, Christopher. *Remembering Survival: Inside a Nazi Slave-Labor Camp*. New York: W.W. Norton, 2011.

Burr, G., and Marion Cohen, eds. *Yesterday's Kitchen: Jewish Communities and their Food before 1939: The Way to a Man's Heart*. London: Vallentine Mitchell, 1993.

Caestecker, Frank, and Bob Moore, eds. *Refugees from Nazi Germany and the Liberal European States*. New York: Berghahn Books, 2010.

Camino, Linda, and Ruth M. Krufeld, eds. *Reconstructing Lives, Recapturing Meaning: Refugee Identity, Gender, and Culture Change*. Washington, DC: Gordon and Breach, 1994.
Caplan, Gregory. "Militärische Männlichkeit in der deutsch-jüdischen Geschichte." *Die Philosophin* 22 (2000): 85–100.
Carlebach, Alexander. "The German-Jewish Immigration and Its Influence on Synagogue Life in the USA 1933–1942." *LBI YB* 9 (1964): 351–72.
Caron, Vicki. *Uneasy Asylum: France and the Jewish Refugee Crisis, 1933–1942*. Stanford: Stanford University Press, 1999.
Cesarani, David, and Tony Kushner. *The Internment of Aliens in Twentieth-Century Britain*. London: Frank Cass, 1993.
Cesarani, David, Tony Kushner, and Milton Shain, eds. *Place and Displacement in Jewish History and Memory: Zakor v'Makor*. London: Vallentine Mitchell, 2009.
Chappell, Connery. *Island of Barbed Wire: Internment on the Isle of Man in World War Two*. London: Robert Hale, 1984.
Cluse, Christoph, ed. *The Jews of Europe in the Middle Ages: Proceedings of the International Symposium Held at Speyer 20–25 October 2002*. Turnhout: Brepols, 2004.
Cohen, Felix S. *Immigration and National Welfare*. League for Industrial Democracy. New York, 1940.
Cohen, Susan. *Rescue the Perishing: Eleanor Rathbone and the Refugees*. London: Vallentine Mitchell, 2010.
Cohn, Alfred. "Exiled Physicians in the United States." *American Scholar* 12 (July 1943): 352–61.
Colcord, Joanna. "Refugee Social Workers." *Social Work Today* 7 (December 1939): 37–38.
Congregation Habonim. *Anniversary Yearbook, 1939–1949*. New York: 1949.
Coser, Lewis. *Refugee Scholars in America: Their Cultural Impact and their Experiences*. New Haven: Yale University Press, 1984.
Crawford, Dorothy Lamb. *A Windfall of Musicians: Hitler's Emigres and Exiles in Southern California*. New Haven: Yale University Press, 2011.
Daily Express War Time Cookery Book: Practical Advice and Recipes Specially Prepared for War Time Conditions. London: Daily Express, 1939.
Davie, Maurice R. *Refugees in America*. New York: Harper and Brothers, 1947.
———, and Samuel Koenig. *The Refugees are Now Americans*. New York Public Affairs Committee: Committee for the Study of Recent Immigration from Europe. New York, 1945.
Diemling, Maria, and Guiseppe Veltri, eds. *The Jewish Body: Corporeality, Society, and Identity in Renaissance and Early Modern Period*. London: Brill, 2009.
Diner, Hasia. *Lower East Side Memories: A Jewish Place in America*. Princeton: Princeton University Press, 2000.
———. *Hungering for America: Italian, Irish, and Jewish Foodways in the Age of Migration*. Cambridge: Harvard University Press, 2001.

Dobkowski, Michael. *Jewish American Volunteer Organizations*. Westport, CT: Greenwood, 1986.

Dorner, Jane. *Fashion in the Twenties and Thirties*. London: Allan, 1973.

Dove, Richard, ed. *"Totally Un-English?" Britain's Internment of "Enemy Aliens" in Two World Wars*. Yearbook of the Research Centre for German and Austrian Exile Studies 7 (Amsterdam: Rodopi, 2005).

Dwork, Debórah, and Robert Jan van Pelt. *Flight from the Reich: Refugee Jews, 1933–1946*. New York: W. W. Norton, 2009.

Edgcomb, Gabrielle Simon. *From Swastika to Jim Crow: Refugee Scholars at Black Colleges*. Malabar, FL: Krieger Publication, 1993.

Edsall, David, and Tracy Putnam. "The Émigré Physician in America." *Journal of the American Medical Association* 117 (November 1941): 1881–88.

Elazar, Daniel, and Morton Weinfeld, eds. *Still Moving: Recent Jewish Migration in Comparative Perspective*. Edison, NJ: Transaction Publishers, 1999.

Elon, Amos. *Founder: A Portrait of the First Rothschild and His Time*. New York: Penguin, 1996.

Emanuel, Muriel, and Vera Gissing. *Nicholas Winton and the Rescued Generation: Save One Life, Save the World*. London: Vallentine Mitchell, 2002.

Endelman, Todd. *Radical Assimilation in English Jewish History, 1656–1945*. Bloomington: Indiana University Press, 1990.

Engel, Sophie. "Refugees from Germany in English Literature and Art." *Jewish Forum* 22 (March 1939): 20.

Fair-Schulz, Axel, and Mario Kessler, eds. *German Scholars in Exile: New Studies in Intellectual History*. Lanham, MD: Lexington Books, 2011.

Fast, Vera K. *Children's Exodus: A History of the Kindertransport*. London: I. B. Tauris, 2011.

Feiner, Shmuel, and Natalie Naimark-Goldberg. *Cultural Revolution in Berlin: Jews in the Age of Enlightenment*. Chicago: University of Chicago Press, 2011.

Feingold, Henry L. *The Politics of Rescue: The Roosevelt Administration and the Holocaust, 1938–1945*. New Brunswick: Rutgers University Press, 1970.

Fermi, Laura. *Illustrious Immigrants: The Intellectual Migration from Europe*. Chicago: University of Chicago Press, 1968.

Fleck, Christian. *A Transatlantic History of the Social Sciences: Robber Barons, the Third Reich and the Invention of Empirical Social Research*. London: Bloomsbury, 2011.

Foner, Nancy. "West Indians in New York City and London." *International Migration Review* 13 (1979): 284–97.

———. "Immigrant Women and Work in New York City, Then and Now." *Journal of American Ethnic History* 18 (1999): 95–113.

———. *In a New Land: A Comparative View of Immigration*. New York: New York University Press, 2005.

———. "How Exceptional Is New York? Migration and Multi-Culturalism in the Empire City." *Ethnic and Racial Studies* 30, no. 6 (2007): 999–1023.

———, ed. *Across Generations: Immigrant Families in America*. New York: New York University Press, 2009.

Foner, Nancy, and Richard Alba. "Immigrant Religion in the U.S. and Western Europe: Bridge or Barrier to Inclusion?" *International Migration Review* 42 (2008): 360–92.

Fortier, Anne-Marie. *Migrant Belongings: Memory, Space, Identity*. London: Berg, 2000.

Franklin, Joshua. "Victim Soldiers: German-Jewish Refugees in the American Armed Forces during World War II." Honors thesis, Clark University, 2006.

Freeden, Herbert. "Britain's New Citizens." *Congress Weekly* 23 (November 1956): 8–9.

Freud-Kandel, Miri. *Orthodox Judaism in Britain since 1913: An Ideology Foresaken*. London: Vallentine Mitchell, 2006.

Friedman, Saul S. *No Haven for the Oppressed: United States Policy toward Jewish Refugees, 1938–1945*. Detroit: Wayne State University Press, 1973.

Friesel, Evyatar. "Jewish and German-Jewish Historical Views: Problems of a New Synthesis." *LBI YB* 43 (1998): 323–36.

Gabaccia, Donna. *From Sicily to Elizabeth Street: Housing and Social Change among Italian Immigrants*. Albany: State University of New York Press, 1984.

———. *From the Other Side: Women, Gender, and Immigrant Life in the U.S., 1820–1990*. Bloomington: Indiana University Press, 1994.

———. *We Are What We Eat: Ethnic Food and the Making of Americans*. Cambridge: Harvard University Press, 1998.

———. *Italy's Many Diasporas*. Seattle: University of Washington Press, 2000.

Gartner, Lloyd P. *American and British Jews in the Age of Great Migration*. London: Vallentine Mitchell, 2009.

Gay, Peter. *My German Question: Growing Up in Nazi Berlin*. New Haven: Yale University Press, 1998.

Gay, Ruth. *The Jews of Germany: A Historical Portrait*. New Haven: Yale University Press, 1992.

———. *Unfinished People*. New York: W. W. Norton, 1996.

George, Manfred. "Müssen Sie Washington heißen?" *Aufbau* (August 6, 1943).

German-Jewish Aid Committee and the Jewish Board of Deputies. *While You Are in England: Helpful Information and Guidance for Every Refugee*. Essex, 1938.

German-Jewish Club. *Aufbau Almanac: The Immigrant's Handbook*. New York, 1941.

Gershon, Karen, ed. *We Came as Children: A Collective Autobiography of Refugees*. London: Victor Gollancz, 1966.

Gerson, Judith. "In Between States: National Identity Practices Among German-Jewish Immigrants." *Political Psychology* 22, no. 1 (2001): 179–98.

———, and Diane Wolf, eds. *Sociology Confronts the Holocaust: Memories and Identities in Jewish Diasporas*. Durham: Duke University Press, 2007.

Gilbertson, Greta A. "Women's Labor and Enclave Employment: The Case of Dominican and Colombian Women in New York City." *International Migration Review* 3, no. 29 (Autumn 1995): 657–70.

Gillerman, Sharon. *Germans into Jews: Remaking the Jewish Social Body in the Weimar Republic*. Stanford: Stanford University Press, 2009.
Gillman, Peter, and Leni Gillman. *"Collar the Lot!" How Britain Interned and Expelled Its Wartime Refugees*. London: Quartet Books, 1980.
Glanz, Rudolf. "German-Jewish Names in America." *Jewish Social Studies* 23, no. 3 (July 1961): 143–69.
Glenn, Susan A. *Daughters of the Shtetl: Life and Labor in the Immigrant Generation*. Ithaca: Cornell University Press, 1991.
Godley, A. C. "Enterprise and Culture: Jewish Immigrants in London and New York, 1880–1914." Ph.D. dissertation, London School of Economics, 1993.
Godley, Andrew C. *Jewish Immigrant Entrepreneurship in London and New York, 1881–1914: Enterprise and Culture*. London: Palgrave, 2001.
Gottlieb, Amy Zahl. *Men of Vision: Anglo-Jewry's Aid to Victims of the Nazi Regime, 1933–1945*. London: Weidenfeld and Nicolson, 1998.
Gotzmann, Andreas, Rainer Liedtke, and Till van Rahden, eds. *Juden, Bürger, Deutsche: Zur Geschichte von Vielfalt und Differenz, 1800–1933*. Tübingen: Mohr Siebeck, 2001.
Grady, Tim. *The German-Jewish Soldiers of the First World War in History and Memory*. Liverpool: Liverpool University Press, 2012.
Green, Nancy. "The Comparative Method and Poststructural Structuralism—New Perspectives for Migration Studies." *Journal of American Ethnic History* 13 (Summer 1994): 3–22.
———. *Ready to Wear, Ready to Work: A Century of Industry and Immigrants in Paris and New York*. Durham: Duke University Press, 1997.
Greenspan, Henry. *On Listening to Holocaust Survivors: Recounting and Life History*. Westport, CT: Praeger, 1998.
———. *On Listening to Holocaust Survivors: Beyond Testimony*. Minneapolis: Paragon House, 2010.
Grenville, Anthony, ed. *German-Speaking Exiles in Great Britain*. Yearbook of the Research Centre for German and Austrian Exile Studies, Vol. 2. Amsterdam: Rodopi, 2000.
———. *Refugees from the Third Reich in Britain*. Yearbook of the Research Centre for German and Austrian Exile Studies, Vol. 4. Amsterdam: Rodopi, 2002.
———. *Jewish Refugees from Nazi Germany and Austria in Britain, 1933–1970: Their Image in AJR Information*. London: Vallentine Mitchell, 2010.
Grenville, Anthony, and Marian Malet, eds. *Changing Countries: The Experience and Achievement of German-speaking Exiles from Hitler in Britain, 1933 to Today: A Study Based on Thirty-Four Interviews*. London: Libris, 2002.
Grenville, Anthony, and Andrea Reiter, eds. *"I Didn't Want to Float: I Wanted to Belong to Something": Refugee Organizations in Britain, 1933–1945*. Yearbook of the Research Centre for German and Austrian Exile Studies, Vol. 10. Amsterdam: Rodopi, 2008.

Grossman, Atina. "German Women Doctors from Berlin in New York: Maternity and Modernity in Weimar and in Exile." *Feminist Studies* 19 (1993): 65–88.

———. "Versions of Home: German Jewish Refugee Papers: Out of the Closet and into the Archives." *New German Critique* 90 (Fall 2003): 95–122.

———. "German Jews as Provincial Cosmopolitans: Reflections from the Upper West Side." *LBI YB* (2008): 157–68.

Grossman, Kurt. *The Contribution of the German Immigrants to American Life: Economic and Cultural Capacity of the Newcomers.* American Jewish Joint Distribution Committee, New York, 1939.

———. *Emigration: Geschichte der Hitler-Flüchtlinge 1933–1945.* Frankfurt, Europäische Verlagsanstalt, 1969.

Groth, Michael. *The Road to New York: The Emigration of Berlin Journalists, 1933–1945.* Munich: K. G. Saur, 1984.

Guske, Iris. *Trauma and Attachment in the Kindertransport Context: German-Jewish Child Refugees' Accounts of Displacement and Acculturation in Britain.* Newcastle: Cambridge Scholars, 2009.

Haesler, Alfred A. *The Lifeboat Is Full: Switzerland and the Refugees, 1933–1945.* New York: Funk and Wagnalls, 1969.

Hammel, Andrea, and Anthony Grenville, eds. *Refugee Archives: Theory and Practice.* Yearbook of the Research Centre for German and Austrian Exile Studies, Vol. 9. Amsterdam: Rodopi, 2007.

Hammel, Andrea, and Bea Lewkowitz, eds. *Kindertransport to Britain, New Perspectives.* Amsterdam/New York: Rodopi, 2012.

Hannam, Charles. *Almost an Englishman.* London: Deutsch, 1979.

Harris, Mark J., and Deborah Oppenheimer, eds. *Into the Arms of Strangers: Stories of the Kindertransport.* London: Bloomsbury, 2000.

Heilberg, Freda. "Experiences, Attitudes, and Problems of German-Jewish Refugees." *Jewish Social Services Quarterly* 15, no. 3 (March 1939): 322–27.

Heilbut, Anthony. *Exiled in Paradise: German Refugee Artists and Intellectuals in America from the 1930s to the Present.* New York: Viking Press, 1983.

Helfer, Martha, and William C. Donahue, eds. *Nexus I: Essays in German-Jewish Studies.* Camden, NJ: Camden House, 2011.

Hill, Paula. "Anglo Jewry and the Refugee Children, 1938–1945." Ph.D. dissertation, University of London, 2002.

Hoerder, Dirk, and Jörg Nagler, eds. *People in Transit: German Migrations in Comparative Perspective, 1820–1930.* Cambridge: Cambridge University Press, 1995.

Holfter, Gisela M. B., ed. *German-Speaking Exiles in Ireland, 1933–1945.* Amsterdam: Rodopi, 2006.

Holmes, Colin, ed. *Immigrants and Minorities in British Society.* London: Allen and Unwin, 1977.

Huder, Walter, Claus-Dieter Krohn, et al. *Jüdische Emigration: zwischen Assimilation und Verfolgung, Akkulturation und jüdischer Identität.* Munich: Edition Text und Kritik, 2001.

Israel, Jonathan. *European Jewry in the Age of Mercantilism, 1550–1750*. Oxford: Clarendon Press, 1985.
Jackman, Jarrell, and Carla Borden, eds. *The Muses Flee Hitler: Cultural Transfer and Adaptation, 1930–1945*. Washington, DC: Smithsonian, 1983.
Jason, Philip K., and Iris Posner, eds. *Don't Wave Goodbye: The Children's Flight from Nazi Persecution to American Freedom*. Westport, CT: Praeger, 2004.
Joppke, Christian. *Immigration and the Nation-State: The United States, Germany, and Great Britain*. Oxford: Oxford University Press, 1999.
Joselit, Jenna Weissman. *The Wonders of America: Reinventing Jewish Culture 1880–1950*. New York: Hill and Wang, 1994.
———. *A Perfect Fit: Clothes, Character, and the Promise of America*. New York: Metropolitan Books, 2001.
Joselit, Jenna Weissman, and Susan Braunstein, eds. *Getting Comfortable in New York: The American Jewish Home, 1880–1950*. New York: Jewish Museum, 1990.
Joseph, Samuel. "Survey of Jewish Immigration to the United States." *Jewish Social Services Quarterly* (March 1939): 299–304.
Kaplan, Marion. *The Making of the Jewish Middle Class: Women, Family and Identity in Imperial Germany*. New York: Oxford University Press, 1991.
———. *Between Dignity and Despair: Jewish Life in Nazi Germany*. New York: Oxford University Press, 1998.
———. "Friendship on the Margins: Jewish Social Relations in Imperial Germany." *Central European History* 34, no. 4 (2001): 471–501.
———. *Dominican Haven: The Jewish Refugee Settlement in Sosúa, 1940–1945*. New York: Museum of Jewish Heritage, 2008.
Kapp, Yvonne, and Margaret Mynatt. *British Policy and the Refugees, 1933–1941*. London: Frank Cass, 1997.
Katz, Jacob. *Out of the Ghetto: The Social Background of Jewish Emancipation, 1770–1870*. Cambridge: Harvard University Press, 1973.
Kennedy, George, and Allen Bell. *Humanity and the Refugees*. Jewish Historical Society of England. 1939.
Keogh, Dermot. *Jews in Twentieth-Century Ireland: Refugees, Anti-Semitism, and the Holocaust*. Cork, Ireland: Cork University Press, 1998.
Kerr, Judith. *The Other Way Round*. London: Putnam, 1975.
Kershen, Anne, and Jonathan A. Romain. *Tradition and Change: A History of Reform Judaism in Britain, 1840–1995*. London: Vallentine Mitchell, 1995.
Khandelwal, Madhulika. *Food and the Migrant Experience*. London: Ashgate, 2002.
Kirchheimer, Manfred, and Gloria DeVidas Kirchheimer, eds. *We Were So Beloved: Autobiography of a German-Jewish Community*. Pittsburgh: University of Pittsburgh Press, 1997.
Kochan, Miriam. *Britain's Internees in the Second World War*. London: Macmillan, 1983.
Korn, Bertram Wallace. *German-Jewish Intellectual Influences on American Jewish Life, 1842–1972*. Syracuse: Syracuse University Press, 1972.

Kranzler, David. *Japanese, Nazis, and Jews: The Jewish Refugee Community of Shanghai, 1938–1945.* New York: Yeshiva University Press, 1976.

Kröger, Marianne, and Andrea Hammel. "Child Exiles: A New Research Area?" *SHOFAR* 23, no. 1 (Fall 2004): 8–20.

Krohn, Claus Dieter. *Wissenschaft im Exil: deutsche Sozial- und Wirtschaftswissenschaftler in den USA und die New School for Social Research.* Frankfurt am Main: Campus, 1987.

———. *Intellectuals in Exile: Refugee Scholars and the New School for Social Research.* Amherst: University of Massachusetts Press, 1993.

———, and Hans Ulrich Esslinger, eds. *Die Emigration Deutschsprachiger Wirtschaftswissenschaftler nach 1933.* Stuttgart: Universität Hohenheim, 1992.

Kugelmass, J. Alvin. "Name-Changing and What It Gets You: Twenty-five Who Did It." *Commentary* 14 (August 1952): 145–50.

Kushner, Tony. *The Persistence of Prejudice: Anti-Semitism in British Society during the Second World War.* Manchester: Manchester University Press, 1989.

———. *The Holocaust and the Liberal Imagination: A Social and Cultural History.* Oxford: Blackwell, 1994.

———. *Remembering Refugees: Then and Now.* Manchester: Manchester University Press, 2007.

Kushner, Tony, and Katharine Knox. *Refugees in an Age of Genocide: Global, National, and Local Perspectives during the Twentieth Century.* London: Frank Cass, 1999.

Kushner, Tony, and Nadia Valman, eds. *Remembering Cable Street: Fascism and Anti-Fascism in British Society.* London: Vallentine Mitchell, 2000.

Kwiet, Konrad. "The Second Time Around: Re-Acculturation of German-Jewish Refugees in Australia." *The Journal of Holocaust Education* 10, no. 1 (June 2001): 34–49.

LaCapra, Dominick. *Representing the Holocaust: History, Theory, Trauma.* Ithaca: Cornell University Press, 1994.

Lafitte, Francois. *The Interment of Aliens.* London: Penguin, 1940.

Lai, Him Mark. *Becoming Chinese American: A History of Communities and Institutions.* Walnut Creek, CA: Alta Mira Press, 2004.

Langer, Lawrence L. *Holocaust Testimonies: The Ruins of Memory.* New Haven: Yale University Press, 1991.

Langman, Anne. "The Problem of the Refugee Physician." Master's thesis, New York School of Social Work, Columbia University, June 1940.

Laqueur, Walter. *Generation Exodus: The Fate of Young Jewish Refugees from Nazi Germany.* Hanover, NH: University Press of New England, 2001.

Leigh, Charles. *The Autobiography of a Jewish Refugee.* London: Charles Leigh, 1990.

Leighton-Langer, Peter. *The King's Own Loyal Enemy Aliens: German and Austrian Refugees in Britain's Armed Forces, 1939–1945.* London: Vallentine Mitchell, 2006.

Leiper, Henry Smith. "Those German Refugees." *Current History* 50 (May 1939): 19–22.

Leverton, Bertha, and Shmuel Lowensohn, eds. *I Came Alone: The Stories of the Kindertransports.* Lewes: Book Guild, 1990.

Levine, Rhonda F. *Class, Networks, and Identity: Replanting Jewish Lives from Nazi Germany to Rural New York.* Lanham, MD: Rowman and Littlefield, 2001.

Levy, Herbert. *Voices from the Past.* Lewes: Temple House, 1995.

Liedtke, Rainer. *Jewish Welfare in Hamburg and Manchester, 1850–1914.* New York: Oxford University Press, 1998.

Liedtke, Rainer, and David Rechter, eds. *Towards Normality? Acculturation and Modern German Jewry.* Tübingen: Mohr Siebeck, 2003.

Lipman, V. D. *A Social History of the Jews of Britain, 1850–1950.* London: Watts, 1954.

London, Louise. *Whitehall and the Jews, 1933 . . . 1948: British Immigration Policy, Jewish Refugees, and the Holocaust.* Cambridge: Cambridge University Press, 2000.

Lowenstein, Judith. "Vocational Adjustment of Jewish Immigrant Women and Girls Assisted by the New York Section of the National Council for Jewish Women." Master's thesis, New York School of Social Work, Columbia University, 1938.

Lowenstein, Sharon R. *Token Refuge: The Story of the Jewish Refugee Shelter at Oswego, 1944–1946.* Bloomington: Indiana University Press, 1986.

Lowenstein, Steven M. *Frankfurt on the Hudson: The German-Jewish Community of Washington Heights, 1933–1983: Its Structure and Culture.* Detroit: Wayne State University Press, 1989.

Lowenthal, Ernst F., ed. *Philo-Atlas: Handbuch für die jüdische Auswanderung.* Berlin: Philo-Verlag, 1938.

Lucassen, Jan, and Leo Lucassen, eds. *Migration, Migration History, History: Old Paradigms and New Perspectives.* New York: Peter Lang, 1997.

Maass, Ernest. "Integration and Name Changing among Jewish Refugees from Central Europe in the United States." *Names* 6, no. 3 (September 1958): 129–71.

Marrus, Michael. *The Unwanted: European Refugees and the Twentieth Century.* New York: Oxford University Press, 1985.

Mauch, Christof, and Joe Salmons, eds. *German-Jewish Identities in America.* Madison: University of Wisconsin Press, 2003.

Medawar, Jean, and David Pyke. *Hitler's Gift: Scientists who Fled Nazi Germany.* London: Richard Cohen, 2000.

Mendes-Flohr, Paul. *German Jews: A Dual Identity.* New Haven: Yale University Press, 1999.

Meyer, Michael. *Response to Modernity: A History of the Reform Movement in Judaism.* New York: Oxford University Press, 1988.

Meyer, Michael, et al., eds. *German-Jewish History in Modern Times, Volumes 1–4.* New York: Columbia University Press, 1996–98.

Meyer-Erlach, Georg. "Die 60 häufigsten jüdischen Familiennamen." *Jüdische Familienforschung-Mitteilungen* 8 (Berlin, December 1932): 500–503.

Milbank, Caroline Rennolds. *New York Fashion: The Evolution of American Style.* New York: Harry N. Abrams, 1989.

Min, Pyong Gap. *Changes and Conflicts: Korean Immigrant Families in New York.* Boston: Allyn and Bacon, 1998.

Moon, Seungsook. "Immigration and Mothering: Case Studies from Two Generations of Korean Immigrant Women." *Gender and Society* 17 (December 2003): 854–56.

Morris, Katherine. *Odyssey of Exile: Jewish Women Flee the Nazis for Brazil.* Detroit: Wayne State University Press, 1996.

Morse, Arthur. *While Six Million Died: A Chronicle of American Apathy.* New York: Random House, 1967.

Mosse, George L. *German Jews beyond Judaism.* Bloomington: Indiana University Press, 1985.

Mosse, Werner E., and Julius Carlebach, eds. *Second Chance: Two Centuries of German-Speaking Jews in the United Kingdom.* Tübingen: Mohr Siebeck, 1991.

Niven, William, and James Jordan, eds. *Politics and Culture in Twentieth-Century Germany* Rochester: Camden House, 2003.

Orellana, Marjorie Faulstich, Lisa Dorner, and Lucila Pulido. "Accessing Assets: Immigrant Youth's Work as Family Translators or Para-phrasers." *Social Problems* 50, no. 4 (2003): 505–24.

Pegelow, Thomas. "'German Jews,' 'National Jews,' 'Jewish Volk,' 'Racial Jews'? The Constitution and Contestation of 'Jewishness' in Newspapers of Nazi Germany, 1933–1938." *Central European History* 35, no. 2 (2002): 195–221.

———, and Evyatar Friesel. "'Jewish and German-Jewish Historical Views: Problems of a New Synthesis." *Leo Baeck Institute Year Book* 43 (1998): 323.

Pessar, Patricia. "On the Homefront and in the Workplace: Integrating Immigrant Women into Feminist Discourse." *Anthropological Quarterly* 1, no. 68 (January 1995): 37–47.

Peterson Kent, Donald. *The Refugee Intellectual: The Americanization of the Immigrants of 1933–1941.* New York: Columbia University Press, 1953.

Pfanner, Helmut, F., ed. *Exile in New York: German and Austrian Writers after 1933.* Detroit: Wayne State University Press, 1983.

Pollak, Felix. "Felix Pollak: An Autobiographical Sketch." *Northeast Series* 5, no. 5 (Winter 1991): 11–24.

Pooley, Colin, and Ian Whyte, eds. *Migrants, Emigrants, and Immigrants: A Social History of Migration.* London: Routledge, 1991.

Proudfoot, Malcolm Jarvis. *European Refugees, 1939–52: A Study in Forced Population Movement.* Evanston: Northwestern University Press, 1956.

Quack, Sibylle, ed. *Between Sorrow and Strength: Women Refugees of the Nazi Period.* Cambridge: Cambridge University Press, 1995.

———. *Zuflucht Amerika: Zur Sozialgeschichte der Emigration deutsch-jüdischer Frauen in die USA 1933–1945.* Bonn: Dietz, 1995.

Radt, Jenny. *Die Juden in New York*. Berlin: Schocken, 1937.
Ramati, Alexander. *Barbed Wire on the Isle of Man: The Wartime British Internment of Jews*. New York: Harcourt Brace Jovanovich, 1980.
Rapport, Nigel, and Andrew Dawson. *Migrants of Identity: Perceptions of Home in a World of Movement*. Oxford: Berg, 1998.
Reinharz, Jehuda. *Fatherland or Promised Land: The Dilemma of the German Jew, 1893–1914*. Ann Arbor: University of Michigan Press, 1975.
Rejak, Sebastian. *Jewish Identities in Poland and America: The Impact of the Shoah on Religion and Ethnicity*. London: Vallentine Mitchell, 2011.
Reutlinger, Andrew S. "Reflections on the Anglo-American Jewish Experience: Immigrants, Workers, and Entrepreneurs in New York and London, 1870–1914." *American Jewish Historical Quarterly* 66 (1977): 473–84.
Ristaino, Marcia R. *Port of Last Resort: The Diaspora Communities of Shanghai*. Stanford: Stanford University Press, 2001.
Robison, Sophia M. *Refugees at Work*. Committee for Selected Social Studies. New York: King's Crown Press, 1942.
Rose, Paul Lawrence. *German Question–Jewish Question*. Princeton: Princeton University Press, 1992.
Rose, Sonya O. *Which People's War? National Identity and Citizenship in Wartime Britain, 1939–1945*. Oxford: Oxford University Press, 2003.
Roseman, Mark, Nils Roemer, and Neil Gregor, eds. *German History from the Margins, 1800 to the Present*. Bloomington: Indiana University Press, 2006.
Ross, James Rodman. *Escape to Shanghai: A Jewish Community in China*. New York: Maxwell Macmillan, 1994.
Rubinstein, William D. *The Myth of Rescue: Why the Democracies Could Not Have Saved More Jews from the Nazis*. New York: Routledge, 1999.
Ruderman, David B. *Early Modern Jewry: A New Cultural History*. Princeton: Princeton University Press, 2010.
Rumbaut, Ruben G. and Alejandro Portes, eds. *Ethnicities: Children of Immigrants in America*. Berkeley: University of California Press, 2001.
Ryan, Louise. "Family Matters: Emigration, Familial Networks, and Irish Women in Britain." *Sociological Review* 52 (2004): 351–70.
Saenger, Gerhart. *Today's Refugees, Tomorrow's Citizens: A Story of Americanization*. New York: Harper and Brothers, 1941.
Scherzer, Kenneth. *The Unbounded Community*. Chapel Hill: University of North Carolina Press, 1992.
Schmid, Monika. *First Language Attrition, Use, and Maintenance: The Case of German Jews in Anglophone Countries*. Philadelphia: J. Benjamins, 2002.
———. *Language Attrition*. Cambridge: Cambridge University Press, 2011.
Scholem, Gershom. "Jews and Germans." *Commentary* 42 (November 1966): 31–40.
Schreier, Barbara. *Becoming American Women: Clothing and the Jewish Immigrant Experience, 1880–1920*. Chicago: Chicago Historical Society, 1994.

Schrover, Marlou, and Floris Vermeulen. "Immigrant Organizations." *Journal of Ethnic and Migration Studies* 31 (2005): 823–32.

Schüler-Springorum, Stefanie. *Die jüdische Minderheit in Königsberg/Preussen, 1871–1945.* Göttingen: Vandenhoeck and Ruprecht, 1996.

Schwartz, Hans Martin. *USA als Einwanderungsland, Jüdische Wirklichkeit Heute, eine Schriftenreihe.* 5 Berlin: 1938.

Segura, Denise A. "Ambivalence or Continuity? Motherhood and Employment among Chicanas and Mexican Immigrant Women Workers." *Aztlan* 20 (1991): 119–50.

Seller, Maxine. *We Built Up Our Lives: Education and Community among Jewish Refugees Interned by Britain in World War Two.* Westport, CT: Greenwood, 2001.

Shapiro, Frank. *Haven in Africa.* Jerusalem: Gefen, 2002.

Shaw, Stanford J. *Turkey and the Holocaust: Turkey's Role in Rescuing Turkish and European Jewry from Nazi Persecution, 1933–1945.* New York: New York University Press, 1993.

Shepherd, Naomi. *A Refuge from Darkness: Wilfrid Israel and the Rescue of the Jews.* New York: Pantheon, 1984.

Sherman, A. J. *Island Refuge: Britain and Refugees from the Third Reich, 1933–1939.* Berkeley: University of California Press, 1973.

Silverman, Lisa. *Becoming Austrians: Jews and Culture between the World Wars.* New York: Oxford University Press, 2012.

Simpson, Sir John Hope. *The Refugee Problem: Report of a Survey.* London, 1939.

Snowman, Daniel. *The Hitler Émigrés: The Cultural Impact on Britain of Refugees from Nazism.* London: Chatto and Windus, 2002.

Snyder, Robert W. *Crossing Broadway: Washington Heights and the Promise of New York City.* Ithaca: Cornell University Press, 2014.

Sonnert, Gerhard, and Gerald James Holton. *What Happened to the Children Who Fled Nazi Persecution.* New York: Palgrave Macmillan, 2006.

Spector, Scott. "Forget Assimilation: Introducing Subjectivity to German-Jewish History." *Jewish History* 20, no. 2/3 (2006): 349–61.

Spitzer, Leo. *Hotel Bolivia: The Culture of Memory in a Refuge from Nazism.* New York: Hill and Wang, 1998.

Srebrnik, Henry Felix. *London Jews and British Communism, 1935–1945.* London: Vallentine Mitchell, 1995.

Stent, Ronald. *A Bespattered Page? The Internment of His Majesty's "Most Loyal Enemy Aliens."* London: Deutsch, 1980.

Stevens, Austin. *The Dispossessed: German Refugees in Britain.* London: Barrie and Jenkins, 1975.

Stock, Ernest. "Washington Heights' 'Fourth Reich.'" *Commentary* 11 (June 1951): 581–8.

Stone, Dan. *Responses to Nazism in Britain 1933–1939: Before War and Holocaust.* Basingstoke: Palgrave Macmillan, 2003.

Strauss, Herbert. "The Immigration and Acculturation of the German Jew in the United States of America." *LBI YB* 16 (1971): 63–94.

———. "Jewish Emigration from Germany: Nazi Policies and Jewish Responses I." *LBI YB* 25 (1980): 313–58.

———, ed. *Jewish Immigrants of the Nazi Period in the USA*. Volumes 1–6. New York: K. G. Saur, 1981.

Suarez-Orozco, Carola, and Marcelo M. Suarez-Orozco. *Children of Immigration*. Cambridge: Harvard University Press, 2001.

Sugarman, Martin. *Fighting Back: British Jewry's Contribution in the Second World War*. London: Vallentine Mitchell, 2010.

Tartakower, Arieh. "The Jewish Refugees: A Sociological Study." *Jewish Social Studies* 4 (1942): 311–48.

———, and Kurt Grossman. *The Jewish Refugee*. Institute of Jewish Affairs of the American Jewish Congress and World Jewish Congress. New York, 1944.

Taylor, Derek. *Chief Rabbi Hertz: The Wars of the Lord*. London: Vallentine Mitchell, 2014.

Timms, Edward, and Andrea Hammel, eds. *The German-Jewish Dilemma: From the Enlightenment to the Shoah*. Lewiston, NY: Edwin Mellen Press, 1999.

Timms, Edward, and Jon Hughes, eds. *Intellectual Migration and Cultural Transformation: Refugees from National Socialism in the English-speaking World*. Vienna: Springer, 2003.

Toch, Michael. *Peasants and Jews in Medieval Germany*. Aldershot: Ashgate, 2003.

———. *The Economic History of European Jews: Late Antiquity and Early Middle Ages*. Boston: Brill, 2012.

Traub, Michael. *Die jüdische Auswanderung aus Deutschland: Westeuropa, Übersee, Palästina*. Berlin: Jüdische Rundschau, 1936.

Turner, Barry. *And the Policeman Smiled: 10,000 Children Escape from Nazi Europe*. London: Bloomsbury, 1990.

Van Rahden, Till. *Juden und andere Breslauer: Die Beziehungen zwischen Juden, Protestanten und Katholiken in einer deutschen Grossstadt von 1860 bis 1925*. Göttingen: Vandenhoeck and Ruprecht, 1999.

———. "Jews and the Ambivalences of Civil Society in Germany, 1800–1933: Assessment and Reassessment." *Journal of Modern History* 77, no. 4 (December 2005): 1024–47.

Vermeiden, Floris. "Organizational Patterns: Surinamese and Turkish Associations in Amsterdam, 1960–1990." *Journal of Ethnic and Migration Studies* 31 (2005): 951–97.

Vogel, Ruth. "The Meaning of the Day Nursery to the Refugee Parent." Master's thesis, New York School of Social Work, Columbia University, June 1941.

Wallace, Ian, ed. *German-speaking Exiles in Great Britain*. Yearbook of the Research Centre for German and Austrian Exile Studies, Vol. 1 (Amsterdam: Rodopi, 1999).

Wasserstein, Bernard. *Britain and the Jews of Europe, 1939–1945*. London: Oxford University Press, 1979.
Westheimer, Ruth K. *Musically Speaking: A Life through Song*. Philadelphia: University of Pennsylvania, 2003.
Westphal, Uwe. *Berliner Konfektion und Mode: Die Zerstörung einer Tradition, 1836–1939*. Berlin: Edition Hentrick, 1986.
Wolfenden, Barbara. *Little Holocaust Survivors: And the English School that Saved Them*. Westport, CT: Greenwood World, 2008.
Wyman, David S. *Paper Walls: America and the Refugee Crisis, 1938–1941*. Amherst: University of Massachusetts Press, 1968.
———. *The Abandonment of the Jews: America and the Holocaust, 1941–1945*. New York: Pantheon, 1984.
Zecker, Robert. "Where Everyone Goes to Meet Everyone Else: The Translocal Creation of a Slovak Immigrant Community." *Journal of Social History* 2, no. 38 (Winter 2004): 423–53.
Zucker, Bat-Ami. *In Search of Refuge: Jews and U.S. Consuls in Nazi Germany, 1933–1941*. London: Vallentine Mitchell, 2001.
———. *Cecilia Razovsky and the American-Jewish Women's Rescue Operations in the Second World War*. London: Vallentine Mitchell, 2008.
Zunz, Leopold. *Namen der Juden. Eine geschichtliche Untersuchung*. Reprint of 1837 Leipzig edition, Hildesheim, 1971.

Index

Academic Assistance Council, 8, 118
accents, 91n1, 97, 97n36, 98, 100–102, 104–109, 105n69, 116
Acland, Sir Richard, 124
advertisements, 1, 23, 28, 34, 37, 38, 39, 40, 42, 43, 44map1.5, 57, 58, 60, 62, 71, 74, 75, 87, 128, 129, 135, 60n70, 124n26
African Americans. *See* race and racism
air raids, bombing of London in, 28, 31, 32, 32map1.3, 32n54, 33, 35, 40, 45, 54, 57, 59, 63, 69, 73, 82, 101, 106, 110, 116, 124, 126, 145, 150, 151, 151imageC.3, 152, 153, 154, 155, 156
Ambrose, Kenneth (formerly Kurt Abrahamsohn), 52, 66, 69, 70, 73, 81–82, 97, 99, 112, 141
American Friends Service Committee, 127
American Jewish Joint Distribution Committee, 127
American Jews, 15, 23, 37, 40, 43, 60, 63, 65, 75, 76, 80, 83, 84, 107, 118, 126, 127–128, 132, 134, 139, 146, 147, 156
"Americanization," 61, 80, 102, 142, 145
Americans, refugee experiences with "real," 62, 76, 79, 81, 89, 101, 104, 111, 112, 113, 114

Amsterdam, Netherlands, 8, 10, 17, 24, 81, 152
"Anglicization," 106, 120
Anglo-Jewry, 15, 19, 23, 26, 28, 67, 92, 115, 117–120, 126, 132, 138, 138n7, 142, 146, 149, 157
anti-German sentiment, 85, 88, 108, 121, 145, 150, 153, 155
antisemitism
  in Germany, 2, 3, 5, 6, 7, 9, 65. *See also* Germany, Jewish life under Nazi rule; race and racism, *Volk* and Nazi racial categories
  in Great Britain, 14–15, 26–27, 29n48, 30, 67, 71, 119–120, 142, 149
  in United States, 7, 20, 83–84, 88, 142, 145, 153
Apt, Rudolf, 58, 96
armed forces. *See* military service, refugee
Aronsfeld, C. C., 17
arrival, upon
  in Great Britain, 8–9, 17–23, 27, 34, 45, 58, 70, 75, 92, 95, 97, 109, 110, 116, 118, 137, 154–155
  in United States, 10, 18–23, 40, 43, 53, 61, 71, 73, 74, 79, 100, 114, 138, 143, 144, 155, 157
asylum, British tradition of, 14, 17, 20, 138

209

Aufbau. See newspapers and newsletters, refugee-published
Aufbau Almanac: The Immigrant's Handbook, 59, 61, 71, 77, 87, 98, 104n67, 112, 139, 145
Australia, 8, 14, 14n58, 31
Austrians, xiin6, 2n6, 7, 9, 21, 35, 53, 100, 115, 121, 122, 128, 153n8

Battle of Cable Street, 27, 120
Baum, Walter, 18, 23, 40, 43, 53, 73, 77, 100, 103n64, 107–108, 115
Berlin, Germany, 3n15, 5n21, 11, 11n43, 19, 23, 37, 38, 44map1.5, 47n3, 57, 87, 133, 134, 135n72
Bickart, Elli, 26, 107
Bickart, Otto, 55n39, 79
Blitz, London. *See* air raids, bombing of London in
Bloomsbury House, 26, 29, 36, 54, 118–119, 120, 125, 127. *See also* Woburn House
Board of Deputies of British Jews, 67n7, 118
body language. *See* manners and mannerisms
bombings. *See* air raids, bombing of London in
books, 4, 25, 41, 44map1.5, 99, 99n47, 123
Boston Committee on Medical Emigres, 127–128
Boston, MA, 109, 127
Brazil, 14, 14n58
Breslau, Germany, 11n43, 40
Britain's New Citizens: The Story of the Refugees from Germany and Austria, 23, 109, 110
British Broadcasting Company (BBC), 98, 105
British Committee for the Jews of Germany, 9

British Ministry of Food, 58n54
British Ministry of Information, 32n54
Britons, refugee interactions with "real," 21, 24, 29, 35, 49, 68, 81, 91, 93, 105, 107, 110, 141, 152, 154, 157
Buenos Aires, Argentina, xii, 11, 158
businesses, refugee-owned, 29, 42–43, 44map1.5, 51, 57–58, 60, 71, 74, 75, 99, 123

"café society," 76
Cambridge College, 96
Canada, 14, 14n59, 31
Catskills, 129
Central Association of German Citizens of Jewish Faith. *See* Germany, Jewish life prior to 1933 in
Central British Fund for German-Jewry, 35
Central British Relief Fund, 118
children, refugee
 babies, 80, 80n63, 85
 day care for, 53, 139
 evacuated out of London, 26, 31, 52, 58, 94, 106, 152
 foster families, living with, 9, 21, 22, 26–27, 36, 52, 58–59, 69, 78, 88, 95–97, 137, 147, 153, 155
 grandparent/grandchild dynamics, 53–55, 54n37, 78, 97–98, 103
 hostels or group homes for, 9, 21–22, 36, 52, 58, 69, 94
 internment of, 31, 52, 94
 Kindertransport (children's transports), 9–10, 14, 14n57, 21–22, 26, 27, 36, 52, 70, 94, 95, 96–97, 105, 116, 119, 147, 152, 153, 155
 parent/child dynamics, 4, 9, 18, 31, 43, 47, 52–55, 63, 70, 73,

74, 78, 80, 88, 96, 97, 101–102, 105–106, 129, 139, 152, 154
play, opportunities for, 57, 123, 130
schools, boarding, 9, 22, 69, 70, 78, 96, 106
schools, local, 53, 54, 69–70, 71, 73, 78, 95, 96–97, 102, 128
teenagers, 9, 10, 23, 29, 31, 53, 54, 70, 106, 108, 133, 142
cinema. *See* leisure, film
citizenship and naturalization
  German, 2–6, 117, 140
  U.K., 9, 23, 33, 68, 121, 122, 126–127, 141, 142, 143, 157
  U.S., 18, 20, 41, 127, 140, 146
Clara De Hirsch Home, 22
clothing. *See* dress, refugee
coffee (*Kaffee*), 29, 57, 60, 62
Cohn, Julius, 79, 98, 107, 110, 113
Cologne, Germany, 2, 3, 11, 11n43
Communists, 124–125
Congress, U.S., 10, 127, 128
Cuba, 10, 16n67, 20
culture shock, 29, 147
Czechoslovakia, 2n6, 11n42

dating and courtship, 53, 78, 101, 157
Davidsohn, Cantor Magnus, 133
department stores, 29, 35, 36, 73, 82
Disraeli, Prime Minister Benjamin, 142
domestic service, refugees in, 9, 10, 25, 26, 28map1.2, 31, 34–36, 43, 45, 48, 49, 50, 51, 56, 57, 66, 67, 72, 78, 92–93, 94, 100, 105, 107, 109, 110, 116, 120, 152, 153–154
Dominican Republic, 10, 14, 14n58
dress, refugee, 1, 3, 4, 5, 64–77, 74n36, 88, 89, 92, 108, 118, 144, 154
  religious attire. *See* Jewish religious practices

driving lessons, 129

Eastern European Jews (*Ostjuden*), 11n41, 13, 23, 26, 37, 60, 60n66, 76, 146
education. *See* children, refugee, schools
Ehrenberg, Eva, 70, 112
Ehrenberg, Gottfried (later George Elton), 78, 82
Ehrenberg, Ludwig (later Lewis Elton), 69, 78, 82
Ehrenberg, Victor, 69
elderly, 49, 54, 55, 63, 80, 97, 98, 99, 103, 130. *See also* children, grandparent/grandchild dynamics
Embassy Theater, 28map1.2, 124
Emergency Committee in Aid of Displaced Foreign Scholars and Medical Scientists, 9, 128
employment, refugee, 8, 12, 14, 20, 25, 26, 34–36, 42–45, 44map1.5, 48–51, 54, 57, 67, 72–74, 78, 80, 81, 84, 86, 92–94, 97, 98, 100, 109, 110, 116, 118, 121, 124, 127, 149, 150, 152–154. *See also* domestic service, refugees in; retraining, job; unemployment
employment restrictions, 10, 30, 34, 35, 36, 56, 67, 73, 81, 94, 121, 149, 152
"enemy aliens," refugee status as, 28map1.2, 29–31, 33, 41, 45, 69, 69n14, 92, 108–109, 151, 152, 155. *See also* internment of refugees
evacuations out of London, 8, 28, 31, 36, 45, 57, 63, 116, 126, 155, 156. *See also* air raids; children, evacuated out of London

Federation of Synagogues, 118

First World War, 4, 5, 5n23, 51, 131, 140, 140n18, 141
Florida, 129
food, 21, 24–26, 28map1.2, 30, 49, 55–63, 73, 121, 129, 146, 153–154
Frankfurt am Main, Germany, 2, 3, 3n14, 5n22, 11, 11n43, 19, 38, 44map1.5, 55, 79, 132, 133, 134
Freeden, Herbert, 142
Friedmann, Lilly, 19, 68
friendship, 22, 33, 40, 47, 53, 55–57, 61–63, 66, 78, 79, 81, 85, 94, 96, 103, 105, 106, 107, 108, 110, 113, 114, 116, 124, 129, 133, 154, 156, 157, 157n12

Gay, Peter (formerly Peter Fröhlich), 33, 103
gender, 2, 2n1, 3n16, 13, 47–53, 47n2, 103
George, Manfred, 138–139
German-Jewish Aid Committee, 29, 67, 109, 118–119, 120
German-Jewish Children's Aid, 127
Germany, Jewish life prior to 1933, 2–5, 2n2, 2n5, 3n14, 3n16, 23, 26, 38, 48, 53n32, 60, 65–66, 86, 111, 117, 132, 134, 140, 140n18, 147
Germany, Jewish life under Nazi rule in, 2n2, 6–9, 11n43, 35, 48, 49, 51, 53, 55, 66, 70, 83, 84, 86–87, 91n2, 117, 140, 141, 144, 146
Germany, postwar, 122, 125, 131, 131n55
Goddard, Hannah, 105
Grebler, Anne Marie, 71
Grebler, Leo, 50, 60, 76, 79, 107, 108, 111, 113, 139, 144, 145, 147
Grenfell, David, Labour MP, 124

Grossman, Atina, 15, 146
Gutman, Ilse, 23, 54

Hamburg, Germany, 2, 3, 3n14, 11n43, 13, 13n50, 16
Hampstead Public Library, 30
Haskalah, 3, 3n15
hats, 3, 65, 66, 69, 70, 73, 74, 76, 77
Hebrew Orphans Asylum, 22
Hebrew Sheltering and Immigrant Aid Society (HIAS), 22, 127
Heiman, Inge, 22, 61, 98
Holocaust, 6, 8, 8n31, 16, 16n66, 55, 63, 120, 147
Home Office, UK, 7, 8n33, 26, 58, 141, 149, 154
hotels, refugee-frequented, 21–22, 23, 36, 40, 59, 62n82, 68, 92, 98, 129
homes, refugee
  beds and bedding, 22, 24, 25, 27, 41–42, 49, 59, 66, 124
  furniture and décor, 4, 6, 21, 24, 41–42, 43, 48, 154
  heating and cooling, 21, 25, 27, 76–77
  kitchen and dining, 21, 23, 24–25, 27, 37, 40–42, 48, 58, 61
Houses of Parliament, UK, 7, 20, 119, 120, 122, 142, 163

immigration quotas, 7, 9, 154
India, 14, 14n58
internment of refugees, 8, 28map1.2, 29, 30–33, 31n51, 36, 45, 50, 52, 54, 57, 58, 63, 69, 81, 93, 93n11, 97, 106, 110, 120, 124, 125, 134, 141, 151, 152, 155
invasion, threat of Nazi, 88, 94, 114, 116, 150, 154
Isle of Man. *See* internment of refugees
Israel. *See* Palestine

Italian immigrants, xii, 13, 55, 81, 83, 84, 85, 145
Italophobia, 81

Jacoby, Ilse, 24, 40, 49, 56, 62, 69
Japanese Americans, internment of, 21n15, 41, 108n87, 152, 155–156
Jewish Refugee Committee. *See* German-Jewish Aid Committee
Jewish religious practices
  Bar Mitzvah, 91
  beards, 76
  bible study, 133
  cantor, 133, 134
  head-covering, 76
  Kosher (*Kashrut*), 4, 26, 57, 60, 129, 131, 146
  liturgy, 3n16, 91, 132
  marriage wigs, 76
  religious school, 134
  See also synagogues
Jewish holidays
  Rosh Hashanah, 38n78, 39table1.1, 125, 129
  Sabbath (*Shabbat*), 26, 76
  Sukkot, 134
  Yom Kippur, 125, 129
Jewish Social Service Association, German Department, 127
Johnson, Peter William (formerly Wolfgang Joseph), 94
Judaism, denominations of
  Conservative, 91, 132, 133, 134
  English Liberal Movement, 28map1.2, 118, 121, 132, 133–134
  Liberale, 5, 91, 132–133, 133n64, 134
  Modern Orthodox, 3, 23, 132
  Orthodox, 23, 23n29, 43, 76, 91, 121, 132, 133, 134, 144, 147

Progressive, 118, 132
Reform, 3, 3n16, 132, 133, 134.
  See also synagogues, London; synagogues, New York

Kashrut. See Jewish religious practices, Kosher
Kahn, Liselotte, 42, 43, 61, 74
Katz, Rudolf, 40, 61, 62, 77, 87, 145, 146
Kerr, Alfred, 34, 98
Kerr, Judith, 21, 52, 92, 96, 97
Kindertransport (children's transports). *See* children, refugee
King's Cross Station, 19
Kitchener Camp, 70
Kleine Bühne (The Little Stage), 123
knitting, 124
Kohen, Resi, 78
Konditoreien (confectionary bakeries), 60
Koppel, Anne, 62, 70, 95, 137
Koppel, Harold, 144

Lady Gollanz, 78
Laky, Bridget Stross, 72–73, 144
language acquisition, 92–95, 97–98, 103–104, 106–107, 116, 118, 129
language, slang, 74n36, 93, 94, 100, 101, 107, 112
languages, refugee-spoken
  English, 11, 43, 47, 54, 92–97, 100, 102–109, 112, 116, 121, 137, 152
  German, 1, 5, 34, 55, 91, 91n2, 92, 98–100, 103–106, 116, 123, 126, 155, 156
  Hebrew, 6, 47, 91
  Yiddish, 5, 91, 91n1, 105, 106
Leigh, Charles (formerly Karl Levinsohn), 25, 58, 59, 69, 78, 82, 94

leisure activities
  art exhibits, 123, 124
  beach, 62, 129
  cabaret, 123, 123n24, 126, 131
  card games, 61, 131
  cinema, 56, 74, 95, 102
  concerts, attending, 121, 123, 124, 134
  dancing, 129, 131, 62n82
  hiking, 40, 129 (*see also* sports)
  jazz music, 129
  lectures, 21, 96, 121, 124, 126, 128, 129, 132, 134
  poetry, 111, 124, 129
  theater, 4, 85, 96, 123, 124
lift. *See* packing for emigration
Lisbon, Portugal, 10, 17, 20, 85, 138
Liverpool Street Station, 19, 21, 21n19
London, East End of, 11, 12, 21, 23, 25–28, 28n44, 31, 37, 120, 146
London, Northwest
  Belsize Park, 24, 28, 31, 32map1.3, 122
  Belsize Square, 29, 36, 132, 133, 134 (*see also* synagogues, London)
  Downshire Hill, 28map1.2, 122
  Fairhazel Gardens, 28map1.2, 57
  Finchley Road, 28map1.2, 121, 132
  Fitzjohn's Avenue, 28map1.2, 56
  Hampstead, London, 23, 24map1.1, 25, 28, 28map1.2, 29–31, 32map1.3, 45, 56, 126, 134, 151imageC.3
  St. John's Wood, 132, 133
  Swiss Cottage, 23, 24, 28, 28map1.2, 29, 32map1.3, 45, 57, 124, 133
London Committee of Deputies, 118
London Underground, 32map1.3, 33, 56
luggage. *See* packing for emigration

MI5, 124–125
magazines, 43, 72, 93, 100–101
masculinity. *See* gender
manners and mannerisms, American
  friendliness, 111, 113, 115
  informality, 61, 62, 73, 74, 74n37, 87–89, 111, 115, 154
  innocence, 114, 115
  kindness, 112, 115
  politeness, 112
  small talk, 111
  superficiality of, 71, 112, 115
  voice, volume and tone of, 107, 108, 115
manners and mannerisms, British
  kindness, 27, 58, 95, 141, 142
  formality, xin2, 109, 110, 154
  politeness, 67, 94, 109, 110
  small talk, 109, 110
  traditional, xin2
  understatement of, 67, 92, 115
  voice, volume of, 67, 109, 110, 115
manners and mannerisms, German Jewish
  formality, 1, 53, 65, 67, 68, 73, 74, 75, 88, 110, 115
  "German look," 40, 114
  voice, volume of, 57, 70, 92, 106, 114, 115
Marks & Spencer, 35, 36, 82
Maybaum, Rabbi Ignaz, 132, 138
"melting pot," United States as, 12, 18–20, 82, 138, 142–145, 157
military service, refugee
  basic training, 100
  camaraderie and sense of belonging, 69, 79, 93, 101, 141, 143, 153
  citizenship, as a path to, 41, 122, 143
  Germany, serving with Allies in, 100–101, 143
  Intelligence Corps, 152, 153

Pioneer Corps, 33, 36, 50, 69, 78, 93, 152
South Pacific, 55
translator role, 101, 153
Mistress and Maid: General Information for the Use of Domestic Refugees and Their Employers, 109, 110
Montagu, Lily, 133
Mosse, Werner, 12
Movement for the Care of Children from Germany, 9
movies. *See* leisure, film
Munich, Germany, 87
Munk, Rabbi Elijah, 134
music, 5, 26, 94n14, 123, 124, 128, 129, 132, 133, 133n64

name changes, 5, 5n22, 77–86, 80n63, 81–85, 82n71, 88, 152
nation and "nationhood," meanings of, 2n2, 3–5, 11, 15, 19, 20, 51, 115, 140, 141, 142, 144, 146, 152
National Coordinating Committee for the Aid to Refugees and Emigrants Coming from Germany (NCC), 127
National Council of Jewish Women, 127, 189
National Refugee Service, 127
Native Americans, 21n15, 142, 144
"New World," United States as the, 18, 19, 44map1.5, 128
newspapers, American and British, 29, 93, 103, 119
newspapers and newsletters, refugee-published
  AJR Information, 1, 15, 16, 68, 117, 120–121, 126–127, 129, 130figure5.1, 151, 156, 157
  Aufbau, 1, 16, 38, 39table1.1, 41, 42, 43, 59, 60, 61, 62, 71, 74, 75, 98, 101, 128–130, 130figure5.1, 131figure5.2, 134, 135, 139, 143, 145, 157
  FDKB Nachrichten, 16, 23, 31, 33, 35, 36, 57, 58, 122–125, 130figure5.1
  Jewish Way, 11n43
New York City, Outer Boroughs
  Bronx, 23, 37map1.4, 38, 39table1.1, 40, 107, 108, 135
  Brooklyn, 18, 37map1.4, 38, 39table1.1, 40, 43, 55, 60, 108, 129, 135, 145
  Queens, 1, 37, 37map1.4, 38, 39table1.1, 40, 42, 99, 108
  Staten Island, 18, 37map1.4, 129
New York City, Manhattan
  Central Park, 40, 129
  Harlem, 39table1.1, 108
  midtown, 22, 39table1.1, 134
  Lower East Side, 11, 12, 13, 37, 37map1.4, 37n75, 43, 60, 60n66
  Upper West Side, 1, 37, 37map1.4, 38, 39table1.1, 40, 43, 62, 75, 99, 128, 129, 139n12
  Washington Heights, 1, 11, 11n40, 11n42, 37, 37map1.4, 38, 39table1.1, 40, 42–45, 44map1.5, 60, 61, 72, 74, 75, 79, 80, 85, 87, 98–100, 101, 102, 103, 128, 129, 131, 134, 144, 147, 156
  Yorkville, 37map1.4, 60, 74, 99n47, 131

organizations, refugee-formed, New York
  American Federation of Jews from Central Europe, 130–131, 131n55
  German American League for Culture Activities and Leisure, 131
  Immigrant Jewish War Veterans, 131
  Maccabi Athletic Club, 44map1.5, 131

organizations, refugee-formed, New York (*continued*)
  New World Club, 44map1.5, 128–129, 143
  Prospect Unity Club, 44map1.5, 131
  Selfhelp of Émigrés from Germany, 11, 129–130
organizations, refugee-formed, London
  Association of Jewish Refugees, 11, 28map1.2, 30, 48, 109, 120–122, 125, 126, 128, 132
  Club 43, 28map1.2, 125–126
  Council of Jews from Germany, 121
  Free German Institute (*Freie Deutsche Hochschule*), 124
  Free German League of Culture (*Freier Deutscher Kulturbund or FDKB*), 23, 28map1.2, 36, 57, 121–125, 124n25. See also Newspapers and Newsletters, refugee-published
  PEN Group of German Writers in England, 126
  Section 1943 of B'nai B'rith (later Leo Baeck Lodge), 28map1.2, 126
Ostjuden. See Eastern European Jews

packing for emigration
  "lift" container, 6, 41, 48
  luggage or suitcase, 21, 66, 68, 69, 118, 137
  trunk, 24, 66, 77
Palestine (Israel), xi, 8, 9, 10, 11, 20, 70, 91, 125, 126–127, 129, 147, 150, 157, 158. See also Zionism
Paris, France, 10, 17, 32, 65n1, 81, 138, 150
Pearl Harbor, 108, 150, 152
Pioneer Corps. See military service, refugee
Placement Committee for German and Austrian Musicians, 128

Pleasantville College School, 22
Poland, 2n6, 7, 8, 8n31, 11n41, 30, 91n1
police officers, 17, 23, 30, 74, 77, 110
Pond, Oliver, 93
postwar era, 28, 48, 122, 125, 156, 138n8
psychological issues
  anxiety, 31, 32, 62–63, 113–114, 126–127
  depression, 48, 62–63, 103
  nervous breakdown, 130
  suicide, 130
  trauma, 16n66, 31, 63, 96, 114

queues, waiting in, 25, 67, 92, 119

race and racism
  African Americans, 21n15, 98, 129, 142n25, 144, 145
  diversity in Britain, lack of, 20, 115, 142, 143, 144
  diversity in Britain, postwar, 15, 142n25, 144, 157
  diversity in United States, 76, 98, 143–145
  Japanese (*see* Japanese Americans, internment of)
  Jews, 2n2, 8, 19, 20, 125, 140, 142, 142n25, 143 (*see also* antisemitism)
  Southern Europeans, 145
  Volk and Nazi racial categories, 2n2, 8, 14, 19, 125, 140, 146
radio, 29, 33, 92, 98, 103, 105, 108
Ramapo Mountain, 129
Rathbone, Eleanor, 21n16, 78
Reichmann, Eva, 49, 78, 93
restaurants, refugee-frequented
  American, 62
  café, 29, 57, 92, 155
  cafeterias, 61–62

canteen, at New Liberal Synagogue, 134
"Continental" restaurants, 29, 57, 58, 123
delicatessens, 60, 60n66, 63
pubs, 94
retraining, job, 7, 26, 36, 68, 92, 93, 118, 124n26. *See also* employment, refugee
Roosevelt, Eleanor, 10
Roosevelt, Franklin Delano, 81, 85, 127
Rosenstock, Werner, 23, 110, 138
Rosenthal, Siegfried, 100–101

Sabor, Gerda, 76, 99
Saenger, Gerhart, 18, 22, 53, 86, 87, 102, 111, 114, 115, 129, 134, 140
Salzberger, Rabbi Dr. Georg, 132–133
Samson, Susanne, 92
Schwab, Alice (formerly Liesel Rosenthal), 21, 35, 56, 78, 82, 92, 94, 110
seamstress and sewing, 6, 48, 54, 75. *See also* tailoring
Second World War
  Battle of Britain, 32, 33, 45, 106, 124, 150, 151, 153, 154. *See also* air raids, bombing of London in
  outbreak of, 8, 9, 20, 28, 34, 56, 68, 70, 78, 91, 92, 150, 157, 158
  "Phoney" war, 31
  rationing, 58, 59, 69, 152, 153
  "victory gardens," 58
  war effort, refugee contributions to, 34, 54, 58, 69, 101, 122, 141, 150, 152, 153. *See also* military service, refugee
  war-time restrictions, on movement and goods, 30, 41, 58, 93, 121
Shanghai, China, 8, 10, 11, 14, 14n58, 20, 158
Shomre Hadath, 127

sleep. *See* homes, refugee, bed and bedding
social classes
  distinctions between, 25, 67, 104, 105, 108, 111
  lower, 3
  middle, 3, 4, 5, 23, 25, 26, 37, 38, 48, 51, 65, 66, 67, 91, 105, 125
  fluidity of, 3, 67, 108, 111, 144
  service, 9
  stratification of, xi, 105, 108
  transcend, ability to, 110, 111, 112
  upper, 53, 67, 85, 86, 96, 104, 112
  working, 23, 27, 67, 105, 111
Society for the Protection of Science and Learning, 8, 118
sports
  baseball, 102, 111
  clubs, 128, 129, 131
  exercise, 60, 123
  football (soccer), 40, 129
  football, U.S., 83, 102
  handball, 129
  ping pong, 40, 129
  skiing, 129
  swimming, 40, 129
stamp-collecting, 128
Stock, Ernest, (formerly Ernst) 41, 60, 79, 99, 100, 102, 103, 108, 113, 114, 139, 153
Strauss, Herbert, 146
suitcases. *See* packing for emigration
Swarensky, Rabbi Manfred, 19
synagogues, refugee
  London, 28map1.2, 29, 36, 132–134, 132n58
  New York, 44map1.5, 72, 134–135

tailoring, 27, 35, 66, 70, 74, 75. *See also* seamstress and sewing
tea (*Tee*), 25, 57, 58, 60, 62, 87n82
Tergit, Gabriele, 25, 48, 56, 66, 68, 96, 109, 141

theater. *See* leisure
titles, use of, 85–89
Today's Refugees, Tomorrow's Citizens, 18, 139, 140

Uhlman, Fred, 122
unemployment, refugee, 26, 29, 34, 49, 50, 67, 86, 92, 93, 94, 100, 103, 124, 153
United Synagogue, 118

Vienna, Austria, 37, 75, 87
visas, acquiring exit or entrance, 6, 7, 9, 10, 19–20, 34, 45, 48, 52, 53, 54, 63, 67, 80, 92

WASP, 74n37, 108
Wagner-Rogers Bill, 10, 155
Walter, Marianne, 70, 78, 110, 114
Washington Heights. *See* New York City, Manhattan
weather, 17, 18, 19, 76, 77, 110, 111, 112
"While You are in England: Helpful Information and Guidance for Every Refugee," 67, 71, 92, 104, 109, 110, 120, 137
White, Graham, Labour MP, 124
White, Irene, 146
Woburn House, 25, 29, 34, 54, 92, 118–120, 125, 127. *See also* Bloomsbury House
work. *See* employment, refugee, retraining, job; unemployment, refugee
World War I. *See* First World War
World War II. *See* Second World War

Yiddish. *See* languages, refugee-spoken
Y.W.H.A., 129

Zionism, xin2, 121

www.ingramcontent.com/pod-product-compliance
Lightning Source LLC
Chambersburg PA
CBHW030649230426
43665CB00011B/1011